D1568912

Managing Doctors

Managing Doctors

Alan Sheldon

DOW JONES-IRWIN
Homewood, Illinois 60430

This publication is designed to provide accurate and authoritative information in regard to the subject matter covered. It is sold with the understanding that the publisher is not engaged in rendering legal, accounting, or other professional service. If legal advice or other expert assistance is required, the services of a competent professional person should be sought.

From a Declaration of Principles jointly adopted by a Committee of the American Bar Association and a Committee of Publishers.

ISBN 0-87094-646-3

Library of Congress Catalog Card No. 86-70965

Printed in the United States of America

1 2 3 4 5 6 7 8 9 0 B 3 2 1 0 9 8 7 6

In memory of
Louis Sheldon L.M.S.S.A.
General Practitioner

PREFACE

The very title of this book will be provocative to some, irritating (at the least) to others. But it is a fact that health care delivery organizations[1] and their managers are facing a stringent competitive environment in which their fates are dependent on their capacity to make difficult strategic choices and manage key operational issues—cost, quality, productivity—effectively. To do this requires influencing physician behavior as a key element to their success or failure, in other words, managing doctors.

This book attempts to identify the reasons this state of affairs has arisen and to suggest what must be managed and how effective management may be achieved. It is based on many years of consulting and research, as well as an exhaustive literature review. In particular, two personal unpublished studies are cited. One, the practice pattern impact study, was an intensive look at how physicians at one teaching hospital saw an impending and unwanted change (see Chapter 7 for details). The other, the 10-hospital study, involved interviewing a small sample of doctors (and the chief executive officers) at each of 10 hospitals across the country[2] (five not-for-profit, five Health Corporation of America for-profit) about the state of management-physician relationships at those hospitals and the future of health care.

Chapter 1 describes the changing health care scene, and how the evolving environment has created challenges for both health care delivery organizations and doctors. Chapter 2 outlines the

---

[1]I use the terms health care delivery organization, health organization, and organization synonymously to avoid the clumsy reiteration of a lengthy phrase.

[2]The names of these hospitals have been disguised in this book.

strategic and organizational issues that must be faced. In Chapter 3 the changing relationship between doctor, patient, and organization is described, and what is legitimate for managers to manage is discussed. Chapter 4 deals with physician influence in the health organization and how doctors are and may be organized, including physician unions. Chapter 5 suggests ways in which physicians' loyalty and devotion may be attracted. Management's delicate role in traditionally medical areas (cost, quality, and recruitment) is discussed in Chapter 6. Chapter 7 deals with the problems of managing change and conflict, assessing their impact, and monitoring physician relations. Chapter 8 discusses the differences among doctors and among organizational settings from a management point of view. Chapter 9 goes into the details of management style and skills that may be effective or ineffective in working with physicians. Chapter 10 suggests that the future will bring a radical change in the nature of doctoring.

This book is addressed to the issue of managing physicians in their relationship to health care delivery organizations. There are many different kinds of health delivery organizations with which physicians work. They include teaching hospitals, community hospitals, hospital groups, health maintenance organizations, independent practice associations, neighborhood health centers, and group practices, among others. It is the intent of this book to deal with the generic issues of working with physicians in any kind of health delivery organization, as well as to give attention to the specific problems of the different kinds of health delivery organizations.

This book is, I believe, unique in bringing together material usually found in disparate places. As a physician myself, I feel privileged that my medical and managerial colleagues in practice have been willing to share their views, attitudes, and concerns with me.

ACKNOWLEDGMENTS

My grateful thanks to The Pew Memorial Trust for providing some of the financial support that made this book possible. Also to Dr. Diana Barrett and the Health Corporation of America for major support of the 10-hospital study.

Alan Sheldon

CONTENTS

CHAPTER ONE

The Changing Health Care Scene 1

Introduction and Argument. The Past Environment—Organizations. The Past Environment—The Physician. The Future Health Care Environment.

CHAPTER TWO

What Must Be Managed? Strategic and Organizational Imperatives 20

Strategic Imperatives. Organizational Imperatives. The Hospital and the Physician. The HMO and the Doctor.

CHAPTER THREE

What Can Be Managed? The Changing Relationship between Physician, Patient, and Organization 34

Physician and Organization. Doctor and Patient. Why Doctors Enter Medicine: The Experience and Its Shaping. Traditional Physician Values. Self-Control or Other Correction? Plupractice, Malfeasance, and Error.

CHAPTER FOUR

Managing Voice, Governance, and Structure: Physician Unions 67

The Issue of Physician Involvement. Governance and the Board. Organizational Structure. Physician Voice. Informing and Involving. The Influential Doctor. Toward True Partnership. Physician Unions:

Background and an Example. Physician Unions: Arguments for and against. When Can the Doctor Organize?

CHAPTER FIVE

Managing Loyalty and Devotion 106

Loyalty and Devotion—The Basic Issues: *A Case Study*. The 10-Hospital Study—What Doctors Say, What CEOs Do. Value Chain Analysis.

CHAPTER SIX

Management's Role in Medical Matters: Managing Quality, Cost, and Recruitment 131

Quality and Cost as Competitive Issues. Managing Quality. Managing Cost. Changing Physician Behavior—The Problem. Changing Physician Behavior—Approaches. Compensation and Financial Incentives as a Tool for Change. Goals and Processes for Physician Behavior-Change Programs: *Summary of M.D. Behavior-Change Programs*. Recruitment.

CHAPTER SEVEN

Managing Change and Conflict: Monitoring Physician Response 175

Managing Change and Conflict. Practice Pattern Impact Assessment: *A Case Study*. Physician-Management Relations Monitoring (PMRM).

CHAPTER EIGHT

Sorts and Settings 202

Doctors Are Not Alike. Settings and Their Managerial Characteristics. Organizational Preparation.

CHAPTER NINE

Management Style and Management Skills: Lay and Physician Managers 224

Management Style and Skills for the Lay Manager. The Physician Manager.

CHAPTER TEN

The Future of Health Care: The End of Doctoring? 243

REFERENCES 260

INDEX 263

CHAPTER ONE

The Changing Health Care Scene

They that be whole need not a physician, but they that are sick.

Matthew 9:12

INTRODUCTION AND ARGUMENT

All health care delivery organizations face essentially the same issue, how to manage in a highly competitive, cost-conscious health environment. The form that this issue takes, as it shapes the fate of any type of, or particular example of, health care delivery organization will obviously be different. Hospitals, especially acute general hospitals, face a more difficult future than do health maintenance organizations (HMOs) for example, because hospital days per thousand are dropping sharply, as are occupancy rates, and they are projected to do so further by 1990.[1] (Fee-for-service patient days per thousand were 728 in 1980, 550 in 1985, and are projected to drop to 490 by 1990.) But all health care providers have to find distinctive characteristics that will attract consumers, strategically placing the organizations in their most appropriate niche in the market, and at the same time all must manage their internal affairs to provide cost-effective quality care that appeals to the chosen market segment. This results in a series of strategic and organizational imperatives that must be faced by any health care delivery organization.

The traditional convergence of health organization and physician interests, dating from the time when the hospital was the doctor's workshop, ceased to exist decades ago as hospitals have sought to cut costs and relate to communities, while doctors have tried to maintain income and the sacrosanct physician-patient relationship. The diverging and complex nature of the

[1]K. S. Abramowitz, *The Future of Health Care Delivery in America: Strategic Analysis/Financial Forecast* (New York: Bernstein Research, 1985).

doctor-hospital relationship today is reflected in the fact that hospitals still obviously want the doctor's patient—especially with dropping occupancy—but they want some patients and not others, for a while and not longer, and with this done but not that, but you must not make it too expensive, and you must get the patients out fast. These divergences are not peculiar to hospitals. HMOs are also caught in a cost-price squeeze as salaries escalate while competition presents the possibility of premium increases. So HMOs must improve productivity and ask the doctor to do more, probably for less.

When interests were identical, physician behavior did not need managing. But now health organizations must influence doctors' behavior, in other words manage them, if they are to survive, let alone be successful competitively, in a manner and to an extent not hitherto required. Moreover, this is becoming necessary at a time of great transition in which the physician still has much power (70 percent of doctors and patients in one study acknowledged that the doctor still determines patient choice of hospital)[2], while traditional professional autonomy erodes, and the physician shifts from entrepreneur to employee with growing industrialization. Perhaps the future doctor, bred in an organizational matrix, will know no different situation, but the present generation, experiencing change, still finds bureaucracy stultifying.

As organizations face ever more stringent managerial demands, physicians face an uncertain and changing future that is altering their role in relation both to patients and to organizations and, for older physicians at least, creating much unsettledness and unhappiness. Physicians must practice a different kind of medicine than that for which they were trained, often in settings that did not exist when they started their training.

Failure to manage the doctor in this transitional period can be catastrophic to the health organization, for the doctor can make the difference between profit and loss if he/she chooses to take patients—especially private pay patients—elsewhere.

One physician summed it up:

> I think the central theme in a situation like this is that you want to make your hospital a strong and viable institution. In theory what is good for the

---

[2]Alan Sheldon, "Practice Pattern Impact Study," unpublished study, 1985.

> institution should be good for the physician . . . practicing there. That is less true in today's environment than it was in the past, obviously. This hospital 20 years ago was a fairly outstanding institution with respect to health care delivery. Physicians got a little greedy, made this a closed shop, invited individuals in, cut them off at the knees, that sort of thing. Those days are gone now. You have two HMOs in the area. You have private practice. You have tremendous anxiety with the physician. There are many conflicts and real threats.

It is only too easy in such a troubled time to seek villains to blame. What is happening is not caused by bad doctors, greedy corporations looking out for the health care dollar, stultifying government bureaucracies with their regulations, grasping lawyers, or careless consumers. It is an inevitable process not unlike that which transformed the crafts into industry at the beginning of this century. As it has become possible to measure what is done in health care (e.g., protocols) and to replace human with technological processes (e.g., the computer), the art of medicine is giving way to the industry of health care. Thus, the unhappy and often paranoid (with reason) physician.

Will the care obtained from the health organization of tomorrow be better or worse than that of yesterday? To some degree that will depend on the success of managing the process. In general, standards probably will rise, and so standard care will, on the whole, get better. Abuses may be less frequent, care will be cheaper, and quality overall will improve. But as is true of any industrialized process, care will be less tailored to the individual, and some people and problems will suffer from diminished knowledge. A different kind of doctor will enter medicine: there will be more entrepreneurs, more academicians and researchers perhaps, and certainly more bureaucrats; fewer of the caring, hardworking, traditional physicians who were idealized.

The health organization–doctor relationship is complicated, not only by the increasing divergence referred to above, but also by the fact that the new strategic directions the organization must take to survive and be successful bring it inevitably into direct competition with the doctor. Hospitals, for example, may secure patient flows through contracts with physicians to supply ambulatory care, but this will not help them with revenues, and therefore the hospitals must move into ownership of ambulatory facilities.

As physicians' patterns of practice and interests diverge from the interests and needs of health care organizations, there are potentially both maladaptive and adaptive outcomes. Clearly unacceptable is the continuation of historical physician independence, doctors continuing to behave as though totally autonomous where convenient, ignoring hospital concerns. Equally maladaptive is any attempt to regulate and rule physicians into compliance. This has been tried with little success in other countries, even in the face of significant doctor unemployment (tens of thousands in Italy and Holland). Regulation will inevitably result, when tried (and surely it will be), in a further hardening of physician attitudes, in an increased formation of physician unions, and in more physicians moving into direct competition with institutions, trends already in progress. Any attempt to influence, manipulate, or govern physician behavior will be seen by some as an abridgement of autonomy and medical judgment. More concretely, the result of any attempt to direct behavior toward some organizational standard will inevitably reduce physician income (or lifestyle). To what extent this can be accomplished without some form of replacement of income—or protest—is an interesting question. Already, physician incomes are plateauing or dropping in the United States. Moreover, what constitutes appropriate behavior raises important questions. Should major deviations from organizational standards be reduced, or should the more common minor ones be the goal? Should deviation from a standard or the basic pattern of practice itself be the target?[3]

The implication for the management of physicians is that health organizations are going to have to find new ways to involve the physician in the institution, to select physicians for the institution, to train physicians, and to organize and pay physicians. While the fate of the organization may be in the hands of the manager, the doctor will still be crucial. Physicians will have to be involved in strategy determination, for if they do not accept new directions in the institution, they will not remain within it. Physicians will have to be managed successfully in operational

[3] J. E. Wenberg, "Factors Governing Utilization of Hospital Services," *Hospital Practice,* September 1979, pp. 115–27.

tasks, for failure to manage them will result in an uncontrolled organization.

THE PAST ENVIRONMENT—ORGANIZATIONS

A major shift toward corporate organization has already started in part because of capital needs, in part because of economic incentives for cost-efficient service.[4] There has been consolidation into investor-owned and not-for-profit health care chains with an expansion of ambulatory care. Profit-making hospital chains have grown from 72,000 beds to 122,000 in the five-year period ending in 1981.[5]

It takes no crystal ball to predict that pressure on medical costs will increase. In part this is because the population over 65 (now 11 percent and accounting for 30 percent of all medical expenditures) will rise to 18 percent by early in the next century. Moreover, new technology is appearing that will make ever more extraordinary medical feats possible, many of them at ever more extraordinary prices. Medical care "having been defended from government interference by physicians" may now be slipping from physician control in another direction altogether.[6]

The pressure on costs has resulted in not only the emergence of the for-profits with their supposedly superior management techniques, but also in the extraordinary growth of multihospital systems. Proprietary multihospital systems have grown from 66,000 beds in 1980 to 101,000 in 1985,[7] and estimates suggest that over three quarters of the hospital beds in the United States will be in some form of multihospital system very shortly.

The last decade has seen also the emergence of alternative health care systems, in part because of the pressures of prepayment and in part because of changing consumer attitudes. HMOs, Independent Practice Associations (IPAs), and PPOs

---

[4]W. Dunn, "For-Profit Perspective," *Group Practice Journal*, May–June 1984, pp. 1–8.

[5]P. Starr, *The Social Transformation of American Medicine* (New York: Basic Books, 1982).

[6]H. H. Hiatt, "The Coming of Corporate Medicine," *Harvard Business Review*, January–February 1984, pp. 4–7.

[7]Abramowitz, *Future of Health Care Delivery.*

(Preferred Provider Organizations) now represent not only adjuncts to hospitals but compete with them, as HMOs seek low-cost beds.

Like HMOs, freestanding ambulatory surgery centers are not particularly new, given that outpatient surgical procedures were fairly common as early as 1909.[8] However, in 1968, the first *independent* ambulatory facility was founded in Providence, Rhode Island. Initially dominated by physicians and antihospital, ambulatory centers are shifting toward nonphysician entrepreneur management and competing essentially with hospital emergency rooms, though many have close functional ties to inpatient facilities. Urgent care centers are like general practitioners' offices, a variation being the occupational medical clinic operating from an industrial base. Some facilities are hybrids providing both urgent and primary care. They attract patients from emergency rooms and from physicians' offices.

Ambulatory care in essence is shifting from hospital settings to independent, freestanding facilities. This trend is not simply a function of health care costs, but also of technological advances that make outpatient care more feasible, less expensive, and safer, as well as of social factors such as convenience and access. Anesthesia advances, for example, let patients go home much sooner without problems, and many new, noninvasive diagnostic techniques are ambulatory. The trend towards healthy lifestyles also emphasizes ambulatory alternatives. The incursion of venture capital has supported such innovations, especially when they are potentially lucrative. (Hospitals are more expensive and therefore less attractive.) New health insurance policies are finally providing economic incentives to use ambulatory care such as PPOs.

However, another reason for ambulatory expansion is the fact that many of these emergency centers are recognized under state law as physicians' offices and therefore are less regulated and so less expensive to operate and less expensive to patronize than are hospital departments.[9] Up from 150 in 1980, in 1982 there were at least 620 urgent care centers, and this did not include surgicenters, birthing centers, or surgery suites in physi-

---

[8]J. Moxley and P. Roeder, "New Opportunities for Out-of-Hospital Health Services," *New England Journal of Medicine* 310, no. 3 (January 19, 1984), pp. 193–97.

[9]E. Friedman, "Slicing the Pie Thinner," *Hospitals*, October 16, 1982, pp. 62–74.

cians' offices. In fact, hospitals may well add more expense if they do not also drop inpatient capacity.[10] Hospitals may support physician staffed/owned ambulatory alternatives as a financial inducement to doctors (guaranteeing physicians an annual income) rather than as a cost-reducing measure.

HMOs have emerged as a leader among the alternative delivery systems in containing health care costs. Most investment studies support the belief that HMOs will continue to expand their penetration into all major metropolitan areas.[11] (The term HMO is used generically for any company that integrates the delivery and financing of health care services.) A hybrid of a health services organization and an insurance company, an HMO creates value by managing health care delivery in a quality system that is responsive to cost controls, and varies by size and delivery model (see Chapter 8).

While HMOs have been around for more than 40 years—Kaiser and Group Health Association both started before World War II—their recent popularity has been a function of an infusion of federal dollars because of the belief, probably correct, that HMOs save money over traditional forms of health care. However, studies to date have been surprisingly unable to discover *why* HMOs save money. Total costs, both premiums and out-of-pocket expenditures, are often 10 to 40 percent lower in HMOs than in conventional health insurance plans, and most of the cost differences are attributable to hospitalization rates, about 30 percent lower than those of conventionally insured populations (due almost entirely to lower admission rates). There is no evidence that HMOs reduce admissions in discretionary or unnecessary categories; rather, the data suggest lower admission rates across the board.[12] There are three possible interpretations of these data. An effective HMO may limit discretionary use across the board; self-selection may have the effect that healthier people come into HMOs; or HMOs may be skimping while conventional insurance plans overtreat discretionary

---

[10] R. H. Egdahl, "Physicians and the Containment of Health Care Costs," *New England Journal of Medicine* 304 (1981), pp. 900–01.

[11] *The Health Maintenance Organization Industry,* Basic Report 84-67A (W. Blair and Company, 1984).

[12] H. S. Luft, "Addressing the Evidence on HMO Performance," *Milbank Memorial Fund Quarterly/Health in Societies* 58, no. 4 (1980), pp. 501–31.

cases. Costs for HMO enrollees have grown at a slightly lower rate than the increase for people with conventional insurance coverage due to this reduction in hospitalization rates. Higher levels of preventive care in HMOs may reflect the more extensive coverage that they offer.[13,14] This obviously has great implications for managers of HMOs, especially in relation to physicians, because there is little guidance from studies to date as to what needs to be managed successfully.

HMOs are less costly than conventional delivery systems. And prepaid group practices are less costly than IPAs, largely because the former have a yet lower hospitalization rate, but why this is so is also unknown. Perhaps partly it is because those who are already ill tend to pick an IPA, because they have a private physician and wish to maintain the physician-patient relationship.

Prospective reimbursement systems will inevitably extend to include physician payments and ambulatory expenses, resulting not only in a declining physician income, but also in the necessity for hospitals to extend their aegis over ambulatory alternatives. Surgicenters, freestanding diagnostic centers, and so forth, now are able (especially with the advent of noninvasive technologies), to carry out much of what used to be done within a hospital. It thus becomes quite feasible for unhappy physicians not only to shift their patients from one hospital to another, but also to take their patients away from hospitals altogether.

Teaching hospitals are in trouble as they seek funding for their expensive high technologies and teaching programs. While they recognize the need to move into low-cost health care provision, there is resistance from the kinds of physicians attracted to teaching hospitals because such physicians' practices would thereby be changed or their membership would be diluted.

The need to attract private patients and provide a stream of revenue is inevitably exacerbating two-tier medicine, usually in those hospitals in a city with high proportions of indigent patients. The further development of a two-tier system seems highly

---

[13]H. S. Luft, "How Do Health Maintenance Organizations Achieve 'Savings'?" *New England Journal of Medicine* 298, no. 24 (June 15, 1978), pp. 1336–342.

[14]F. D. Wolinsky, "The Performance of Health Maintenance Organizations: An Analytic Review," *Millbank Memorial Fund Quarterly* 58, no. 4 (1980), pp. 537–80.

likely because cost containment must limit the availability of new medical technology. Will the affluent subsidize access by the poor or will tiers develop that provide needed services but vary in amenities and access to unneeded but desired services? In particular, the very old very sick, the very poor, and the discretionary do create rationing dilemmas. One solution proposed is a reduction in the number of medical students being educated and specialists being trained, and in the rate of technology development.[15]

THE PAST ENVIRONMENT—THE PHYSICIAN

Between 1965 and 1980, the capacity in American medical schools doubled, resulting in an expected increase of 23 percent in the number of active physicians between 1980 and 1990. The impact has already been felt in physicians' appointment books. Total patient visits for all physicians were down 19 percent between 1974 and 1982.[16] Family practitioners, the largest category of primary care physicians, experienced a 25 percent decline in appointments over the same period, and this trend will probably continue. In 1982, the median weekly patient visit rate dropped from 126 to 108 for all office-based physicians, because of competition from primary care outreach and freestanding emergency centers.[17] With a physician glut, more internists and family practitioners are practicing in ambulatory alternative centers, which are replacing part-timers and moonlighters with full-time physicians who are given a piece of the action. This is particularly attracting older physicians or younger doctors just starting out, because neither group wants the expense of setting up or continuing a practice, or the administrative, malpractice, and paperwork hassles.

Further pressure on the traditional fee-for-service practice is coming from medicare cutbacks and employer concerns about costs, resulting in the formation of business-sponsored health care coalitions. While third-party payment was still the source of

---

[15]Egdahl, "Physicians and the Containment of Health Care Costs."

[16]*Health Maintenance Organization Industry.*

[17]H. Eisenberg, "And Other Competition You Will Face in 1983," *Medical Economics,* January 10, 1983, pp. 239–48.

two thirds of the typical office-based practitioner's income in 1984,[18] medicare patients accounted for 17 percent of the office-based physician's income, preferred provider arrangements are discounting care, and the advisory council on social security proposes that doctors be paid according to a national fee schedule. Both medicare and medicaid are trying risk contracts with physicians, and even Blue Cross and Blue Shield are contracting directly with doctors who agree to accept reimbursement as payment in full. The overall result has been to diminish the fee-for-service market and therefore alter the traditional relationship between the patient and the physician, a relationship further affected by society's demystification of doctors and technological successes.[19]

A Lou Harris study[20] reported that physicians saw many changes in medical practice coming but few positive developments for physicians. Physicians believed that there would be a physician surplus, that increased competition would lead to changed styles and services (though not to reduced physician fees, already in fact occurring), and that physicians are paying more attention to personal and nonprofessional concerns than did their predecessors. These findings were confirmed in the 10-hospital study (see Preface) which also found that lifestyle is more important for many physicians than it used to be and that many physicians choose to join an HMO rather than go into private practice with its excessive demands. Half of all the physicians surveyed by Harris felt sufficient doubts about the future of medical practice that they would not recommend it as highly as they would have 10 years earlier. Again this is confirmed in the 10-hospital study, where one third of 100 physicians interviewed stated that they would not enter medicine again or recommend it, and a further one third would have great doubts about doing so. Many physicians are concerned about the loss of autonomy that they are experiencing, which they attribute to regulatory interference and external intervention.

---

[18]K. Hunt, "Do They Finally Have the Guns to Kill Fee for Service?" *Medical Economics,* April 2, 1984, pp. 145–60.

[19]D. E. Rogers, *American Medicine: Challenges for the 1980s* (Cambridge, Mass.: Ballinger, 1978).

[20]L. Harris, *Medical Practice in the 1980s: Physicians Look at Their Changing Profession* (Menlo Park, Calif.: Henry J. Kaiser Family Foundation, 1981).

While self-employed, office-based solo practice remains the norm, there has been a steady attrition over time as a result of a growing trend toward salaried employment and hospital and group-based practice. More women are entering medicine, with rather different values from their male counterparts. Physicians, somewhat ironically, were quite responsive to the introduction of physician assistants and nurse practitioners. Ironically, because this, too, has contributed to the weakening of the physician-patient relationship.

Many physicians have either joined or are considering joining an IPA or HMO. Younger physicians, such as residents, seem likely to be more attracted to HMOs than do physicians already in practice. This in spite of the fact that doctors also believe HMOs provide inferior doctor-patient relationships, inconvenient office locations, and patient dissatisfaction with service. While closed-panel HMOs were seen to be more cost effective and financially viable than IPAs, they were perceived to be more likely to provide a lower quality of care and of physicians. But HMOs are attractive because they provide immediate employment without the need for capital and are free of administrative burdens on the physicians, though they offer fewer incentives for individual initiative, relatively low income, and less autonomy.

With HMOs serving over 12 million enrollees, and with penetrations of upwards of 25 percent in a number of major metropolitan areas, together with the satisfaction of HMO enrollees reported above, it is not surprising that physicians, under the pressure of a professional glut and growing competition from their fellows, are finding HMOs more attractive. While perceptions of lower quality persist, in fact, studies do seem to demonstrate at least parallel quality with fee-for-service alternatives. The HMO industry has become strong and established and in a sense legitimate, for the AMA gave its imprimatur in a 1980 report on HMOs that concluded "the HMO approach appears to have the potential to provide health care of acceptable quality and lower total cost to enrollees." At least one report confirms these physician beliefs, in that there will be a continuing trend toward hospital-based physicians and alternative delivery systems, which will mean a decline in physician influence and in fee for service.[21] Fiscal constraints and greater use of prescribed

[21]A. Anderson, *Health Care in the 1990s* (HCHA: Trends and Strategies, 1984).

patient-care protocols portend less autonomy for tomorrow's physician, more frequent conflicts with hospitals, and an anticipated decline in professional satisfaction derived from practice.

The frustration of physicians implied in these projections is captured in a major article in the *Boston Globe* published in June 1985: "Feeling threatened by the national trend toward for-profit medical care and by long-term frustrations with major government and insurance health care financing programs, a group of Massachusetts doctors plans to announce today an effort to form a new labor union for physicians."[22]

The trend toward unionization is marked, and as is true of IPAs, unionization is an attempt to organize, to seek conditions of work satisfactory to physicians. But in a sense it is whistling in the dark, for what is happening to physicians can no longer be reversed. The combination of excessive "production" of physicians, together with cost pressures and competition not only among health organizations but also among physicians themselves, is producing changes in medical practice that inevitably will reduce the autonomy and the free exercise of judgment that once provided the skill and fun in medical practice. Where physicians once had only the patient's interest at heart, now they must satisfy their organization's interests also, and which shall prevail?

The drop in the median weekly patient visit rate for office-based doctors further indicates increased competition between doctors.[23] Competition is also coming from primary care outreach family practices and PPOs, as well as from freestanding emergency centers or convenience clinics.[24] With more competition, physician organizations will become smaller and not be able to maintain their cash flow, so they will be acquired or have to become multi-institutional.[25] Such competition increases because

---

[22]J. Foreman, "Doctors Announce Plan to Form Massachusetts Labor Union," *Boston Globe,* Tuesday, June 15, 1985.

[23]H. Eisenberg, "Competition You Will Face in 1983," *Medical Economics,* January 10, 1983, pp. 239–48.

[24]Friedman, "Slicing the Pie Thinner."

[25]L. Kaiser, "Competition: Past, Present, Future," *Group Practice Journal,* January–February 1984, pp. 14–19.

there are more physicians, and a maldistribution of them, as well as declining dollars, price competition, and aggregation of the patient base. Group practices may have a competitive edge because of the high involvement of physicians within them, and therefore they may provide a model for the organization of the future.[26] Group practices are closest (at least for physicians) to the traditional independent fee-for-service form of practice.

Physician autonomy is being eroded not only in individual practice, but also in terms of the doctor's influence over the rationing of medical care.[27] Doctors traditionally have made judgments as to priorities and need, but centralized budgeting procedures have limited the resources available under insurance plans in most countries. Formerly, access to health care was limited by waiting time, by limited sites, or by bureaucratic barriers. While such implicit rationing limited expenditures, it was not necessarily rational. With a shift to explicit rationing, there is also a shift from the physician's judgment determining priorities to the organization or bureaucracy determining priorities. Bureaucratic medical settings put the physician under pressure to sacrifice the interests of the patient to satisfy organizational needs.

One outspoken critic of current trends, especially of for-profits, believes that health is a basic right of citizens and a public rather than private good which therefore historically was subsidized by public funds.[28] The consumer is heavily dependent on the advice and judgment of the physician. Private health care corporations use technology that was often developed at public expense, and use and sell publicly subsidized services allocated through the decisions of physicians rather than consumers, and paid for through third-party insurance. He believes, therefore, in the possibility of abuse. For-profits are in business to increase sales. (So, today, is the hospital, because it needs revenue to expand services to remain in business.) Doctors cannot afford to

---

[26]D. Ottensmeyer, "The Prototype Physician Organization," *Group Practice Journal,* January–February 1984, pp. 10–11.

[27]D. Mechanic, "The Growth of Medical Technology and Bureaucracy: Implications for Medical Care," *Milbank Memorial Fund Quarterly* 1977, pp. 61–78.

[28]A. S. Relman, "The New Medical Industrial Complex," *New England Journal of Medicine* 103 (1980), pp. 963–70.

have any actual or potential economic conflict of interest. The public must perceive the doctor as an honest, disinterested trustee. The AMA should proscribe any kind of profit association with the health care market. This critic is especially concerned about cream skimming, the elimination of unprofitable services, the exclusion of unprofitable patients, and the elimination of educational programs. He argues that economic interest and medical judgment must remain separate for the public to have continuing confidence in the medical profession. Physicians should have no financial benefits whatsoever other than those derived from their own professional services. For-profits that view each physician as a business partner may make for good working relationships but sound the wrong note for a private market in which the hospital is the seller, the physician is the purchasing agent for the patient, and the public pays the bill.

It is true that physicians have long opposed obtaining financial gain from patient care. Indeed, this has long been a tenet of the Hospital Corporation of America's corporate values. But as the pill changed attitudes towards sexuality and virginity, so have changes in the health care environment and particularly in the nature of reimbursement, begun to change physician attitudes even in this core area. Indeed, it is only logical that if physicians should share risk, they should also share gain when it comes to the physician-organization relationship.

THE FUTURE HEALTH CARE ENVIRONMENT

The first HMO was founded in 1929, but its first half century of existence had little influence on the U.S. health care system. In 1980, only 10 million people, or 4 percent of the population, were members of the 240 extant HMO plans, and 40 percent of these belonged to the Kaiser Permanente Medical Care program.[29] The reason for that lack of popularity is oddly enough the very same reason that HMOs are now popular—they offered cost effectiveness through reduced system access to a price-sensitive population. As costs in general have skyrocketed, employers have be-

[29]Abramowitz, *Future of Health Care Delivery.* Much of this section is based on his forecasts.

come appalled at their health care benefit figure and so have passed the burden in the form of higher employee cost sharing. The cost-sensitive employers and employees have fostered HMO growth which has accelerated and is likely to exceed the most optimistic forecasts.

By 1990, 75 million people, or 30 percent of the population, will be members of HMOs, Abramowitz estimates. This contrasts with the National Industrial Council for HMO Development's lower estimate of 15 percent penetration. If PPOs are included, close to 70 percent of the population will be members of an organized health care delivery system by 1990. At least 10 HMOs will operate in each major city within two to three years, and three will operate in smaller cities. The four major hospital management companies will have at least 10 HMOs by 1986, and most of the eight major insurance carriers will have at least 5.

Many HMOs will be tempted to enter the medicare market of 28 million beneficiaries and the medicaid market of 22 million because of the attraction of risk contracts. Most HMOs will offer PPO as well as HMO products.

Proprietary multihospital systems are expected to control 90 percent of all proprietary beds and 17.4 percent of all acute care beds in the United States by 1990. Their strengths lie in their multiple locations, and their starts in geographic locations with lower costs per admission on the average, as well as where they are sole or dominant hospital. Their large cash flows attracting debt and equity capital, and their management expertise have enabled them to diversify rapidly, taking advantage of attractive opportunities. While proprietary systems, like the nonprofits, will be affected by declining hospital utilization and by the shift to HMOs and PPOs, they are in an excellent position to take advantage of these emerging trends and move defensively.

Traditionally health insurance carriers have reimbursed on a cost-plus basis without any attempt to monitor utilization or quality of services rendered because of the reverence given the physician-patient relationship. However, there is much competition in the health insurance field, for example from the nearly 400 HMOs and from the major hospital management companies which are moving rapidly into insurance. The response is the "managed care plan" which retains fee-for-service medicine but imposes mandatory preadmission certification through coordination with nurses and physician backup, or concurrent review of hospital utilization and discharge planning. Length of stay is predetermined and monitored. Hospital days have already been reduced 15 percent to 25 percent through these means and will drop further. Managed care has no influence on prices and therefore is less cost effective than HMOs, but will probably evolve into formal or informal PPOs. In addition, in the future, corporations will increase the extent to which they self-insure, and in these instances insurance carriers will merely be claims administrators.

The major insurance carriers are also moving rapidly into HMOs. Blue Cross already has 75 plans and 2.5 million members. CIGNA, Prudential, John Hancock, and Metropolitan also are active, and a joint venture established by Aetna and the Voluntary Hospitals of America (VHA) involves setting up a national network of HMOs based on the 400 member hospitals with 110,000 beds belonging to VHA.

The U.S. health care system will undergo a radical transformation to a wide array of economically based delivery systems that are truly competitive and completely deregulated. The new systems will control utilization, ensure quality, and restrain pricing. National health care expenditures will decline from 10.6 percent of GNP in 1985 to 9.1 percent in 1990 as increases in health expenditures slow from 42 percent in 1982 to 37 percent by 1990.[30] Hospitals may have priced themselves out of the market for routine care, and many of their services will move into outpatient and home settings. Hospital occupancy will decline from 75 percent in 1980 to 60 percent in 1985 to 50 percent at best by 1990, assuming that no hospitals close. As government and private insurance payers focus on cost savings, hospital reimbursement and profitability will be dramatically altered. HMOs and PPOs will probably grow much faster than suspected, and the hospital industry will contract sharply. Capacity was overbuilt in the past on the faulty assumption that 4.5 beds per thousand were needed, whereas a more accurate figure is 3.5 beds per thousand now. As a result of this overbuilding, the country is supporting a hospital system one-quarter larger than needed.

---

[30]Abramowitz, *Future of Health Care Delivery.*

A massive hospital price war is predicted, probably by 1987. As profit margins decline, even well-managed proprietary hospital companies will suffer. With gross hospital revenues per patient day now approaching $650 nationally, hospitals have effectively priced themselves out of the market. These projections are based on current trends. Length of stay has already declined for medicare patients from 9 to 7.5 days and for private-pay patients from 5.8 to 5.4 days. This is because of the introduction by the Health Care Financing Administration (HCFA) of the prospective payment system for medicaid patients, which is now believed to be likely to become global. Abramowitz is perhaps unduly sanguine about the likely effect of HCFA's risk contracts as it has been the experience of providers that rates tend to be ratcheted down by risk contracts, and what may seem attractive now is going to be a burden in the future.

Insurance companies will learn rapidly how to control system utilization and provider pricing, and employees will increasingly share the cost of health insurance with employers, increasing employees' cost sensitivity, these factors together providing additional pressures to reduce hospital utilization.

HMOs, while growing themselves, will evolve into hybrids involving individual practice associations that meet consumer demands for convenient access and reduce capital needs. The existing multihospital systems, while continuing to grow, will diversify into total health care systems. The Hospital Corporation of America, for example, already owns 18 percent of Beverly Enterprises, the leading nursing home chain with 700 facilities and revenues of $1.5 billion. Health care delivery will no longer be the province of traditional providers as corporations will self-insure, and insurance carriers diversify into health care delivery. The 3,400 nonprofit community hospitals are poorly positioned for the future, and their continued existence is in doubt. The voluntary nonprofit has survived in the past through medicare cost reimbursement, private insurance charge reimbursement, state price controls, philanthropy, and low-cost, tax-exempt bond financing. But medicare is converting to fixed-rate DRGs (Diagnosis Related Grouping), insurance carriers are demanding discounts, state rate review is dying, philanthropy is disappearing, and tax-exempt bonds are coming under increased scrutiny. Teaching and indigent care will no longer be cross-subsidized by private buyers or supported through cost reimbursement or philanthropy.

Perhaps 10 percent of the hospitals in the United States will go bankrupt by 1990. Those companies that can create and market a high-quality, cost-effective, competitively priced health care delivery system will benefit. Such a system will be highly vertically integrated, with self-operated clinics and hospitals that will be close to 100 percent utilized and will encourage higher physician productivity and effectively service the majority of patients. The majority of present health care providers will face very significant problems. The average freestanding for-profit or not-for-profit community hospital in even a modestly competitive area will be squeezed by HMOs and PPOs and have little access to capital within two to three years. In other words, while it has been true for some time that the smaller community hospital in a competitive setting could not survive except by joining a multihospital system or by altering its product from acute care, it will also become true that hospitals in what seem to be noncompetitive situations will increasingly feel the effects of competition from ambulatory health care alternatives that may be started by entrepreneurs or by physicians themselves.

Successful competitors must be structured to diversify, for competition will be "the name of the game."[31] However, physicians' recommendations will still influence patients' choice of institution, and private-pay patients will remain a significant proportion of the marketplace, so physicians will still be enormously important. Physicians will be selected by patients more often on the basis of where the physician has admitting privileges and the cost and quality of the institution's services. It becomes important, therefore, for hospitals and their medical staffs to work together to build a reputation that enhances their position in this competitive marketplace. Hospitals must foster financial partnerships with physicians and ensure doctors' cooperation if they are to make needed strategic changes and control operating factors such as cost and productivity.

In conclusion, health organizations are facing major change. The nature of the tasks that they have to perform to survive, to be viable, to be successful competitively has changed and will

---

[31] Anderson, *Health Care in the 1990s.*

continue to change. Successful performance of these tasks necessitates an altered relationship with physicians in which physicians must be managed successfully. At the same time, the pressures on physicians mean that physician sensitivity will be enhanced to a point where inadvertent actions on the part of hospitals are likely to be misinterpreted. So such management must go hand in hand with extraordinary sensitivity to the vulnerability and concerns of physicians.

CHAPTER TWO

What Must Be Managed? Strategic and Organizational Imperatives

I find the medicine worse than the malady.

John Fletcher

STRATEGIC IMPERATIVES

If health organizations and physicians had the same interests and wanted the same things, there would be no need to manage physicians. It is only when physicians incline to behaviors that differ from those organizations require or desire that management becomes necessary. What is it, then, that health organizations want or need, and where might differences in interest arise such that management is required?

Health organizations, in general terms, must either reduce costs or enhance revenues to be competitive, but as each choice may have but short-run efficacy, both are probably required for success. Hospitals that do both are more likely to have a lower cost per admission, greater earnings, higher quality of care, and less cost shifting among payers and other groups.[1] These goals require new and different strategies from those exercised in the past, and substantial changes in physical practice patterns and behavior.

What kinds of strategic changes are required to achieve these ends? Possible generic strategies lie in the areas of cost leadership, differentiation, and focus.[2] In health care delivery what this means is that a health organization must become the low-cost provider in a given area to obtain competitive leadership. Or it must develop a series of services that are significantly

[1] P. Campbell, "Hospital-Physician Relations in a New Era—An Exploratory Study" (Boston: mimeo, 1985).

[2] M. E. Porter, *Competitive Advantage* (New York: Free Press, 1985).

different from those of its competitors, or are perceived to be so, if the organization is to maintain or enhance its competitive position. The focus strategy means that a health organization can choose to limit what it does and specialize in a particular area rather than provide services across the board. This is indeed the strategy of choice of many smaller hospitals that are unable to compete with larger ones because they have insufficient size and scale to become cost leaders and insufficient resources to provide differentiated services across the board.

Each of these strategic choices carries implications for the physicians associated with the health organization. To become cost leaders in today's reimbursement environment means inevitably expanding into ambulatory care aggressively as well as paying particular attention to internal operating costs. Ambulatory services must be offered at hours and in places convenient to the marketplace, not to the professional.

Expansion requires capital and the building of new facilities or their acquisition through merger or joint venture. The exercise of a differentiated strategy, not necessarily mutually exclusive with cost leadership, involves the development of distinctive services. Many teaching hospitals have specialized expertise in a number of technical areas that lend themselves to this strategy. Moreover, as quality becomes an ever more important issue not only in the avoidance of litigation, but also in the marketing of health care, a differentiated strategy may involve the provision of lower-cost services within a particular quality market segment.

Henry Ford Hospital in Detroit is implementing a lower-cost, high-quality strategy in its market area through aggressive expansion into very comprehensive, high quality, large ambulatory facilities. In addition, it is pursuing its traditional focus strategy in the provision of high-technology care. As hospitals move toward low-cost ambulatory systems, they have to recruit physicians with quite different practice patterns and practice styles from those they have traditionally engaged. Moreover, existing physicians must change their patterns or be isolated from the emerging low-cost system. What this suggests is the need to move toward a dual organizational model in which the low-cost system is separated organizationally and financially from the high-technology system, with each selling its services to a distinct and separate market segment. If this organizational change is not made, neither strategy will be successfully pursued for it will prove impossible to lower costs in the low-cost system, or to keep physicians motivated within it, while the pressures for low-cost care will begin to destroy the high-technology system.

The successful health organization will be the one that can create and market a high-quality, cost-effective, competitively priced delivery system.[3] The system of the future will be highly vertically integrated, with self-operated clinics and hospitals that will be close to 100 percent utilized as contrasted with the 50 to 60 percent occupancy characteristic of hospitals today. The system will encourage higher physician productivity and will effectively service the majority of patients. Incremental demand will be met through contractual arrangements with nonsystem parties for a 20 to 30 percent markup per patient payment.

Most present health care providers will face very significant problems. The average freestanding community hospital, whether for profit or not for profit, in even a modestly competitive area, will be squeezed by HMOs and PPOs and have little access to capital within the next three years. The small community general hospital will probably become defunct as an isolated entity. Small multihospital systems in areas with little geographic concentration or insurance capability will be only slightly better off. The average physician will suffer a 10 to 30 percent decline in compensation, while the marginal or low-quality physician will be forced out of practice. Small hospitals, small insurance carriers, and small local HMOs will no longer be able to survive. The inefficient fee-for-service system is said to be dead[4] and will be succeeded by a far more cost-effective competitive system. Recruitment, retention, and management of physicians are key marketing issues for hospital managers. Hospital strategies will include aggressive competition for doctors, diversifying into a broader mix of services, and developing captive distribution systems to control patient flow and promote institutional services.[5]

---

[3] K. S. Abramowitz, *The Future of Health Care Delivery in America: Strategic Analysis/Financial Forecast* (Bernstein Research, 1985).

[4] Ibid.

[5] J. C. Goldsmith, *Can Hospitals Survive? The New Competitive Health Market.* (Homewood, Ill.: Dow Jones-Irwin, 1981).

The number one management concern over the next 10 years will be the continued financial viability of health care delivery organizations. Access to and availability of capital and decreasing inpatient census are major concerns, as are competition and the changing nature and stringency of reimbursement/payment systems. Therefore, strategic planning and analysis become critical in establishing organizational missions and goals, in evaluating markets and competitive positions, and in making decisions about the appropriate mix of products and services to be offered.[6]

A strategic plan must establish the future direction of the institution by specifying objectives and time tables needed to realize organizational goals. Strategic planning must become integral to management, and plans must be assessed continually. Successful competitors must be structured to form joint ventures to reach new markets, share risks, obtain capital, and diversify revenue sources, and to do so quickly when the opportunities arise. New ventures must be organized in manageable, accountable segments. Financial performance of individual segments must be measured within the operation and across the operation. Needs and risks must be evaluated, and the proper legal and corporate organizational structure adopted. Calculated risks are required for success in the new competitive environment. Some form of networking will become desirable, if not essential, whether taking the form of contract management and direct leasing, or affiliation, actual merger, or acquisition. The need for new structures is dictated by the fact that successful systems will provide a range of services that are geographically and organizationally decentralized, and that involve hospitals as well as ambulatory alternatives. Such systems will not only require new corporate and organizational structures, but also new kinds of relationships between managers and physicians. The future belongs to such networks of organizations.[7]

One result is that services obtained will be governed by the individual's ability to pay, in other words, multiple tiers of service will develop. Providers should monitor and anticipate

---

[6]A. Anderson, *Health Care in the 1990s* (HCHA: Trends and Strategies, 1984).

[7]L. R. Kaiser, "Competition, Past, Present, Future," *Group Practice Journal*, January-February 1984, pp. 14-20.

changes in their patient mix. Hospitals must reexamine their missions and determine how they will finance increased charity care. New ventures must be explored that will subsidize needed but unprofitable community services. Pluralistic solutions for care of the indigent uninsured must be sought.

An example is Northern General, a large urban hospital that traditionally provides much of the needed care within the city for the indigent and is affiliated with a local medical school. The Northern General system already contains within it a variety of ambulatory alternatives such as nursing homes and freestanding clinics, but is struggling with two key issues: how to develop structures that will adequately link these services in a real system, and how to bring about a change in the attitude of physicians working within the system, used as they are to traditional medical school criteria for performance and promotion. Academically oriented, high-technology physicians concerned with research and teaching find it difficult to adapt to the developing low-cost approaches now espoused. And as management seeks remunerative market segments, physicians with traditional attitudes toward charity cases worry about whether the indigent will continue to be cared for as they were in the past. This is resulting in physicians seeking a new kind of relationship with management in which doctors participate more in the overall direction of the system as well as in the specifics of new organizational efforts. However, doctors both want more of a voice and resent the time that this increased voice will take away from their practices.

The need to enhance revenues requires diversification, whether through expansion of health care services such as the acquisition of ambulatory facilities, or of non–health care services such as investments in revenue-producing ventures. Diversification inevitably means a dilution of the original institution's mission and purpose. It means a dilution of managerial and professional effort over the larger scale implied in diversification.

In many institutions, the majority of physicians have played a small role, if any, in the determination and implementation of strategic direction, given that few hospitals made major alterations in strategic direction up to the last decade. With the strategic choices now facing health organizations, and their enormous implications for the institution's future and its relationship to physicians, seeking the advice and support of physicians is critical if such strategic initiatives are to be successfully carried out. Physicians still retain enough power to slow down, if not snuff out, strategic redirection. It is also becoming important for physicians to be educated concerning the nuances of the environment to which the organization's board and top management are responding, that is, for physicians to achieve some strategic grasp. If they do not understand the environment or alternative strategies, how can doctors understand, let alone support, strategic redirection and actions that may appear inimical to their private practice?

ORGANIZATIONAL IMPERATIVES

Organizational imperatives are those internal tasks that hospitals must manage to survive and to be successful competitively. These include the management of cost, productivity, quality (both human and technical), patient mix, and volume, so that costs can be minimized and revenues maximized. In an era of dropping occupancy, the health organization has to be particularly concerned with keeping its loyal physicians and attracting new ones. Moreover, it is not enough to concentrate on volume, for patient mix and the share of physician practice are as important. It is much more possible to influence physicians who give an institution a high share of their practice, than those giving a low share. Indeed, health organizations might well find it valuable to start to pay attention to designing the practice profiles of their physicians, by means such as selective recruitment practices and selective incentives, rather than taking these practices for granted.

Managing loyalty and devotion therefore becomes crucial, and is the topic of Chapter 5. In addition to getting and keeping doctors, influencing what they do while they are in the institution is equally important, and this is the subject of Chapter 6. Conflicts are important, for these often involve matters of particular concern to physicians, or reflect their relationships with others in the organization, and can affect the organization's performance indirectly if not directly. Such conflicts tend to arise over issues of physician control and power over their own work conditions or those of others, practice style, and physician autonomy. The basic issue is whether the physician is vested to choose in the interests of the patient, or in the interests of the organization, and how these interests may be reconciled when divergent.

While the DRG system may not endure, some such form of reimbursement will no doubt prevail. Cost shifting as a response to reducing profitability will no longer work, and thus, cost pressures on the health organization will increase. Health delivery organizations must therefore determine and understand their underlying cost structures. Cost accounting must be given high priority, and systems created to accumulate cost data. Identification and understanding of costs is the key to pricing and expansion decisions. Determining incremental or marginal costs is essential for decision making. Actual costs must be monitored against established standards, and cost benefit studies must be conducted.[8]

Services will have to be assessed for their overall profitability, and some must be eliminated or altered. Inevitably, health organizations and their medical staffs will be pitted against one another in some of these arrangements, and so organization and physician must collaborate to find innovative ways of treating patients within prescribed financial limits. Standards must be established and closely monitored to ensure the quality of patient care. Because physicians continue to be the most influential factor in the patient's choice of hospital (as discussed above), it will be crucial for organizations to work with their physicians as these organizations face competitive and marketing challenges.

Freestanding outpatient centers will compete successfully with hospitals. Therefore, health organizations must analyze markets, customers, and competitors as well as their own competitive strengths and weaknesses to develop and deliver competitive services and products, and design appropriate corporate structures that integrate the full range of services to be offered. Providers must segment markets and introduce product-line management into their delivery systems, developing those services that they can deliver most cost effectively and profitably.

---

[8]Anderson, *Health Care in the 1990s.*

They must develop adequate referral sources to attract patients into their system through such strategies as affiliations with HMOs or PPOs, partnerships, joint ventures, or wholly owned ambulatory systems. Marketing programs must, however, be sensitive to the potential for negative reaction from the patient and the physician. Pricing will be critical to success. Systems will essentially have two types of patients—those who enter as a result of a contract with a PPO or HMO and those who are free to choose a facility each time they require treatment. Each health organization must determine how to position itself in the competitive market, as consumers will have incentives to purchase care through a variety of new arrangements.

Productivity will become crucial and should be based on standards, incentives, and disincentives, which will have to be established for employee (including physician) performance on an individual and departmental basis. Productivity measures should include effective scheduling of use of ancillary departments to ease employment during peak volume periods. While in the short run, productivity may take the form of increased efficiency, in the long run, physician practice patterns will become important and have to be managed.

Competition will not only be on the basis of cost but also of quality, and health organizations must define acceptable levels of quality and services and implement adequate monitoring systems. Health organizations and their physicians will have to develop more specialized patient care protocols and educate both doctors and support personnel concerning these protocols. These trends may well present moral and ethical dilemmas which, though debated at a national level, will manifest themselves in concrete form in the particular health delivery organization. Each organization must therefore develop mechanisms for anticipating and dealing with these situations as they arise, and the design of incentives must not only foster productivity and efficiency, but also deal with the ethical implications of these managerial concerns.

The physician surplus will affect health organizations in terms of recruitment, cost of care, and quality of service. Organizations will more often employ physicians directly, and so compensation arrangements that are competitive must be negotiated. Compensation packages must be attractive and varied and should include nonpecuniary benefits. Physicians want to work with qualified colleagues; opportunities for continuing education and expanding skills must also be forthcoming. As incomes decrease, physicians may become (indeed are becoming) more interested in financial partnerships, which must be fostered to ensure physician cooperation in maintaining institutional solvency. Those physicians with an interest in and concern for the business of medicine should aggressively be recruited and involved in the institution's management. Health organizations and their staffs must collaborate with doctors on the criteria to be used in the recruitment and/or limiting of physicians, and policies should be developed to guide the allocation of limited resources to patients on the basis of diagnosis, prognosis, or other measurable indicators.

THE HOSPITAL AND THE PHYSICIAN

The preceding discussion dealt with the many strategic and organizational issues facing health delivery organizations. One proposed major strategy for hospitals is to integrate forward into ambulatory care,[9] but in so doing they may directly compete with their own medical staffs' practices which themselves are under increasing competitive pressure. Indeed, many teaching hospital primary-care practices often started with subsidies such as from the Johnson Foundation, have found that as these subsidies disappear, they have had to shift from a focus on the indigent to the private-pay patient to maintain revenues. Neighborhood health centers have experienced a similar phenomenon. This brings them into direct competition with the attending physician referring to the hospital and presents the center with a nearly insoluble competitive dilemma.

Thus the fear, spoken or unspoken, of many physicians, including those working in the for-profit hospital chains such as the Health Corporation of America, that the hospital will choose to recruit full-time physicians to improve its competitive ability. However, hospital-based outpatient medical practices are often high cost, indeed, more costly than private physician practices,

---

[9]Goldsmith, *Can Hospitals Survive?*

which are more likely to substitute technicians for ancillary physicians. This form of competition may diminish if the hospital's objectives can be achieved through a cooperative approach, for the hospital has enormous technical and organizational advantages over even the largest group practice in evaluating and initiating new ventures in primary care. Hospitals should consider making these technical and financial resources available on a joint venture basis to selected members of their medical staffs, allowing the staff to further their professional practices or develop new forms of health care delivery. In other words, hospitals should go into the business of working with physicians in developing ambulatory alternatives.[10]

The Health Corporation of America, for example, provides subsidies for medical office buildings and marketing support for its physicians. So does the Samaritan Hospital Group, which also provides specific marketing studies on request. This is an example of hospitals beginning to study and understand the physician's "value chain."[11] (See Chapter 5.) If a hospital can make it possible for the physician's private practice to function more efficiently or more economically, then the hospital is entering the physician's value chain, and the physician is more likely therefore to develop and maintain loyalty to the hospital. Formal contracts may jeopardize a hospital's tax-exempt status. However, if assistance is offered which, if withdrawn, poses some economic risks to the physician, then possible legal problems may be overcome. But if physicians use hospital resources and admit their patients elsewhere, administrators are justified in refusing to continue the physician's association.

Hospitals have a compelling economic interest in the health and welfare of their physicians. Doctors' practices are the primary feeder system for the hospital, and the success that physicians have in penetrating and holding a share of the marketplace will have a direct bearing on the utilization of the hospital. It has been asserted that hospitals do not need to own or operate their own feeder systems because they can achieve the same result through joint ventures.[12] This assertion, however, is now ques-

---

[10]Ibid.

[11]Porter, *Competitive Advantage.*

[12]Goldsmith, *Can Hospitals Survive?*

tionable, as the prospective payment system makes it difficult to operate hospitals efficiently, and thus to make sufficient excess over revenues to support new ventures.[13] It is more likely, therefore, that hospitals will have to move toward wholly owned ambulatory systems, even though these may not be hospital based. This is what Ford is doing, recognizing that patients will be spending more of their time in ambulatory settings and that more revenues for diagnosis and care will therefore accrue in those ambulatory settings. Rather than making arrangements with HMOs and PPOs (key feeder systems), hospitals will have to run HMOs and PPOs, whether the hospital starts the programs or acquires them.

THE HMO AND THE DOCTOR

The window of opportunity for the traditional HMO is rapidly closing. Born of governmental and employer impatience with rapidly escalating health costs, HMOs offered one real and one theoretical competitive advantage. They are cheaper than hospital-based systems largely because they reduce hospitalization days. They purport to be more effective, because of their emphasis on prevention, but this has never been proved. In fact, prepaid systems such as DRGs reduce hospital days, and therefore, the HMO competitive margin is deceasing. As hybrid forms develop and alternatives such as PPOs proliferate, the pressure is on HMOs to prove that they can be cost effective and produce quality care even as they are squeezed by rising salaries and competitive pressures to hold premiums down. Moreover HMOs have largely penetrated the easy areas, whether major urban markets or amenable employers. As they extend, they have to move to low-density areas where the economics of the HMO are marginal at best, and work with employers who are more skeptical of their benefits.

Employers, chief executives more than their benefits officers, tend to be cautious about the value of HMOs, especially in underserved areas.[14] While smaller employers worry about the

---

[13]Abramowitz, *Future of Health Care Delivery.*

[14]L. Harris, *Employers and HMOs: A Nationwide Survey of Corporate Employers in Areas Served by Health Maintenance Organizations* (Menlo Park, Calif.: Henry J. Kaiser Foundation, 1980).

perceived burden of cost administration and prepaid benefits, larger employers worry about the quality of care delivered by HMOs, especially the quality of the physicians and the hospitals used, as well as about employee satisfaction. IPAs are seen as higher quality than HMOs. HMOs are perceived as inferior to fee for service as regards convenience and location of physician offices and hospitals, quality of physicians, and employee satisfaction, though employers recognize that traditional HMOs are effective as cost containment.

While 57 percent of members are satisfied with HMOs, and only 3 percent talk about not renewing, members level substantial criticisms at HMOs. Members are concerned about the perceived quality of doctors, impersonal service, and the time it takes to get an appointment.[15] In other words, they are concerned about the human aspects of quality. After geographic mobility, these quality issues are most often given as the reasons for leaving an HMO. Those who are not members of HMOs worry about being free to choose their doctor or hospital, and also about the quality of HMO doctors.

In addition, while HMOs stress their advantages in providing coverage 24 hours a day, seven days a week, and in providing preventive care and a one-stop shop for all care, in practice these attributes are not always available. Not all HMO centers are open all the time. Many have sketchy preventive services. Appointments to see specialists may take weeks.

Critical to the future of HMOs is the development of effective relationships with employers, not only with regard to marketing, but also follow-through. Physicians could also be involved more extensively than is customarily the practice because communication between marketing and physicians is often inadequate. Marketers tend to exaggerate benefits, leaving the physician to be the "bad guy" who must deny them to the angry member. Marketers, too, tend to gloss over inadequacies that turn patients off.

The selection, training, and quality of physicians, whether recruited as employees of HMOs or contracted with IPAs, is important. IPAs in particular must learn to identify favorable practice patterns of individual doctors or physician groups so that

---

[15]L. Harris, *American Attitudes Toward Health Maintenance Organizations* (Menlo Park, Calif.: Henry J. Kaiser Foundation, 1980).

they may selectively contract with those doctors willing to provide high-quality, cost-effective medicine. Moreover, IPAs must develop practice profiles so that they can recruit and retain doctors and give these physicians a high share of the IPA's practice, because if only 3 percent of a physician's patients belong to an IPA, he or she is not going to be amenable to cost- or quality-control measures.

While it is true that the physician glut is making it more likely that physicians will find HMOs attractive, the future growth of most HMOs is likely to be in smaller urban or rural settings where recruitment of physicians is by no means easy.[16] Many HMOs are beginning to find that their ability to recruit an adequate flow of high-quality doctors limits their expansion. HMOs must design and manage arrangements and incentives, whether at the organizational, physician, or patient level, that will produce cost-effective quality care of a competitive nature, i.e., one that will enable them to compete on price. This is not as easy as it might sound, for it involves understanding what quality attributes are desired by actual or potential members, as well as dealing with such technical aspects of quality as appropriate hospitalization levels. Hospitalization rates are already dropping and occasionally producing a revolving-door phenomenon that is potentially harmful to patients.

HMOs must learn to understand and manage growth, especially from a small base. Growth is essential for HMOs, for, as is true of hospitals, they require relatively large numbers of members to provide revenues that will enable them to offer the variety of services required to remain competitive. As is the case with the smaller hospital, the smaller HMO will probably cease to exist, and only major chains will endure in tomorrow's competitive environment. Yet growth, especially from a small base, stretches staff capacities because HMOs cannot afford to overstaff during growth phases. Not only does this produce recurring stress on lay and professional staff, but conflicts in values regarding growth may also develop between managers and professionals. Doctors and nurses value stability because it enhances the capability to provide quality care. Growth reduces this capability and therefore the opportunity for professional satisfaction

---

[16]F. D. Wolinsky, "The Performance of Health Maintenance Organizations: An Analytic Review," *NMFQ* 58, no. 4, pp. 537–80.

in their work. "Midwest" is a case in point. An aggressively growing, successful HMO, "Midwest" recognized the need to provide additional centers in the metropolitan marketplace in which it competed, as well as to extend the range and nature of its services, especially in the provision of out-of-hours care. Yet the result of this managerial aggressiveness was that physicians felt less and less in control of the medicine that they practiced, and questioned the strategy of senior management which they understood little and liked less.

In part these value discontinuities come from a failure of HMO top management to adequately involve their physicians at the board or strategic decision-making levels. Few HMOs have more than a nominal number of physicians on their boards. The problem is compounded by the fact that as HMOs grow, they do so by adding centers, rather by enlarging existing centers. Therefore, physicians do not form collegial relationships. This leads to a further managerial imperative: HMOs must discover how to effectively manage a geographically decentralized system of physicians.

The final challenge for HMOs is how to involve physicians as health maintenance organizations convert to for-profit status to obtain capital. Physicians, having entered an HMO because they felt it would free them from the pressures of private practice, resent the pressures to increase productivity and particularly resent the benefits that accrue to top management from for-profit conversion if the physicians do not share in the benefits.[17]

HMOs and IPAs that fail to control costs have but one option, raising the premium to deal with their excess costs. They may find themselves pricing themselves out of the market. Health Watch, an IPA in Rochester, New York, failed after four years of operation for this reason. The plan failed because it was indiscriminately promoted to high-use patients, as well as because it lacked utilization review and risk sharing with physicians. Thus, HMOs, as well as for-profits, face the delicate ethical dilemma that they can make more money if they selectively market to employers with favorable employee profiles—the young or healthy—such as may be found in the high-technology industries.

---

[17] L. Harris, *Medical Practice in the 1980s: Physicians Look at Their Changing Profession* (Menlo Park, Calif.: Henry J. Kaiser Family Foundation, 1981).

CHAPTER THREE

What Can Be Managed? The Changing Relationship between Physician, Patient, and Organization

God and the Doctor we alike adore
But only when in danger, not before;
The danger o'er, both are alike requited,
God is forgotten, and the Doctor slighted.

John Owen

PHYSICIAN AND ORGANIZATION

Until 1912, a random patient with a random illness consulting a random physician did not have a better than 50-50 chance of benefiting from the encounter. The physician's usual role, even until relatively recently, was to diagnose, reduce suffering, advise, and comfort. Where the physician could do little, he had much authority. Thus, it is ironic and almost paradoxical that as the efficacy of medical treatment has improved, the area left for physician judgment, individually or collectively, has narrowed. Where once a physician's judgment about what could be done, what should be done, what it would cost (or regardless of cost), and what could and should not be done was paramount, now it is as often the regulator, the hospital, or the law that makes such judgments. Clinical judgment is being replaced by managerial judgment, as the nature of the relationship of the physician to the patient, and to the organization shifts and the balance changes.[1] In part, this shift comes about from a changing definition of health, in which health care has become a right rather

[1]D. Crane, *The Sanctity of Social Life: Physicians' Treatment of Critically Ill Patients* (New York: Russell Sage Foundation, 1975).

than a privilege and is therefore to be protected by society rather than granted by the physician.[2] It is also paradoxical that as many behaviors have become medicalized, in other words, diagnosed as sickness rather than criminal behavior, and thus fall within the jurisdiction of medicine, the physician's authority has dissolved. The shift away from physician authority is a function of the emerging efficacy of technology, and the phenomenon of growing but critical public expectations, as well as the development of ever more powerful and large medical bureaucracies.[3]

During this transitional period, at least, there will be a number of conflicts among physicians as to what they regard as good medicine and what the patient and organization demand. Peer review cannot deal with these problems, for they are genuine conflicts of interests and values. Medical confidentiality also becomes a problem in bureaucratic organizations because nonphysicians do not share physician values about confidentiality.

The erosion of the physician-patient relationship has been a matter of much speculation.[4] It appears to be a worldwide phenomenon, resulting from multiple changes that some sociologists call proletarianization.[5] There has been a shift from essentially white physicians with training dictated by the AMA and controlling their own work, "owning" their own patients, equipment, and physical plant, and determining hours worked toward nonphysician "ownership." More physicians are minorities and women, the government and other interests affect the scope of the curriculum, work is segmented and directed by organization administrators, patients are clients or members of an organization, technology is owned by the organization and operated by nonphysicians, the plant itself is owned by people other than the physician, and hours of work are directed by the organization.

Some suggest that the physician will become a historical anachronism, for the six major tasks performed by doctors, i.e.,

---

[2]R. Fox, "The Medicalization and Demedicalization of American Society," *Daedaulus*, Winter 1977, pp. 9–22.

[3]D. Mechanic, *The Growth of Bureaucratic Medicine* (New York: John Wiley & Sons, 1976).

[4]E. B. Gallagher, ed. *The Doctor-Patient Relationship in the Changing Health Scene* (Washington, D.C.: United States Department of Health, Education, and Welfare, 1976).

[5]J. B. McKinley and J. Arches, "Towards the Proletarianization of Physicians," *International Journal of Health Services* 15, no. 2 (1985), pp. 161–95.

the medical history, the physical exam, ordering ancillaries, diagnostic formulation, treatment determination, and prognosis are all done by machine, supposedly more efficiently and reliably.[6] Others propose that the advent of the computer is as important as the invention of the printing press in the Middle Ages, as it has helped displace the physician monopoly over technical and strategic knowledge, which no longer exists.[7] The emergence of physician unions (Chapter 4) is a symptom of this so-called deprofessionalization which occurs (as in industry) when autonomy, spontaneity, freedom to perform, and identification with the object of labor are no longer vested in the activity of a single individual and there is no longer any dignity to be derived from the act of working itself.

One prerogative of a profession, in addition to individual judgment, is the exercise of collective discipline.[8] Indeed, it is not perhaps going too far to suggest that a profession can only exist if its members are willing to exercise some degree of control over each other, whether at the national or organizational level. A widely publicized relative failure to do this, both at the national and local levels, has additionally affected the physician's long-asserted freedoms. As national and state medical societies failed to regulate gross misbehaviors, the law has had to take over.

One young physician in rural practice wryly commented that he and his colleagues expected, regardless of the quality of their practice, to be sued once every five years. From start to finish, he estimated the average duration of a lawsuit at two years. Therefore, he concluded, he and his colleagues could expect to be under indictment for some 40 percent of their professional careers, more, he pointed out, than the most habitual criminal. This is not simply because of the litigiousness of the American consumer or of the aggressiveness of the American lawyer; it is at least in part due to a failure of physicians' self-control.

---

[6] J. S. Maxmen, "Goodby Dr. Welby," *Social Policy* 3 (1972), pp. 97–106.

[7] M. R. Haug, "The Deprofessionalization of Everyone," *Sociological Focus* 8, no. 3 (August 1975), pp. 197–213.

[8] W. J. Reader, *Professional Men: The Lives of the Professional Classes in Nineteenth Century England* (New York: Basic Books, 1966).

At the hospital level, it is widely acknowledged that peer review will work for the gross case, but not for the small deviation. Even in relatively gross cases, it is difficult for physicians who rely on each other for referrals and live in the same small community to make critical judgments of each other, especially as they may be sued if they cannot prove their assertions. Here is a place indeed for managers to exercise an important influence; if a health organization really cares about the quality of medical practice within its doors, management should be willing to back any physician in court who will take it upon him- or herself to exercise proper peer review functions.

Physicians believe that they themselves are conscientious and are unwilling to have anyone else—administrators or other physicians—tell them when they are not.[9] Doctors make a distinction between "normal mistakes" and "deviant mistakes," and one is not ashamed of the former. The latter is a matter for peer review and correction. However, the nature of the context in which error is acceptable is shifting. Indeed once a "normal mistake" or error was considered inevitable, a result of the exercise of judgment which, not being infallible, could occasionally be incorrect. (An analogy is that the craftsman, in fashioning a handmade chair, would make small errors that contributed to the uniqueness of the ultimate product.) This has, in today's environment and context, become unacceptable. Distinctions between the inevitable errors that accrue from the exercise of judgment and malfeasance (bad or irresponsible medicine) no longer seem to be made in courts of law. Physicians are as liable for the one as for the other.

Thus, medical judgment is displaced by defensive medicine, which pushes up costs. One young general practitioner bitterly noted that when somebody walked into his office with a stomachache, in the past he would give the patient medicine and if it did not work in two weeks, try something else. After a while, if that did not work, he might do some tests. Almost invariably that was good and efficacious medicine. Now, because one in a thousand cases could turn out be be cancer, he runs a $2,000 bat-

---

[9]E. Freidson, *Doctoring Together: A Study of Professional Social Control* (New York: Elsevier, 1975).

tery of tests straight away for every patient. The physician does this because if he made a delayed diagnosis, however justifiable, he would be held responsible. The fun is going out of medicine, and there is little room for the exercise of judgment.

Physicians are not particularly good at evaluating and controlling each other. They are reluctant in part because they feel they have insufficient information to do so. Anyway, they prefer to motivate rather than discipline. As much protective as regulating, the collegium (the physician collectivity) is largely a neutral force in the social control of members' performance. Because performance not only includes the exercise of clinical judgments, but also the completion of records, attendance in an office, etc., it is clear that if such behaviors are to be controlled, managers cannot altogether rely on either the individual physician or the physician collectively.

Yet it is interesting that because medicine is a "dominant profession,"[10] it expects not only authority over its own work but also over that of other professions subordinate to it. Because of this professional autonomy and professional dominance, marketing came late to medicine; marketing assumes that one's point and purpose is to solve the problems of others as defined by those others. In medicine, the customer is only right when the doctor tells him that he is.[11]

Physicians could not be managed because of the damage such an arrangement was believed likely to cause to medical self-respect, dignity, and clinical autonomy. It was believed that physicians should not be subordinated to a manager within a structured management system. Clinical autonomy is defined as involving four components[12]: independent practice, i.e., the use of judgment without the scrutiny of a manager; the right of the client or patient to choose the practitioner and of the practitioner to refuse to treat the client; prime responsibility for patient care; and the profession with primacy. In fact, medicine in Great

[10]E. Freidson, *Professional Dominance: The Social Structure of Medical Care* (New York: Atherton Press, 1970).

[11]M. L. Johnson, "Patients: Receivers or Participants?" in *Conflicts in the National Health Service*, ed. Barnard and Lee (New York: Prodist, 1977), pp. 72–98.

[12]H. Tolliday, "Clinical Autonomy," in *Health Services: Their Nature and Organization, and the Role of Patients, Doctors, Nurses and the Complimentary Professions*, ed. E. Jaques (London: Heinemann, 1978), pp. 32–52.

Britain, as in the United States, has recently come more under managerial scrutiny because of emerging strategic and organizational imperatives, which raises questions about the traditional hands-off approach. Moreover the sacred cow of mutual choice of practitioner and patient may shortly be slaughtered, for there is legislation on the books (in Massachusetts) requiring physicians to accept medicaid patients or lose their licenses. This legislation was prompted by rejection of such patients by medical practitioners who felt they could only treat medicaid patients at less than cost.

Given that many shibboleths once cherished by the physician are now under pressure if not attack, what should not fall under managerial scrutiny? What should not be managed?

Views on this will differ to some degree by the nature of the setting. Physicians and managers in an HMO would give a different answer from those in a hospital. In general, managers still seem willing to leave to physicians' discretion such matters as the kind of patient they admit, the nature of the treatment given to those patients, and recruitment, although managers do have a very great interest in patient mix, in the cost of treatment, in quality, and in the implications of recruitment. While these areas do come under managerial scrutiny, physicians and managers agree (see the 10-hospital study) that it is only where physicians fail that managers should move in and then only to stimulate the physicians, or their organization, to perform properly. In view of the continuing high value physicians place on their autonomy, independence, and self-respect, this would seem appropriate, providing of course, that physicians do take care of these issues themselves, and that there is recourse to management in the event of failure. It therefore becomes incumbent on managers to find ways of effectively influencing physicians and their organizations to do their jobs properly.

However, even this conclusion may be erroneous. It is essentially based on the beliefs of physicians and managers in settings where the relationship of the physician to the organization is one of consultant, i.e., where the physician works with but is not in some important sense directly subject to the management hierarchy. When hospitals were extensions of the physician's office, interests were convergent and the relationship of the physician to the hospital was one of independent cooperation. For the physician, as a consultant, it was convenient to bring patients into the hospital; for the hospital, it was a simple matter to humor the physician. But the environmental pressures noted (Chapter 1) have produced divergence of interest and have revealed inherent strains. Interdependence remains, however, enhancing conflict.

The inherent strains between organizations and physicians include the fact that organizations need predictability to achieve goals, but professionals need freedom to operate in uncertainty. Organizations need goals for survival and effectiveness, but professionals' goals center on treatment of the individual patient. Organizations require coordination and integration of costs, tasks, services, and departments, but professionals need freedom to function within specialized interest areas and loose coordination. Organizations need control and feedback for public accountability, but professionals need individual accountability to patients and peers.[13,14]

Ironically, it is because physicians have been moving closer to health organizations, rather than practicing at arm's length as in the traditional fee-for-service relationship, that such strains are revealed. At the same time that these strains are being revealed, the nature of the intimate aspects of the relationship of the physician to the hospital is altering, for advances in technology require protocols and decision-making rules, leading to greater specialization in function and greater competition between specialties. An example is the "turf" disputes between pathologists, radiologists, and internists over developments in nuclear medicine. As the mix of diseases moves toward the chronic complex conditions associated with aging, different kinds of teams of specialists and providers are required, teams in which the physician plays a smaller part. Clinical decisions are no longer the exclusive domain of the medical profession; boundaries are more permeable, allowing participation by other providers, regulatory groups, and consumers. So there is a greater need for clini-

---

[13] S. M. Shortell, "Hospital Medical Staff Organization: Structure, Process and Outcome," *Hospital Administration* 19 (Spring 1984), pp. 96–106.

[14] S. M. Shortell, "Physician Involvement in Hospital Decision Making," in *The New Health Care for Profit*, ed. B. Gray (Washington, D.C.: National Academy Press, 1983).

cal participation in managerial decision making and of management in clinical decision making.

Where once the nature of the relationship of the physician to the organization was a given—almost all physicians were in fact consultants on the staff, often of several hospitals, with but few being full-time employees—now the nature of the relationship between physicians and hospitals is a matter of choice, often a critical and strategic choice for both. More and more physicians are becoming full-time employees of hospitals and other health care organizations, e.g., HMOs. Alternatively, groups of physicians may form contractual relationships with health care organizations, agreeing to provide designated services for a designated fee. In some instances, managers and physicians seek an adversarial relationship, while other health care organizations are moving toward the idea, if not the actuality, of true partnership.

Each of these arrangements has significant and differing consequences both for physicians and for the organization. With each arrangement, what must be managed differs to some degree, and who legitimately manages the physician also differs. But there is one thing that any manager wishing to manage or to influence physicians must face. In this painful transitional era, physicians are losing many of their historical prerogatives and much of what brought them into medicine in the first place: the exercise of independent judgment and the practice of skills that make for medicine being fun. Physicians are therefore realistically paranoid and, as such, sensitive and suspicious. Innocent actions, however well intentioned, may be misinterpreted. All managers must be aware of this fact.

Where once the doctor-patient relationship was paramount, now each partner in the relationship is beginning to relate primarily to the health organization rather than to the other, as Figure 3-1 shows. It is not surprising that as health managers begin to manage more forcefully, as is their prerogative, their management of organizational concerns is responded to as though they were managing the doctor-patient relationship. And in like fashion, it is easy to mistake the neutral management of organizational concerns for the management of error or abuse, which it certainly is not.

FIGURE 3–1 The Shifting Doctor-Patient-Organization Relationship

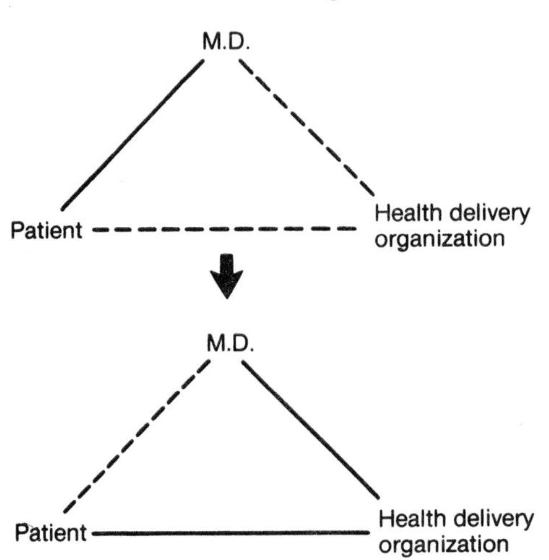

DOCTOR AND PATIENT

Physician authority appears to be questioned worldwide.[15] It is interesting that in Germany[16] apparently there are few malpractice suits, as is also true in Britain where one regional administrator said that he actually attempted to stir up patients to sue because he felt there were insufficient lawsuits to keep the doctors honest! Perhaps the infrequency of malpractice litigation is in part a function of a different legal system than in the United States, in part of the "habit of authority" referred to below. In France there have been infringements, as elsewhere, on the traditional prerogatives of physicians, as the government wished to set new fee tables rather than have physicians decide. This is, of course, analogous to medicare or medicaid setting limits on fees.

---

[15]E. B. Gallagher, ed. *The Doctor-Patient Relationship in the Changing Health Scene* (Washington, D.C.: U.S. Department of Health, Education and Welfare, 1976).

[16]M. Pflanz, "The Two Phases of the Patient-Doctor Relationship and the Changing Welfare State: The Federal Republic of Germany," in *The Doctor-Patient Relationship in the Changing Health Scene,* ed. E. B. Gallagher (Washington, D.C.: U.S. Department of Health, Education and Welfare, 1976).

Doctors resisted, using as argument the "good of the patient and the quality of the patient-doctor relationship."[17]

With the British National Health Service,[18] one of many infringements of autonomy is that patient choice of physician is restricted, as there may well be only a single general practitioner in their particular locality whose list of patients they can join. Moreover, the general practitioner has the right to refuse a patient, so the patient more or less has to be able to get on with the physician! On the other hand, because the GP is paid according to the number of patients on his or her list, there is an incentive for the physician to give in to the patient, particularly to private patients who augment the physician's income.

Two of the major challenges to the traditional role of the physician lie on the one hand, in the bureaucratization of medicine (in other words, the changing relationship of the physician to the organization) and on the other, in the challenge to the physician's authority (i.e., the changing relationship of the physician to the patient).[19] The danger of bureaucratic medical settings,[20, 21] such as the National Health Service or an HMO, is that they put the physician under pressure to sacrifice the interests of the patient to satisfy organizational needs. Responsibility tends to be diffused and the buck is easily passed, for now the organization rather than the individual physician, is felt to be responsible. Bureaucratic structures tend to promote detached relationships and conflicts. While physicians could provide empathy, continuity, and humane care, they tend to give higher priority to bureaucratic and technical functions. Because they are rewarded more

---

[17]C. Herzlich, "Conceptions of the Doctor-Patient Relationship in the French Medical Press," in *The Doctor-Patient Relationship in the Changing Health Scene,* ed. E. B. Gallagher (Washington, D.C.: U.S. Department of Health, Education and Welfare, 1976).

[18]G. V. Stimpson, "Interactions Between Patients and General Practitioners in the United Kingdom," in *The Doctor-Patient Relationship in the Changing Health Scene,* ed. E. B. Gallagher (Washington, D.C.: U.S. Department of Health, Education and Welfare, 1976).

[19]M. R. Haug, "Issues in Patient Acceptance of Physician Authority in Great Britain," in *The Doctor-Patient Relationship in the Changing Health Scene,* ed. E. B. Gallagher (Washington, D.C.: U.S. Department of Health, Education and Welfare, 1976).

[20]D. Mechanic, *The Growth of Bureaucratic Medicine* (New York: John Wiley & Sons, 1976).

[21]D. Mechanic, "The Growth in Medical Technology and Bureaucracy: Implications for Medical Care," *MMGQ,* 1977, pp. 61–78.

for being good managers than for providing humane care, such care tends to be given despite the bureaucracy rather than because of it.

Proletarianization is a step beyond bureaucratization.[22, 23] It means being divested of control of the key prerogatives relating to the location, content, and essentiality of activities which are subordinated to the broader requirements of capitalist control of medical care! In other words, health care is being industrialized, and the physician is becoming just another worker. This will be taken up at greater length in Chapter 10, but key intrusions into traditional physician areas include: work segmented and directed by administrators for organizational ends; patients who are technically clients or members of the organization and whom physicians "share" with other specialists; technology owned by the organization and operated by nonphysicians; physical plant owned and operated by the organization; and regular hours of work and established salaries, which limit outside practice.

There are seven aspects to the deprofessionalization that bureaucratization and proletarianization entail.[24] First, while it is in the use of technical skills that medical practice is usually distinguished from other so-called helping professions, it is these very skills that the computer will replace. Second is the problem of professionals in a bureaucracy that has detrimental effects on professionalization. Third is the change in the organization of medical practice. Fourth, the social position of physicians has changed; they are now members of teams abiding by rules over which they have little control and with penalties for infractions of the rules. Administrators regard themselves and are regarded as full professionals with their own body of knowledge and a supporting ideology. Fifth is the movement toward unionization. Sixth, the physician is as an agent of social control. Seventh, the challenge from outside, such as the do-it-yourself movement.

---

[22]J. B. McKinley, "The Turning Political and Economic Context of the Patient-Physician Encounter," in *The Doctor-Patient Relationship in the Changing Health Scene,* ed. E. B. Gallagher (Washington, D.C.: U.S. Department of Health, Education and Welfare, 1976).

[23]J. B. McKinley and J. Arches, "Towards the Proletarianization of Physicians," *IJHS* 15, no. 2 (1985), pp. 161–95.

[24]M. R. Haug and B. Lavin, "Public Challenge of Physician Authority," *Medical Care* 17 (1979), pp. 844–58.

The physician-patient relationship has been weakened not only by alterations in payment systems that intervene between the patient and the physician, not only by technology in which "god-like tests are replacing god-like physicians as subjects for obeisance and belief,"[25] but also by changes in the attitude of the consumer or patient toward the physician. Neither the expertise nor the good will of the professional are any longer taken on trust, resulting in the "revolt of the client" and the demand for accountability. While this phenomenon is perhaps more marked in the United States, it seems to be worldwide. It is attributed to rising educational levels among the public, and to new divisions of labor redistributing expertise in the human service field. Computerization and aggregation of clients and bureaucratic services further the phenomenon, aided by the trend toward self-care and a preoccupation with healthy lifestyles rather than illness. Many of the tasks of the physician are given over to paraprofessionals or new professionals such as the midwife, the nurse clinician, the ICU nurse, and the physician assistant. Not surprisingly, the older generation is more accepting of physicians; though in all countries younger people tend to be more challenging, individual countries clearly vary in the specifics.

In Britain, physician's role in the National Health Service as public servant places him at more risk, but is balanced to some degree by the great respect for authority also to be found in England.[26] Moreover, in Britain, the physician is gatekeeper to socially valued services such as telephones and housing, which reinforces his or her position. In Russia, physicians are also gatekeepers, signing certificates and validating illness claims and rights to sick leave.[27] The implication of these changes in doctor-patient relationship is that, in the future, transactions between patients and doctors will have to be more cooperative or involve more bargaining than in the past. This perhaps is all to the good. What is less positive is what seems to be happening in HMOs,

---

[25]M. R. Haug, "Issues of Patient Acceptance of Physician Authority in Great Britain," in *The Doctor-Patient Relationship in the Changing Health Scene*, ed. E. B. Gallagher (Washington, D.C.: U.S. Department of Health, Education and Welfare, 1976), pp. 239–54.

[26]A. P. Thornton, *The Habit of Authority* (London: George Allen and Unwin, 1966).

[27]M. R. Haug, "The Erosion of Professional Authority: A Cross-Cultural Inquiry in the Case of the Physician," *MMFQ* 54 (Winter 1976), pp. 83–104.

where physicians feel locked into the doctor-patient relationship, with no choice as to whom they shall see, while having to deal with a greater volume of "difficult" patients than ever before. The organization, faced with competition, is unsympathetic, placing pressure on the physician to do whatever it takes to placate HMO members. Long gone are the days of Lord Horder who once said, "Only the doctor knows what good doctoring is."[28]

As a result of diminished consumer expectations concerning the physician, many established doctors begin to find the contemporary medical scene confusing or threatening; one of the responses to the belief that medicine is in decline and that doctors are losing their traditional autonomy, is to work less and play more or spend more time with the family. Another is to become involved in medical politics, perhaps to retrieve that lost autonomy, but this is often a futile exercise. What is ironic is that doctors continue to be trained as though the old way still existed.

Radical changes are occurring in the role of the physician and in the relationship of physicians to patients. These changes are patchy, faster in some regions than others, faster in some countries than others. But they are inevitable and due to the overall industrialization of medicine with the concomitant deprofessionalization of the doctor.

WHY DOCTORS ENTER MEDICINE: THE EXPERIENCE AND ITS SHAPING

Contrary to the sterotype, relatively few of the physicians questioned in the 10-hospital study, some 100 in all, had doctors in the family, though family influence was by no means an insignificant factor in their choice of profession. Many had had some experience during childhood or adolescence with illness or with doctors that turned them toward medicine. According to that study, for most doctors, what appeals is "the combination of enjoying the science and working with people." If it is not the challenge of science itself that is important, then it is the challenge of solving problems: "every patient, every situation is different, there's always that challenge." For some, medicine is a means of

[28]M. L. Johnson, "Patients: Receivers or Participants," in *Conflicts in the National Health Service*, ed. K. Barnard and K. Lee (New York: Prodist, 1977).

getting away from a situation: "being poor and black and young you have two kids and one is going to be a doctor and one a lawyer." For others it is a way of going toward something: "I had no idea of what I was getting into. There were some monetary things I wanted and I could see no other way of living the life I desired."

Of course, the reasons change during the lengthy process of training. While being one's own boss is important, and status and respect are also, not to be underemphasized is the strong altruistic streak in many physicians that goes along with the intellectual scientific challenge.

Coombs gives a vivid picture of what goes on during medical school.[29] For all the diversity of medical students, most students are unmarried, white, Protestant, first-born or only children between 21 and 23 years of age, and from stable middle-class homes; they have been to college and have taken courses in the biological sciences. They share a common desire to become physicians. Many have not entertained the possibility of another career and have overcome formidable obstacles in gaining admission to medical school, competing successfully for best grades and politicking effectively to impress premedical advisers and medical school admissions committees. They are willing to bear the heavy financial burdens and to sacrifice personal pleasures to achieve goals. Since these students are so highly motivated, the potential of effective socialization is greatly enhanced. Students during medical school, while learning from nurses and basic scientists, regard members of the clinical faculty as their important mentors. The common intense pressure makes the students even more alike than they were on entering.

Students value not only role models among the clinical faculty, but also clinical information in their curriculum, and it is frustrating to them that much time during the first two years is directed toward pursuits that seem oriented more toward careers in scientific research than toward medical practice. Yet, as long as the reward structure of the medical school favors those who excel at research, publishing, and grantsmanship, basic scientists will maintain their strong position in the power structure of the institution. Medical school is not only a teaching institution

---

[29]R. Coombs, *Mastering Medicine: Professional Socialization in Medical School* (New York: Free Press, 1978).

where knowledge and professional doctrines are disseminated, but also an obstacle course where stressful situations frequently require that recruits prove their adaptive ability. The hurdles and emotional obstacles that lie along the career path serve as rites of passage to prove ability, dedication, and emotional vigor. Those who withdraw are not academically incompetent, but succumb to adversity and emotional strain. Female students especially face major adjustments. The typical medical student remains in a relatively dependent adolescent-like situation until he approaches the age of 30. Scant attention is paid to the basic aspects of the socialization process, specifically to the anxieties that confront medical students, for scientific detachment and objective rationality reign supreme. It is not, therefore, surprising that medical students, on graduation, may be inadequate to deal freely and openly with the subjective features of medical care. How is the practitioner to deal successfully with the emotions and feelings of patients and families when personal doubts and inner feelings have not been successfully dealt with?

When they do get to clinical experience, students find that human maladies are not neatly classified as they are in the textbooks. To enhance the probability of clinical success, student physicians usually prefer certain types of patients, i.e., those who are most easily dealt with from a medical and interpersonal standpoint. It is easier to deal with adults than children, with middle-class than lower-class patients, with the organically rather than the emotionally ill, and with the acutely rather than the chronically or terminally ill. For students who are not yet doctors, obtaining the patient's full trust and cooperation may require bluff. Little formal training is offered in developing the interpersonal skills of patient management. So medical students are better trained in the science of medicine than in the art of patient care. There is little uncertainty in the minds of medical students about the doctor's status and role, so their views about doctors don't change much. Good doctors are seen as being technically competent, as dedicated to patients' welfare and to maintaining good relationships with them; bad doctors are viewed as lacking technical competence, having little concern for patients, maintaining poor relationships, and being overly concerned with money and prestige.

The rewards seen by students are a chance to interact with people, feelings of personal accomplishment, interesting and challenging work, opportunities for independence and responsibility, sizable income, and considerable status and prestige. The liabilities are demanding work, the potential intrusion of work into personal life, and problem patients. Students remain romantic in that doctors are placed on a pedestal and are attributed almost superhuman qualities of professional and personal excellence.

Students begin to decide on specialties by narrowing down the field and focusing on the idiosyncratic features of each specialty and its practitioners. Some specialty areas, such as general practice and pediatrics, are easily characterized, while neurology, dermatology, and radiology project an unclear image. The most consistently critical comments are made about specialists who avoid frontline contact with patients. Most admired are doctors who are willing to devote long hours of hard work in face-to-face contact with patients. Status comes to prospective doctors who prove themselves capable of successfully handling the diverse vicissitudes of medical training. Prospective doctors seem propelled by an inner need for career attainment, by a desire to succeed and to achieve occupational prominence.

Medical students are intelligent, resourceful, serious, and self-assured, and such personality traits serve them well in college competition and in medical school. Does total absorption in career development to the relative exclusion of outside interest remain a healthy thing? Is a price paid for such dedication and zeal? While clinicians must have empathy for patients, they cannot identify too closely with their pain and suffering if objectivity is to be maintained, no matter how sympathetic a clinician may be; emotional detachment is a major factor in performing the expected role. Cynicism, however, does not become generalized as a personality trait, but students do tend to become less religiously inclined and more politically interested.

What happens then in residency? Michael Harwood described the experience. "The intern is being pulled for all sides, and his goal is just somehow to create a buffer around himself and survive. You lose whatever humanistic interest you have."[30]

---

[30] M. Harwood, "The Ordeal," *New York Times Magazine*, June 3, 1984.

Medical school graduates immediately find themselves loaded with work, exhausted by grueling shifts and schedules, harried, anguished, and frightened by the reality of being responsible for people who are sick and dying. The process often requires that they bury a lot of their feelings, and they sense themselves changing, growing distant from patients, and sometimes even cold and callous. As schedules ease, however, they know more about medicine, and they can solve increasingly complex problems on their own. Their confidence and excitement about medicine rise, they begin to feel comfortable with patients, and they see their treatments helping patients get well. At that point, they may let their feelings surface again. But individuals differ. Some never recover from the shocks of the first year; some end their training believing the world owes them a debt for their time and trouble. Some never find a comfortable or stimulating niche. Tough as it is, they tend to feel that they would not change the mechanics of what they do, for the system works.

Training once involved apprenticing with an established physician. The system of hospital internships began around the turn of the century, allowing fledgling doctors to learn from a variety of physicians. With complexity in medicine, there came division into specialties regulated by specialty boards with rigorous training standards. Narrower specialty areas meant more requirements for more training. One year before graduation, medical students choose their specialty. By that time, they have had two years of classroom instruction and a year's clinical experience in a medical school hospital.

Most residency programs rotate physicians through different wards or services on a regular schedule, exposing the residents to a variety of cases. Many rotate through public and private hospitals, thus providing different responsibilities and different approaches to hospital medicine. Some residency programs give residents little responsibility and independence, others much. Each training program reflects the personality of the department chairman. The match between student and available residencies occurs in the senior year of medical school. Students rank their priority for application and program directors rank their interest in students. Ninety percent of the 18–19,000 residency slots are filled by the match. The rest are filled by special arrangement.

Internship is when the learning curve is steepest, and when the most unexpected and unpleasant things happen to new doctors all at once. Suddenly, they are responsible for patients. Suddenly, they have to confront death. They wonder if that death occurs because of their lack of knowledge and experience. They begin to notice that the world outside of medicine has unreasonable expectations of what a doctor should be, i.e., faultless, absolutely reliable, accessible at all times. One intern, after a tiring period, commented out loud in an elevator that she was really confused; the passengers' response was that she was not allowed to be confused and that they did not care if she was confused, they did not want to know about it. The new intern is rapidly disabused that things are well defined as in textbooks; in fact, they are not black and white, and there is no right decision. Much comes down to intuition or judgment. The hardest part is knowing that you are going to be wrong some of the time, or worse yet—never knowing whether you were wrong or right. And you find out that doing *this* and *this,* does not necessarily make *that* happen because so many people are so sick that there is little that can be done for them.

The main experience is one of exhaustion. Much of the work takes a long time to do, because the intern is at the beck and call of everyone. Often, the intern is up at night. Despite all of this, studies have shown that although the sense of well-being is affected, clinical performance is not. Such pressure does foster an elitist attitude, impatience, and a belief that one should be treated specially. Efficiency is, therefore, at a premium, and soon it is discovered that personal involvement with patients as human beings interferes with efficiency because it takes time. Moreover, feelings impair good judgment when someone is dying or there is terrible trauma. Somebody else is always needing help beyond the one that has died. You get the information you need and then shut off.

In the middle of the internship year, confidence returns and the pleasures involved in the challenges begin to assume greater importance. Skills are refined, techniques honed. Interns become more adept at managing the hospital's system, at steering it for the benefit of patients. As the doctor learns to perform tasks more quickly, there is more time to spend with patients and to listen to them. Maybe some of the hard surface softens and the intern can feel for patients again. There is a danger in the teaching hospital of insensitivity and of regarding the patient simply as instructional material. Death is a fact of life, too, and attitudes vary broadly as to how heroic measures should be to avoid it.

Residents spend most of their time in the hospital, so most of their friends are doctors and nurses. It is like boot camp. The isolation is professional as well as personal. The hospital may become not only the workplace but also the resident's true spiritual home. The pressures take their toll, particularly on marriages. While counseling may be available, it is often useless. The hospital, in a sense, arrests residents' development, for the experience prolongs adolescent dependent-student status. The resident has to go on pleasing superiors.

The choice of specialty is complex. Doctors do not like those patients who are not going to get well because of age or disease, and also dislike those who will not follow doctor's orders to stop doing those things that will inevitably harm them. They resent those who insist on the doctor's attention at all hours of the day and night, as well. The specialty choice, then, is not only intellectual—which specialty will offer an intellectual challenge—but may also be contingent on areas where patients will not be terribly sick, such as in ophthalmology or dermatology, or where the physician will not be directly responsible for patients, such as radiology and anesthesiology. These specialties allow doctors reasonable hours, few interruptions, and very good livings.

Money is important. Not necessarily out of greed, but because there are student debts outstanding. Moreover, the whole process takes so long that physicians often say at the end of it that they might not have gone into medicine had they fully realized what was involved.

TRADITIONAL PHYSICIAN VALUES[31]

What is important to doctors about doctoring?

> It is the doctor-patient relationship. There has been an evolution. When you are at medical school you treat disease. After you have been in practice

[31]The quotations in this section are all taken from Sheldon, "The 10-Hospital Study," an unpublished report.

> and you know people, then you treat patients and that is a good feeling. To see patients again, the continuity is very important. They develop a trust in you, you develop a love for your patients. You really do.

What else is important?

> Autonomy, that is to say clinical autonomy. To have total control of all affairs is not as important. If I could go to the office and somebody took care of all the details and I could just see patients and be financially rewarded sufficiently, I would be comfortable with that.

Autonomy and independence are the most highly valued attributes of doctoring for most, if not all physicians, though the form it takes may differ slightly from one practitioner to another. Among the factors cited:

> My ability to make my decisions on treating, payment schedules, whether I take payment or not, and my control of my practice.
>
> Control of my own destiny, the lack of government and control, interference with the medical aspect of it.
>
> I couldn't practice rubber stamp medicine, medicine is an art.

Also important are respect and social status. The respect comes from colleagues as well as patients, and income goes along with status.

> You are respected and looked up to as helping people not because you are rich. I do a lot of general practice on people I know and sometimes I do not charge. This develops a good rapport. I like small town attitudes where you are part of the flow of things rather than the big city.

To be respected in one's community for doing a good job is part of the reward, though the income certainly helps. Part of the status is the mystique: "All of us cherish the role of the shaman, the witch doctor role."

While respect is in part authority, and therefore power, that power is very much the power to do good and to "alter the course of events." As one doctor said, "I love to treat someone who can't breathe. I love to do good for people and also for me, as well. It is cultural authority that is important to me, not social authority."

That authority involves "taking control of what I think is right for the patient," and "being able to manage my patients." It is the erosion of this freedom and this power that doctors fear as a result of the changes they are experiencing in medicine. For them, the point of practice is that doctors are their own bosses.

"I am my own boss. I make my own decisions. The gratification of putting people back together and making them function is mine."

Respect comes from people and from relationships with people. One doctor after another comments that it is only with the passing of time that they have learned to value their relationships with their patients. "After 10 years I am beginning to realize what I value most is being able to deal with my patients as friends and getting to develop a relationship with them."

> [Fee for service] gives you more of a better relationship with people, whereas when someone else is paying the bill you lose that relationship. If someone is willing to pay me for my services, fine. If they do not feel my services are of that much value, fine. They would not come back and I would not expect them to. I would rather give my best to the patient.
>
> I cherish the opportunity to enter into the lives of many people and become important to them and have many intense interesting and personal relationships, not only with my patients but my colleagues who are as diverse a group as anyone could wish.
>
> Seeing people, taking care of them, and having a comfortable setting for doing that seems to set the tone.

However, the ability to do something for people is threatened.

> As we become more and more technologically oriented we get removed from that. As computers take on a greater diagnostic role, we become removed from the interpersonal relationships that are established between doctors and patients. In a sense, it is the technology doing the treatment instead of the doctor. And so the doctor becomes merely the agent of the technology, which is the true mediator, rather than the technology being the physician's servant.

Caring, giving quality care are attributes valued by physicians.

> If you do not care, no matter how good you are, you might as well do something else. If you can try hard and have a normal intelligence you should do fine. You should never assume that you can be complacent with yourself. The satisfaction of seeing your work do something good, to enjoy that work and see the benefits of it, is the pleasure.
>
> It has to do with the satisfaction of being with people who are in distress with a certain body of knowledge, combined with a certain attitude about people and a certain optimism that you can make things better, but staying with problems no matter how difficult they are, and most of the time people do get better. The whole tradition of healing and comforting in the context of a discipline where you master some tools of the trade. It is gratifying and I have always had the experience of people appreciating what I do and respecting it. I still think there is room for satisfaction in

work. Perhaps busy practitioners should let go of some patients and do a good job with the people they stay with. Medicine breaks down when you do not work within some limits.

But the gratification of working independently to develop relationships and better the lives of others is breaking down.

I'm getting to the point where difficult problems are tearing on me mentally especially with malpractice.

Having a relationship with patients is becoming more and more adversarial both from a legal expectation standpoint and a financial standpoint. That is the most upsetting thing. I would rather make $30,000 and enjoy my practice and have my patients feel they were getting good service than make $1 million and have them think I was a miserable SOB.

As one doctor sums up,

The particular role of the physician is as much art as science. Being in a position to understand people who are ill from the perspective of the biological, psychological, and sociological. So far a well-trained physician remains the unique person in our society capable of helping in those three dimensions simultaneously, and if anything is done to make physicians become mere biomedical technicians while the psychosocial side of medical care is taken over by social workers or nurse practitioners, that will be a net loss for patients.

It is being a person, a human, not a machine or a computer that spits out medicine and diagnoses. Anything that is going to change the doctor-patient relationship in terms of my ability to deal with them on a one-to-one basis is going to upset me. Anything that takes away my right to handle or deal with patients and their problems in a personal manner is going to upset me. If I have to do it from an administrative standpoint or cost-effective standpoint rather than what I think is best for them, then I am going to be upset. Those are ideals of medicine for me.

The fear of change, and the impact of those changes, extends beyond control over one's own practice to control of the health care team. "There is a loss or fear of loss of management by the physicians. We are health care teams. Who is in charge of the ship? We are told other groups can do it better than we, and that is disturbing."

It is this emphasis on the art of medicine as well as its science, on the humanity of medicine as well as its efficiency, that leads us inevitably to a consideration of error, for the nature of humanity is to err where judgment comes into play. The essence of art is that it is unique, and that is part of its imaginative basis, and in uniqueness lies variation, not conformity. Science is both critical and analytic as well as exploratory and imaginative.[32,33] In the latter it is akin to poetry. "It is in the imaginative grasp of what might be true that lies the incentive for finding out what is true."[34] While this statement was written about science, it might as well have been written about diagnosis. In the imaginative capacity of the individual physician to divine what *might* be wrong lies the possibility of discovering what *is* wrong. Because signs and symptoms are not the uniform manifestations of machines but the colorful language of a hurt body and mind, some degree of divination as well as logic is required to apprehend them. As a poem is a mixture of control and impulse, so diagnosis joins the art of medicine with the science, for the manifestations of illness must be understood at the levels of both logic and spirit.

But the changes in medicine are inimical to error and are driving it out. Some of those changes perhaps accrue from the failures of the individual physician or the collegium to contain error within defensible limits.

SELF-CONTROL OR OTHER CORRECTION?

A profession is an aggregate of people finding identity and sharing values and skills absorbed during a period of intensive training through which all have passed. It is a group of workers joined together by virtue of sharing a particular position in society and common participation in a given division of labor. The medical profession's strength is based on a legally supported monopoly of practice through a system of licensing that bears on the privilege to hospitalize patients and the right to prescribe drugs and order laboratory procedures otherwise virtually inaccessible—the state grants this monopoly. What is invariable is technological or scientific autonomy, for everywhere the medical profession appears to be left fairly free to develop its special area of knowledge and to determine what is scientifically acceptable practice.

Through education, the student is socialized to become a physician and to accept the concomitant responsibilities. The

---

[32]P. D. Medawar, *The Hope of Progress* (London: Methuen and Co., 1972).

[33]P. D. Medawar, *The Art of the Soluble* (London: Methuen and Co., 1967).

[34]I. A. Richards, *Poetries and Sciences* (London: Routledge & Kegan Paul, Rev. ed. 1970).

physician holds the life of a patient in his or her hands and has as a personal responsibility working directly with the patient, which requires that the physician take the blame for bad results. More experience replaces less experience, and it is through experience that errors are reduced. The profession's responsibility extends to raising one generation of specialists after another from professional infancy to professional adulthood, at which time the fledglings are pushed out from the nest and you hope for the best.[35] Education is paramount, and if a change in the way that clinical judgments are made is desired, factoring in such issues as quality and cost, then it is in part through training that such altered values must be inculcated.

It is in the nature of professions that professionals do not readily relinquish any kind of control over their work to outsiders. Instead, they take, or are assumed to take, the responsibility for monitoring themselves individually or as a collectivity, "the collegium."[36] Thus, the National Health Service in Britain built into its managerial structure elaborate mechanisms for ensuring physicians control over clinical practice, and managers in health delivery organizations in the United States acknowledge that their role in managing such clinically relevant areas as quality assurance, cost, and physician recruitment lies in the provision of data, the design of physician-operated systems, and the "nudging" of those systems when they fail to work as planned. Professionals interpret their mandate to control performance as an injunction to maintain high community moral standards; while they may forgive technical error, they punish moral error.[37] Doctors do not expect application of medical knowledge to be perfect—there will always be honest errors—but they do expect compliance with the norms of clinical responsibility. The issues involve ambiguity because professional self-control can mean both the individual professional's ability to handle responsibility and the corporate responsibility of the profession to regulate its internal affairs. If the process of self-education and self-control does not work, who then controls the individual?

---

[35]C. L. Bosk, *Forgive and Remember: Managing Medical Failure* (Chicago: University of Chicago Press, 1979).

[36]E. Freidson, *Doctoring Together: A Study of Professional Social Control* (New York: Elsevier, 1975).

[37]Bosk, *Forgive and Remember.*

The professional is hesitant to establish standards and may punish, but rarely by exclusion. Physicians give the impression that there is a body of knowledge and procedure which may be taken as routine or standard, constituting a set of rules for acceptable performance; deviations from these rules are not likely to be seen as normal mistakes or errors and therefore are not excusable. However, differences of opinion are clearly recognized, given that often there is ambiguous evidence.[38]

The argument in this respect seems to extend only to the adverse potential consequences of technical errors. But personally mishandling patients may also have adverse consequences. A young physician at an HMO was rude to a patient and was castigated by the medical director. The physician felt this was extremely unfair because the circumstances were not fully comprehended, namely that he was overloaded and under pressure from an aggressive patient. Not denying his own rudeness, he felt that it was excusable if not justifiable under the particular circumstances. In the context of an HMO, retention of patients within the system is important; therefore, interpersonal errors are as catastrophic to the system as medical errors and have as great a consequence for the reputation of the organization. But the normal corrective mechanisms, as created and administered by physicians, do not normally take such errors into account. The physician manager concerned here was acting managerially and was responded to as a manager rather than as a supervising clinician.

Doctors evaluate each other on the basis of education, training qualifications, patient reports, colleague gossip, experience, and medical records.[39] The primary information is firsthand experience with a physician's work and the opinion of other physicians. Such information contains many gaps, and so it is difficult for physicians to exert effective control over one another. Much critical information is actually omitted from informal interactions, and many secrets are kept. Physicians as a group do not share information, and medical charts tend to be used after a question is raised rather than before when looking for problems. It is not surprising that, with a complex informal system bolstered by a fear of litigation, physicians rely on the "market-

[38] E. Freidson, *Professional Dominance: The Social Structure of Medical Care* (New York: Atherton Press, 1970).

[39] Ibid.

place" to take care of problems (see Chapter 6). In other words, rather than discipline one another directly, physicians find it easier to use referrals as a disciplinary measure.

Because doctors have a tendency to consider each other as essentially good or essentially bad and largely unchangeable, and because they rely on their firsthand knowledge of each other, it is also not surprising that they find it difficult to work with formal review procedures. They prefer, as in the case of one astute physician manager, Doctor R (discussed further in Chapter 9), to create systems that make it difficult for doctors to err rather than to correct error after the fact. In this respect, Doctor R has taken a leaf from McDonald's in that the design of technology governs behavior.

Doctors tend to reject economic sanctions against their brethren and use two methods of peer control: either the withdrawal of favors and acts of reciprocity where cooperation was optional, or overt complaining and criticism. Doctors prefer to avoid confrontation, thus, a paradox. Because doctors avoid those they wish to criticize and refer patients to those they like, popular colleagues tend to become overloaded quickly, i.e., are punished! This defensive solidarity involves the collective obligation to protect each colleague's independence. However, while the market mechanism for self-correction may work in a traditional fee-for-service structure through referral or nonreferral, it does not work so well in other forms such as group practices or HMOs. In these contexts, the group has imposed on it external bureaucratic controls that reinforce its defensiveness about its freedoms. This augers ill, because there is a trend toward groups rather than solo fee-for-service practices.

Physicians in an organizational setting, such as a group practice, expect management to relieve them of administrative burdens but not to supervise them, except in strictly limited areas such as housekeeping duties. The definition of housekeeping is often a matter of contention and does not extend, for example, to such matters as the keeping of hours or the number of patients seen. Indeed, in a union setting, such as the Group Health Association, a large HMO in Washington, D.C., such matters as hours, pay, and productivity become part of the negotiated contract rather than becoming the subject of managerial discretion. In this instance, it is the physician union that acts as the collegium, not so much controlling its own members as seeking favorable work conditions through negotiation with management.

What is needed is not more management constraints or more administrative systems, but more inventive ways of getting physicians to discipline themselves in the light of public interest or of organizational concerns.[40] In other words, the answer lies in the creation of incentives rather than in attempts to regulate.

Because differences of style are recognized as legitimate, as matters of disagreement, they are removed as serious topics for discussion or control. This underscores autonomy as a value for professionals, while diminishing differences in practice patterns as subjects of public debate or public control, or for that matter, managerial control. This involves *quasi-normative error*, i.e., the stylistic idiosyncracies of different doctors. If a doctor is a responsible ethical colleague, he knows when he has made a hash out of a case, and there is no need therefore to rub his nose in it. If he is not responsible, no one can change him. If his style is simply different, no one *should* change him.

Is the lack of social control due to the uncertainties with which physicians or surgeons deal, and the cognitive framework used by members of the profession, or to the way that physicians are socialized? The answer must be both, and both must be influenced for change to occur.

Physicians tend to be on a cusp between the scientist and the artist. Whether they refer to themselves as one or the other often depends on the circumstances! When faced with a problem for which experience provides an incorrect answer, they may ask for a scientific clinical trial, thus placing correction beyond the manager and in the realm of science. When clinical trials give results that contradict experience, they revert to the paramountcy of the unique individual experience, i.e., to the art of medicine. Either way, they manage to infuriate the manager whose job it is to make decisions under uncertainty, in other words, to use a different kind of judgment.

Professional authority rests in the assertion that professionals should be trusted because they are professionals; the burden of compliance therefore is on the client. In science authority is based upon fact and common rules of evidence and procedure.

---

[40]Ibid.

Doctors assert that it is their particular knowledge of a unique patient as a human being that transcends statistical facts deduced from a scientific study, and they may on occasion be correct. Because of the license given to the doctor—the prescription of drugs, the ability to cut—because of the special knowledge and skill necessary for the occupation, other skills, other disciplines are not legitimate by comparison. This license is the basis of professional dominance. The physician is the ultimate expert on the definition of health and illness, on how to attain the former and cure the latter, and believes that other professions must be subordinate to this. So control over physicians may be difficult, as may be control over diagnostic and therapeutic processes involving others than physicians, as long as physicians retain dominance. Ironically, the erosion of the professional authority of the physician, not only in relation to the patient but also in relation to other professions, has come in part from the physicians' own acceptance of other professions performing some of their work, once the idiosyncratic province of the doctor, for reasons of efficiency and competition. The increased sophistication of patients with regard to the nature of alternative technologies and their efficacy or suitability has further reduced the physician's authority in this regard.

> Individual self-discipline is insufficient. Without collective evaluation and restraint it is a treacherous foundation for responsible social control. It soon degenerates into an anarchy of individual opinions, acceptable because stemming from presumptively conscientious, competent individuals. Collective evaluation is crucial. It must involve the formation of a dynamic consensus among colleagues about the boundaries of discretion formed in the course of constant interaction over differences of opinion about proper performance. Workers must be obligated to keep judgment on this by being accountable to others and within collectively determined boundaries. The collegium must be obliged to do its work well and conscientiously and to be involved in a collective effort to improve the level and direction of everyone's performance.[41]

Given this definition, it is not surprising, therefore, that efforts, whether in Britain or in the United States, have been directed toward strengthening the systems that physicians use within health delivery organizations. Because physicians are

---

[41]Friedson, *Professional Dominance.*

practical, active individuals who do not easily buckle to bureaucratic pressures, certain protections are provided against the overzealous manager who knows more about efficiency than about patient care.[42] In questioning whether managers can control doctors, the issue is not whether managers could do the work, or even give detailed technical instruction. The issue is whether they can understand enough about the work and the specific needs it has to meet to manage performance.

The manager is defined as one accountable for subordinates' work in all aspects, one who can assess the quality and effectiveness of subordinates' work, one who has the authority to make further prescriptions or reassignments of work as necessary, and one who is able to lead subordinates in new developments in approach and practice. A manager must therefore understand the needs and characteristics of developing practice to be able to represent those ideas and views adequately in external discussions and negotiations. If the so-called manager cannot really help with technical problems or judge competence, or lacks a feel for emerging possibilities, then he or she cannot really be a manager. In Britain, even those administrators who said they felt able to manage doctors acknowledged that they did not feel competent to assign clinical cases or to make assessments of clinical as well as general abilities, nor could they carry full accountability for all aspects of the work of doctors. In other words, they could not issue final or binding prescriptions in the face of strongly conflicting views, or make or act upon fine assessments of performance or personal competence, as is generally expected in managerial relationships. They could take action if a doctor went off the rails, but could not tell a doctor about the choice of treatment, which drugs were to be used, or at what rate to clear beds by discharging patients.[43] (The latter assertion has become to some degree questionable.) It is ironic that with the development of protocols,[44] judgment about choice of treatment or use of

[42]Mechanic, *Growth of Bureaucratic Medicine.*

[43]R. Rowbottom, "Professionals in Health and Social Services Organizations," in *Health Services,* ed. E. Jacques (London: Heinemann, 1978).

[44]R. B. Saltman and D. Y. Young, "The Hospital Power Equilibrium: An Alternative View of the Cost Containment Dilemma," *Journal of Health Politics, Policy and Law* 6, no. 3 (Fall 1981), pp. 391–418.

drugs is being shifted from the individual practicing professional to the system. The reimbursement system, along with protocols, as much as professional judgment may well determine length of stay.

It is the belief in England that health service administrators can manage personnel and supply specialists, even though those managed may have some special skills. But until recently, it has not generally been accepted that administrators can manage engineers let alone nurses or physicians. The assumptions behind this are as follows: When a patient arrives in a hospital, he or she expects to be treated by a specific physician, although the specific nurse may not be as important. This specific physician is not employed to execute the policies and programs of the employing authority, but is an independent practitioner with joint clinical autonomy within the broad terms of the contract. The more confident a patient is that the physician has complete freedom, the more trust will develop. A strong therapeutic relationship is therefore linked to independent practice, and this implies the possibility of choice on each side. Independent practice means a voluntarily maintained relationship of trust and cooperation between a specific professional practitioner and a specific patient or client. (HMOs that do not have patient panels in which members can choose individual physicians clearly negate this condition.)

The appointment of a manager immediately stops this individual professional, for behind the manager is a figure, or a whole line of them, each with the power to adjust, direct, or override. When many professionals work together in independent practice, all must be equal colleagues, none subordinate to another. Herein lies a crucial problem of the group practice. As long as a group practice functions in a collegial manner, it fulfills this condition, but is at best an organized anarchy. For in such a collegial structure, each practicing professional essentially has veto power. So it becomes difficult, if not impossible, to make executive decisions. Once there is a shift toward a managerial structure, with a hierarchy of decision-making power, managerial efficiency is gained at a cost to professional collegiality.

Even in a contract relationship, the employing body has no right to impose particular rules or policies, or to demand that particular tasks be accomplished or particular methods allowed, unless they have been the subject of specific contract negotiations. Justification for legitimizing the claim of authority by one professional group over another must turn on questions of knowledge or competence. The group with primacy must have better or broader competence to assess the real needs or problems in the field concerned. While doctors have traditionally claimed primacy, there are many kinds of situations in which this must be questioned. The World Health Organization goal of health care for all, especially as applied to Third World countries, is as likely to involve improvements in public health, water supply, economic development, or nutrition, as in clinical services. The developmentally disabled child may have as many problems in education and socialization as in health.

A subordinate craft or profession can be organized in a separate managerial hierarchy, subject to specific prescriptions for members of the encompassing profession.[45] Members of the subordinate profession can be organized directly under managerial control. But a problem with teamwork between professions is that there is often uncertainty about who is in charge, and the issue becomes one of prime responsibility. The person with prime responsibility must make personal assessments of general need and take the action needed or initiate it, referring as necessary to colleagues or agencies, keeping an awareness of progress, taking further initiative, and making decisions as needed. Is this person any longer the physician? Does the physician have the skills, the knowledge, or even the desire to be the team leader, the manager?

The real reason for retention of clinical autonomy and medical dominance lies in the nature of illness and the form that health care must take to benefit the patient.[46] Because the sick patient is anxious, personalized care is necessary or desirable. Therefore the doctor has been responsible for fashioning care in a relationship of confidence and trust believed to be possible only as long as autonomy exists. This trust is dissipating, and therefore, the grounds for maintaining clinical autonomy have weakened. The failure of physicians to acknowledge organizational

[45]Rowbottom, "Professionals in Health."

[46]H. Tolliday, "Clinical Autonomy."

realities may be the last straw in handing dominance over to management.

PLUPRACTICE, MALFEASANCE, AND ERROR

While patient expectations concerning the doctor have diminished, their expectations concerning medical technology have skyrocketed. Fueled by the unwise claims of researchers, physicians, or health organizations, the public now expects to be symptom-free, and believes, or wishes, that all illness is curable, all disabilities remediable, and all persons perfectable. No babies should be born dead, let alone disabled. No doctor should make mistakes, for mistakes mean bad medicine and bad doctors, and none should exist. In this state of "plupractice," in which doctors are expected to perform without error, the use of clinical autonomy or judgment becomes questionable, because judgment implies the possibility of error. In the context of plupractice, where error is regarded as malfeasance, not as reasonable, any mistake will be punished by litigation. Error is no longer forgivable, for to forgive means that there must be trust, and trust has largely vanished. Why should one trust an (impersonal) organization— and most of us will go to organizations for our health care, or indeed already do so, rather than to (personal) doctors. In turn, how can you care if you are not trusted? So it becomes harder for the physician to practice caring medicine. And so the vicious circle continues, trust being eroded on both sides. Only in rare cases where they have long-standing relationships with physicians, will patients be willing to absolve error. In the one-stop shops, ambulatory settings, and HMOs, contacts are usually brief, episodic, and with different doctors, and no trust can then develop. Under these circumstances, error is not regarded as the all-too-human failure of well-intentioned judgments, but as a result of ignorance, greed, or some other punishable offense. Distrust drives out judgment, and what is left can only be a mechanical approach to medicine. This is sadly inevitable with the shift from the doctor-patient relationship to the patient-organization relationship. Studies confirm a relationship between the likelihood of litigation and the quality of the doctor-patient relationship.

The economic interdependence of physician and health care organization continues, yet as physician and organizational interests diverge, conflict is inevitable. How can conflict be reduced? How can interests be harmonized? The benefits of cooperation and partnership far outweigh the benefits of maintaining conflict.[47] Physicians and managers each have unique professional and managerial competencies that are complementary and each should stay out of the way of the other—a belief certainly strongly held by the managers and physicians interviewed in the 10-hospital study. The conclusion that must be drawn from the evidence adduced in this chapter is that the changes in the doctor-patient-organization relationship are inevitable, and while eventually perhaps benefiting the client, are widely perceived by physicians to be inimical. Eventually, physicians will fall under the aegis of management, with concomitant deprofessionalization, although that day is still some time away. In the meantime, there remain the heightened sensibilities of physicians who respond to the neutral management of organizational concerns with an all too predictable distaste.

---

[47] J. C. Goldsmith, *Can Hospitals Survive? The New Competitive Health Market* (Homewood, Ill.: Dow Jones-Irwin, 1981).

CHAPTER FOUR

Managing Voice, Governance, and Structure: Physician Unions

Physicians are like kings—they brook no contradiction.

John Webster

THE ISSUE OF PHYSICIAN INVOLVEMENT

Physician voice has to do with the nature and extent of physician participation in the governance and management of health organizations. Which doctors should participate, when, and in what? How many doctors should be on the board, who should they be, and should they represent constituencies? How should physicians be involved in management—through involvement in management committees, in elected positions, or by holding paid medical management posts? How should physicians be involved in the organizational structure of tomorrow's health organization? How does a physician become influential?

These questions are not rhetorical. Physicians can undermine strategic redirection if they misunderstand or dislike it. Physicians can undercut the best laid plans for improving quality or cost. Studies demonstrate that greater physician involvement in hospitalwide decision making facilitates cost containment and protects or even enhances quality of care.[1,2]

While the physician and the organization have diverged, it is in their interests to collaborate.[3] Yet the changing relationship of the physician and the health organization leaves both sides uneasy and wondering exactly where they are. Physicians feel less

[1]J. C. Goldsmith, *Can Hospitals Survive? The New Competitive Health Market* (Homewood, Ill.: Dow Jones-Irwin, 1981).

[2]S. Shortell, "Physician Involvement in Hospital Decision Making," in: *The New Health Care for Profit,* ed. B. Gray (Washington, D.C.: National Academy Press, 1983).

[3]Goldsmith, *Can Hospitals Survive?*

powerful than they once were, and are concerned both with their relationship to management and with their own futures. Physician leaders in health organizations are concerned with increasing their voice among members. This is true for small community hospitals, large institutions, group practices, and HMOs.

The physician leadership at Northern General, for example, was concerned that possible restructuring of their hospital as a health care system would leave them with little influence over the system's direction if they became a physician corporation relating solely to the hospital. Concerned also with aggressive lay management, physicians sought to alter the existing traditional governance system in which they had little representation on the board and an ineffective chief of staff. They also worried about preserving traditional services for the indigent in an era when management appeared to be emphasizing lucrative market segments, but felt little power to do so.

Henry Ford Hospital in Detroit, with a full-time salaried staff, has moved aggressively to develop an extensive HMO network and wholly owned ambulatory system. But some physicians felt that promises were made to enhance quality in the marketplace that left them with burdens, and others found it unattractive to shift their high-technology practices to deal with the evolving low-cost system. Astute physician leaders surveyed the concerns of the rank and file doctor and promptly moved to deal with physician dissatisfaction by reconstituting the governance system to involve more of the rank and file. Yet there remained a residue of discontent. This probably had as much to do with the growing size of the institution and the uncontrollable factors affecting medicine, which left doctors feeling powerless, as with anything else. Indeed, a theme running through physician dissatisfaction with organizations is their feeling of lack of control, as much of medicine in general, as of organizations in particular. Still this should not be used as an excuse to avoid the fact that many physicians are largely disenfranchised in the health delivery organizations in which they work.

Group practices, though physician owned and dominated, are not immune. South Clinic is a medical group practice organized as a partnership of physicians (85 partners) and run by a management board of seven doctors. It has a sizable administrative staff and employs many additional physicians. Partners also own the South Medical Foundation, an operating division of which is the Foundation Hospital used by South Clinic doctors. The president of the foundation is also chief executive officer of the hospital. The clinic is run by a management board that originally consisted of the founders and was restricted to physicians. The major department heads have line responsibility for running the departments both in the clinic and the hospital. In the late 1970s, following the death of the hospital administrator, it was felt that a man of stature was required to fill the post. A new, ambitious lay chief executive officer was recruited and made president of the foundation, as well. At that time, the medical director of the clinic was also chairman of the board of trustees. The new man moved rapidly, seeking a series of hospital affiliations, takeovers, and mergers. This activity was supported by foundation management but viewed with skepticism by clinic management (the doctors) who valued such moves only to the extent that they helped the group practice. Indeed, many of the activities were resented because of the consequences they would have for the clinic's physicians. It soon became apparent that physician confidence in the new administrator had eroded to the point that he had become a liability and had to go. This is yet another example of a paradox: even where physicians own their own facility and recognize the need for aggressive lay management, management activities and interests tend to run counter to those of physicians. In the repetitive conflicts that are inevitable in this era of health care, doctors want to have their say.

At a different level, Midland County is a fairly typical small hospital of some 200 beds trying to compete with two larger hospitals in its East Coast town. Originally started by a physician who was unable for reasons of religious prejudice to obtain a position in a neighboring hospital, the hospital had attracted a patchwork quilt of some excellent and some poor doctors. Over the years, there had been a steady upgrading of the medical staff, many of whom had appointments at nearby medical schools. A new chief executive officer hired by Midland felt that the medical staff little understood management and lacked real leadership, and that there was poor communication between the department chairmen and management, which had led to unfortunate misperceptions. The CEO recognized that the role of an unpaid (elected) department chairman in a community hospital staffed wholly by voluntary community physicians is difficult. One of the few sources of power the chairmen had was the recommendation of specialty appointments, though even this was tenuous; the professional committee of the board had the final say. The hospital had a typical medical staff structure with an elected president and a medical executive committee consisting of both department chairmen and elected at-large physicians. Unusual in a hospital of this size was the existence of a paid vice president for medical affairs.

The doctors were equally concerned about their relationship with management. They felt there had been too much independent action without consultation and a proliferation of managers. Lacking input, many attending physicians were no longer angry or aggressive but passive. They would just come into the hospital, treat their patients, and leave. Younger doctors were not supporting the hospital as actively as the older ones were. The pharmacist no longer gave them free drugs. Fewer upper-class and more indigent patients were being admitted.

Private patients worried about who they were going to have to share a room with. The doctors were suspicious of the new CEO and new management, in spite of their overtures, because, as one physician put it, doctors put down roots in a community and stay there but administrators come and go, for to them a job is but a stepping stone. Management goals were felt to be different from those of the doctors. The new CEO was left wondering what he could do to improve relations between the doctors and management.

A very similar question was asked by Tom Dalton, Executive Director of Colding Health Services, an ambulatory health care organization offering both prepaid and fee-for-service care. There were 15 full-time physicians in this small center, seeing 40,000 patients. It was planned to extend the prepaid service and add a number of additional locations beyond the two already in existence. Some of the key issues facing Tom Dalton included: Could or should the medical staff be in control of operations at the two existing locations and future locations? How could the doctors have a more direct say in income distribution and the way other monies are expended? Could doctors incorporate as a separate organization and negotiate with the board over income distribution and other matters? Should they be working for a board of directors? How could the CEO's powers be defined in relation to a physician? How could a better working relationship be created? How could the productivity of physicians be improved?

The history of Colding is illustrative of some typical problems facing managers and doctors trying to work together. Early on, a medical director hired by management developed bylaws for the doctors, who were unwilling to do it for themselves. These bylaws were later seen as irrelevant to the physicians' interests and a result of management's deliberations. The medical director was looked on as a creature of management. (This is true, of course, in many HMOs and IPAs.) After some time had elapsed, the doctors elected their own medical officers in addition to the management-supported medical director. A variety of innovative incentives were tried, including a bonus system tied to increases in gross revenues. But because the bonus was tied to revenue increases, not to costs, it became easy for individual doctors to add revenue by increasing staff! This was soon altered to a plan involving negotiated revenues and costs.

Basically the issues involved developing a set of checks and balances in the relationship between management and the doctors. How could responsibility and power be shared by the two without veering too much toward either extreme? Both the doctors and the director felt that neither a management-dominated institution with physicians serving as hired employees, nor a physician-dominated group practice would be the answer. This dilemma is common in HMOs and IPAs. Most were started by lay management who retained power, seldom put physicians on the board, and placed their own management doctors in positions of power. No wonder the doctors in many staff model HMOs wonder whether they should move to the group model with the advantage of the negotiating power, or to a union such as exists in the Group Health Association in Washington, D.C.

GOVERNANCE AND THE BOARD

In the 1970s, Schulz noted that there was relatively little involvement of physicians on boards and in management. Such involvement was increasing and has continued to do so, particularly in long-range planning and in the budgeting process,[4,5,6] albeit the growth is slow.

With increased emphasis on competitive strategy as the key to survival and success in the future health environment, the functions of and relationships among the three leadership groups in the health delivery organization—boards, management, and doctors—will be critical in the years ahead. Strong governing boards will be needed to guide health organizations in an ever more complex world. In addition to a strong board, working committees will be more common and more used.[7] For efficiency, the board must be limited to a size conducive to deliberate yet timely action. But with greater board involvement in policy decisions regarding strategic planning, capital expenditures, and patient acceptance, the involvement of physicians as voting members becomes increasingly important. This is particularly true in view of the physician perturbations referred to in the preceding chapter, which may undermine strategic actions, however well planned and well intended. It is for these reasons, for example, that physicians in the urban teaching hospital mentioned above were so concerned about being represented on their board.

While there should be a significant representation of physicians with voting rights on the board, these doctors should represent physicians in general and not specific interests, and they should not dominate the board. "It is not good to have an all-physician board anymore than it's good to have an all-lay one. Physicians should have 50 percent of membership, otherwise they get paranoid and become isolated in their view of medical practice," one CEO suggested. Roughly two thirds of hospitals in one survey had physicians on the board; these were often selected by the board and rarely represented the physicians at

---

[4] R. Schulz, "Does Staff Representation Equal Active Participation?" *Hospitals* 46 (Dec. 16, 1972), pp. 51–5.

[5] R. Schulz, "How to Get Doctors Involved in Governance, Management," *Hospital Medical Staff* 5 (June 1976), pp. 1–7.

[6] R. Schulz, D. Grimes, and T. E. Chester, "Physician Participation in Health Services Management: Expectations in United States and Experiences in England," *Millbank Memorial Fund Quarterly* 54 (Winter 1976), pp. 107–27.

[7] A. Anderson, *Health Care in the 1990s* (HCHA: Trends and Strategies, 1984).

large.[8] For-profit hospitals, particularly the Health Corporation of America, tend to be unusual in seeking heavy representation of physicians on the boards of their hospitals. Physicians are becoming better educated and more interested in becoming involved.[9]

With the National Health Service in Britain, given the injunction against managing physicians in the area of clinical responsibilities, the medical executive committee has much broader functions than is common in the United States. This includes responsibility for the budget for medical services and the services of the professions supplementary to medicine. In Britain, physician participation in medical executive committees is widespread and is not restricted to physicians with formal positions such as professors or chairmen. (This is different from the case in many American hospitals, where a common complaint from physicians generally is that the same small number of physicians sit on all committees and control all important processes.) The British system apparently works fairly well, though with reservations. An implication for the United States is that certain expenditure decisions might be delegated to medical staff, and there should be peer review of resource requests.[10] Clinicians should be equal in making medical staff decisions and should be represented by elected spokespersons. Complete commitment to this concept by management and the board is important, and key managers and nurses should also be integrated into clinical divisions in which physician participation should be limited to decisions directly affecting patient care.[11]

Johnson initially proposed the corporate model as the solution to managing a hospital in today's complex environment.[12] The notion was that doctors should become part of the organiza-

---

[8] M. Kessler, "Doctors on Boards: Survey Tracks a Growing Trend," *Hospital Medical Staff*, June 1976, pp. 10-16.

[9] K. Sandrick, "Medical Staff—Administration Relations Under PPS," *Hospitals*, April 16, 1984, pp. 79-82.

[10] H. Howat, "Doctors in Management," *Health and Social Services Journal*, December 1 and 8, 1973, pp. 2881-82 and 2816-2820.

[11] J. Larson, "Physician Participation in a Teaching Hospital's Planning: The English Experience," *H. C. M. Review*, Winter 1980, pp. 69-75.

[12] R. Johnson, "CEO Must Have Authority to Coordinate Governance, Management, Medical Staff," *Hospital Progress*, April 1984, pp. 49-53.

tional structure under the management and governance of the CEO and board rather than apart from it. But in more recent work the author has acknowledged that the corporate model does not function as smoothly in the hospital setting as in industry.[13] While hospital chief executive officers may view the medical staff as part of the hospital's operating structure, the board tends to accept medical staff recommendations without critical examination, and doctors tend to view the administrator as providing a support system, not as somebody to lead and inspire them. Therefore, if the CEO makes strategic moves more rapidly than the medical staff can assimilate, the CEO may be out of a job, particularly in physician-dominated organizations such as large group practices.

For-profits and not-for-profits differ in the nature of their goals, and therefore in the degree to which physician and hospital interests are aligned.[14] As an example, voluntary hospitals, in meeting community objectives, may find some goals conflict with those of physicians while others are not viable financially. However, there are probably more similarities than differences between voluntaries and for-profits in today's regulatory, cost-containment environment. And in both cases, greater participation in governance and management seems to lead to enhanced performance such as lower costs and higher quality of care as measured by morbidity and mortality rates.[15,16]

ORGANIZATIONAL STRUCTURE

Three alternative structural models have been put forward to solve the problem of hospitals being, according to Shortell, incompletely designed organizations. They are incomplete because nonmedical areas are typically organized along *functional* lines, i.e., nursing, finance, personnel, nutrition, housekeeping, and so

---

[13]R. Johnson, "Revisiting the 'Wobbly Three-Legged Stool'." *HCM Review*, Summer 1979, pp. 15–22.

[14]Shortell, "Physician Involvement."

[15]S. Shortell, "Hospital Medical Staff Organization: Structure, Process and Outcome," *Hospital Administration* 19 (Spring 1974), pp. 96–106.

[16]S. Becker, S. Shortell, and D. Newhauser, "Management Practices and Hospital Length of Stay," *Inquiry* 17 (Winter 1980), pp. 318–30.

on, but do not involve the curing component, namely, the medical staff. The physician portion, the traditional medical staff, is typically organized along *divisional* lines, such as surgery, obstetrics, etc., with subspecialists concentrated in each division. While each division contains relevant clinical specialists, it, too, is incomplete, for it does not contain the relevant clinical and administrative support services. This, of course, has resulted in the classic dual hierarchy of authority.

The present environment calls for more physician involvement in hospitalwide decision making, longer appointments for chiefs of staff, full- or part-time paid medical directors, more stringent privilege reviews, and altered bylaws that reflect community needs. To achieve these goals, three models are suggested: the independent-corporate model, the divisional model, and the parallel model.[17]

In the *corporate model*, the hospital is a totally functional organization dealing at arm's length with a totally independent medical staff. It is akin to the group model HMO. It might also be called the condominium model. The ultimate form could be a series of corporations, each independent and contracting with the others to provide a series of services in a space called a hospital. Thus, a series of physician groups would contract with a hospital management group and support groups as well as a real estate group. This, however absurd it might seem, has a number of practical advantages and is being explored. The nature of the relationship of the physician to the other entities is one of contractor, and it is in the contract that all performance specifications must be enumerated. The basic issue for the hospital, if it continues to exist in its present form, is the make or buy decision. If the hospital buys rather than makes, i.e., secures from outside rather than inside, monitoring the contract becomes a matter of paramount concern. If the contractor (the physician group) fails to perform, are there immediate alternatives available to the hospital?

The advantages of this model, are that it supports physician autonomy, because recent legal decisions have shifted the burden of responsibility for quality of care to hospital governing boards and administrations. (Note the Midland example given

---

[17]S. Shortell, "The Medical Staff of the Future: Replanting the Garden," *Frontiers of Health Services Management* 1, no. 3 (1985), pp. 3–48.

earlier.) As an independent legal entity, physician corporations have sole responsibility for their own bylaws, quality assurance, and accreditation; privileges are not dependent on volume or cost effectiveness; and the group can establish whatever criteria it likes for its members. Moreover, such groups would not be part of the hospital and therefore would be independent of any regulations aimed at the health delivery organization.

A crucial element for physicians to consider, however, is the level at which they wish to incorporate. At the urban teaching hospital referred to above, the physicians had to consider whether they would form a separate corporation relating to the hospital, or one relating to the hospital system as a whole. Indeed, once physicians incorporate as a separate legal entity, while the health delivery organization can have little influence over them other than through the contract, the physicians also have little influence over the health delivery organization. In addition, separately incorporated physicians would have to arrange for their own malpractice insurance and would face many of the problems of group practices. The group is also a semiorganized anarchy with any member having effective veto power over executive actions. Thus, if the group wants a new compensation plan and one physician refuses, the plan would be difficult, if not impossible, to implement. Indeed, there seems to be some evidence that it is easier for physicians to get together to form a union, where relatively few decisions have to be made, than to form a corporation. This is because a union negotiates salaries with another entity, while a group disperses its own profits, a more contentious issue.

The divisional model, at the opposite end of the continuum, places all managerial and technical support services within a series of clinically designated divisions. Each division is headed by a physician–clinical specialist who presumably has acquired managerial skills. This is the model adopted by Cleveland Clinic some years back, when faced with a recalcitrant director of nurses and enduring problems with nurse staffing. The clinic reorganized from the traditional model to seven divisions, each headed by a physician and with a clinical nurse director. The change appealed to both the physicians and the nurses, with the latter finding they had greater power both within nursing and in the division.

Some disadvantages became apparent later, when nurses began to realize that in losing their director of nursing, and in subordinating clinic directors to a divisional physician chief, they had lost all input to top management. This problem could be remedied by the creation of a matrix organization in which functional specialists would report both to a new senior nursing manager at the top management level for certain purposes and to the divisional chief for daily operations. (The "certain purposes" might include career development, resource allocation, and specialty consulting.)

Johns Hopkins Medical Center in Baltimore also has a divisional design, as do some other large medical centers. This type of organization, because all services are incorporated into a single management structure, lends itself to a divisional budgeting process. Responsible budgeting is harder to accomplish with the other models or in the traditional structure, for there is no single management structure that can assume responsibility.

For physicians, the major advantage of the divisional model is increased authority and control, for the physicians head the divisions. They may report directly to the president of the health care delivery organization. Where this structure has been adopted, the CEO is often, though not necessarily, a physician. Considerably enhanced management skills and attitudes, as well as time are needed to make this model work, and these are not always forthcoming. It is indeed curious that while much lip service has been paid by managers and by M.D.s to the need for management skills, and though training programs are becoming quite common, it is still rare that clinical chiefs are chosen, even in part, for their managerial abilities. From the hospital's perspective, the divisional model fosters integration across the variety of support services needed to provide clinical care. However, it should be recognized that divisional organization tends to diminish functional specialization, which may become a problem in the long run in terms of career development. The divisional model lends itself to DRGs for the divisions can be organized around clusters of DRGs. The disadvantage to the hospital is loss of control by hospital administration, especially by nurses.

The third alternative is the parallel model. The parallel organization consists of a series of relatively permanent committees meant to deal with the major strategic issues facing both the hospital and the medical staff. Clearly this structure will be time-consuming and will usurp some of the daily operating responsibilities of the traditional medical staff, though it may be more effective as a mechanism for involving physicians in the overall management process than are traditional structures.

The advantage of the parallel model is that physicians have more significant input into those issues that affect their long-run future. It is time-consuming, and those who serve in the parallel organization may well be self-selected and lose credibility with their peers. Obviously, the parallel organization should not replace the traditional system. It is also difficult to see how this model differs from any approach that seeks the wider involvement of physicians in strategic planning task forces or committees within the traditional structure.

Because these models are designed for hospitals, they do not address the issue of medical staff organization in relation to health system development. Ford in Detroit, for example, is experiencing difficulties in relating those physicians who work in its satellite systems to those working in the central hospital. Each of Ford's facilities is organized within a traditional structure, but because of geographic distance and time, there is relatively little contact between the physician groups. In addition, doctors in the satellite system, because they are associated with the evolution of a low-cost ambulatory system, tend to be viewed as practicing less highly specialized, and therefore lower-status, medicine.

The same problem is faced by the multisite HMO that has departments in which members rarely, if ever, see each other. The problem will be compounded as hospitals cease to be the focus and become merely one facet of health delivery systems. What structures will suffice for geographically dispersed doctors? Should there be a medical director at each site? Should there be someone in charge of a specialty at each site? With whom is management to talk about resource allocation and performance problems?

Where there are multiple strategies there must be multiple structures. If a health organization decides to simultaneously pursue being a low-cost system and a high-technology focus provider, never the twain shall meet! A single structure, a single set of processes to govern doctors functioning in dissimilar systems will never work. High-technology doctors have different values, goals, and careers for they seek rewards and status among their academic colleagues, while service providers look for their rewards in patient care and in income or time off. No single department can satisfy both with a single incentive system. Dual systems must be created to take care of these two very different kinds of doctors operating in quite different kinds of environments, although within the same health system.

There is no easy answer to the multisite HMO structural problem. Because HMOs are relatively small, any given department may have but a few physicians at any particular site. However, HMO physicians tend to be young and therefore at an early stage of professional development, so colleagues are enormously important to them. It does seem valuable to have departments that cut across the HMO, to facilitate bringing together physicians within a department, as well as to have meetings of the entire medical staff from time to time. But here, as in any geographically decentralized system, face-to-face meetings involve a cost in time and loss of productivity. One potential solution lies in the realm of communications technology which offers the possibility of linkups either through computers or through teleconferencing. Regular communications could certainly take place through a computer network, while meetings could relatively easily be teleconferenced, using satellite or cable links, probably at lower cost than if the doctors had to travel. While department chairmen within an HMO should take care of recruitment, professional development, and resource allocation, physician managers at the site should integrate care within a given facility, reporting through the management structure to the medical director.

Structure should follow strategy. While the models described are certainly valid alternatives for any health delivery organization to consider, the particular structure adopted should be a function of the unique strategy of that organization rather than some absolute pattern that all should follow.

PHYSICIAN VOICE

The 10-hospital study, carried out at 5 for-profit and 5 not-for-profit hospitals in a variety of regions of the United States, sought the opinions of a sample of doctors at each hospital as well as of the CEOs. A number of questions were asked about physician voice (see Chapter 7 for details): Were there physicians on the board? What management committees existed and were physicians represented on the committees? Did managers sit on physician committees? Were physician managers paid, and was there a medical director or vice president for medical affairs? Were physicians satisfied with the amount of influence they had in general, and in particular over hospital goals and direction, capital projects, clinically related activities, allocation of physical and staff resources, and the work setting? Were there conflicts between physicians and managers, and if so, how were they resolved? Did physicians feel that they were appropriately informed and educated so that they could have an adequate voice?

While the study was mainly intended to obtain qualitative information, crude numerical ratings were made on a hospital-by-hospital basis and showed that satisfaction with physician influence varied quite significantly from one hospital to another. On a scale of one (low) through five (high), ratings varied from roughly 2.7 through 4.3. There was, interestingly enough, no particular correlation between satisfaction and being adequately educated and informed, or between satisfaction and influence. Those hospitals in which physicians expressed the least and the most satisfaction with their influence were *both* rated highest in physician satisfaction with adequacy of information. This confirms what is often found in consulting: when managers and physicians complain about communication, they usually mean not the passive reception of information but the exercise of influence. Thus, hospitals that may be very good at passing on information do not necessarily provide channels for physicians to exercise power.

A frequent comment in many of the hospitals was that information was often passed on from management through the formal channels of the medical executive committee and the department chairmen. Chairmen varied extremely in their willingness or capacity to act as information conduits, many being quite inadequate in so doing.

There was no great variation among hospitals surveyed in terms of governance or medical structure, though it was noteworthy that the for-profits had greater representation of physicians on the board than did the not-for-profits. Moreover, in the not-for-profits, physician representatives on the board tended to be officers rather than at-large attending physicians who were more often representatives in the for-profits. Indeed, a frequent complaint of at-large physicians was that there was inadequate representation of their views and interests in the board or in medical and management committees. Physicians felt strongly that M.D. board members should represent physicians at large. There was also a strong feeling that medical executive committees that lacked at-large representation essentially disenfranchised a significant proportion of the medical staff. Satisfaction with physician voice also obviously varied from physician to physician, and those with formal positions tended to be better satisfied than those with at-large positions.

Physicians in smaller hospitals neither had nor wished to have a paid physician manager, such as a medical director or vice president for medical affairs. It was only in the larger hospitals (300 to 400 beds and up) that such a position became an issue. Even then, in those hospitals lacking a physician manager, doctors had mixed and ambivalent feelings about the position, as they also had about whether chairmen should be full-time and paid. A number of smaller hospitals still had part-time chairmen, many of whom were unpaid. There was a strongly held view that the moment a chairman, whether part- or full-time, began to be paid, he became a captive of management and would therefore attend to management's interests rather than to those of the physicians. Indeed, in one smaller community hospital, the part-time paid chairman of the Ob/Gyn department negotiated a contractual arrangement on behalf of his department only to have the agreement rejected by his own physicians who felt that the contract involved conflict of interest because management paid part of the chairman's salary.

There was no systematic or marked variation in physician influence across hospitals; for-profit hospitals had no better or worse record than voluntaries. Although not altogether surprisingly, physician influence tended to be greater in smaller hospitals than in larger ones. Few hospitals had managers regularly sitting in on physician departmental meetings or physicians attending management committee meetings on a regular basis. However, most hospitals did have some physician representation on long-range-planning and capital-budgeting committees where these existed, but usually these physicians were appointed rather than at large and tended to be department chairmen. This is important because physicians expressed great concern over management actions that they felt were competitive. As an example, at one community hospital a physician was brought into a local town to increase referrals and was given benefits that caused the other doctors to wonder whether they should have resigned and reapplied to the hospital! The complaining physicians failed to note, however, that it might have taken such excessive inducements to secure a capable physician in that rural setting. As one doctor in the study put it,

> A current example is the hospital's entry into recruitment for the area to widen their base or protect the fringe area. They just recruited a family physician without consulting the Department of Family Practice. They did work through a medical needs assessment committee, but signed the contract offering this physician substantial benefits to open a practice without him having met members of the family practice department. I do not think [the department is] opposed to the concept but they will have to offer coverage to this person without having chosen or had input. They chose a board certified internist and said he was a family practitioner which is not the mentality of family practice.

In this instance, the hospital was felt to consult only those physicians, not necessarily representative, who were most likely to be sympathetic to management's wishes. This was true in areas other than recruitment, as well. Psychiatry, for example, felt relatively powerless as compared with pathology. And management did not think through the medical ramifications of managerial decisions in physicians' eyes. The chairman of psychiatry commented:

> In psychiatry in the last few years there has been discussion of psychiatry's problems without ever bringing a psychiatrist into the discussions, especially as regards emergency room coverage. That is why we are now a department. We have to be in the committee structure. But a number of hours were spent in committees and task forces without asking a psychiatrist to any of the meetings. It seems like a waste of time. We finally said we were tired of reading the minutes and helping come up with a solution. They could benefit in terms of program development from having more voice from office-based physicians.

This physician felt that the committee structure in the hospital

> leaves something to be desired because of who is on the committee. If the committees are not representative of the staff in terms of composition then

> there is an imbalance. The hospital-based physicians and surgeons are on lots of committees. They complain that they have all the work to do, which they do, but only because they're viewed as the workers. One physician is on six committees and 50 physicians are on none.

This was not a single physician talking—others echoed the sentiment that the doctors the hospital consulted were not representative. A recurring source of anger and frustration among physicians at many hospitals was management "selling" an idea to its selected sympathetic docs, often bypassing formal mechanisms or preempting them.

Even where there were physicians on the board, medical skepticism about some executive decisions ran high. At another hospital, one doctor said,

> If there is any physician input into [those] situations, I do not know about it. You wonder if there is any physician input, and if you check into decisions along those lines, you find out that there is very little, if any. Those decisions are made by administration. [Management] may conceive of an idea and then proceed to try to sell that idea. Even if they cannot sell it, they go ahead and institute it.

INFORMING AND INVOLVING

There does seem to generally be a relationship between favorable evaluation of physician influence and opinions concerning the adequacy of the influence structure and process. If physicians are represented on the board, if they sit on the major committees and management sits on theirs, if management is open to physician influence and accessible, in short, if they are *involved*, then physicians usually feel positive about the appropriateness and extent of their voice. A favorable attitude does not mean that physicians always get what they want. In fact, it often goes along with a tough management that confronts doctors squarely with the facts of life about competition and gives them a reasoned, prompt, and just response to their requests, even if that response is "no."

Informing physicians is a complex issue. In many instances additional or different mechanisms are needed. In some hospitals,

> there has been a glut of information. We had a meeting with the medical staff last week. In addition to the quarterly meeting, we're going to have

quarterly dinners and newsletters. The system does not always work because there are so many committees. Sometimes there's duplication of effort, sometimes working at odds. We're trying to do something about it.

Many physicians felt that

we are mostly informed after the fact. If we were made more acutely aware of the need to be a little more discretionary as far as, for example, the number of blood tests that were ordered or diagnostic procedures, there's probably a lot that we could do to order fewer tests.

Many felt that information could be better.

We are reasonably informed but it could be more. There are things going on that one would like to know a little more about. The board gets our minutes . . . but we never see theirs. I don't know why that should be. There may be a reason, but I think if we knew what they were thinking one would perhaps have more input. At the moment we rely on our physician trustees to give information, and that does not work very well.

But often it was the fault of the doctors themselves. "The doctor today does not want to take the time to listen and/or read. That's why physicians here are on committees. Our multiple communication tools are not sufficient."

And what did doctors do if they did not like what went on?

It is a combination of sitting around and bitching. We have a large section of bitchers who, if they are not involved in a project, bitch about not knowing anything. But those who are actively involved go directly to the source. It would be nice [as this CEO said] to be able to let the bitchers know they could come and see me and get directly involved, but it is a slow evolutionary process.

The problem of informing is probably insoluble. Dissatisfaction with communication as expressed by physicians is often, as stated above, as much a function of lack of influence as a lack of information. Indeed, any significant efforts to improve communication, whether written or verbal, whether through individual or group processes, usually provoke the response that physicians are inundated. Efforts are not always welcomed, nor will they necessarily result in improved satisfaction ratings. Yet they probably need to be made. Such problems must be lived with as much as solved. The trouble is that where communication is ineffective, problems can be considerable. Often management is at fault for not understanding physicians (see Chapter 3). Physicians are rational activists. They are trained and function with a sense of immediacy. Problems cannot be put on the back shelf. Management and trustees have to respond in that way. If physicians say they want a nuclear magnetic resonance machine tomorrow, the board has to say we will make a decision on that issue after we study it, and we will have the decision for you in March. Then they have to produce that decision in March. Medical staff unrest is strictly on the basis of unfulfilled promises. It is okay for the answer to be "no," although the administration and the board are reluctant to say no. So they say "maybe," and that is worse than no.

Management should not develop significant programs or processes

without input from the individuals involved. For example, the current administrator thinks nothing of deciding to open up the outpatient for extended hours, conceptually a good idea, but in its mechanics a poor approach. He did not tell anybody. He just decided to do it. And that means a tremendous change in the patterns of physicians because the physician is in his office during the afternoons or early evenings when the outpatient department is supposed to be open!

The cost of limiting involvement can be severe.

The management team still feels it is easier to make decisions without getting the physicians involved. For example, the hospital had to react to fiscal pressures, and took a look at some numbers, and felt that nursing staffing levels were higher than they needed to be, so they let go some nursing positions and did not fill empty ones. They did not say that they were going to cut a certain percentage of the hospital staff and get together physicians and nurses and discuss it. So now some doctors feel there is a nursing staff shortage in some critical areas of the hospital and are putting administration on the defensive about some of these post facto decisions. And of course, quality of care becomes an issue.

Informing and involving are time-consuming and tedious, but necessary. Whom do you involve? The loyal? The obscure? The high admitter or the low admitter who should be admitting more? The participant who always fulfills his duties or the nonparticipant who never does? These are interesting questions, but without definite answers other than the use of that rare commodity, managerial judgment.

Yet doctors are quick to appreciate that while management may often fail in its duty to inform and educate the physicians adequately, physicians also tend to be an apathetic lot.

The doctor today does not want to take the time to listen and/or read. In general, physicians are totally apathetic and always have been so. In gen-

> eral, any physician just wants to practice his medicine and really does not give a crack about the management of the hospital or anything else. It is just a total apathy.

So management is faced with a dilemma: it is always the same small group of physicians who respond to management's efforts to reach out, and it is always the same large group of apathetic physicians who will be the first to complain about an action that affects their interests. This apathy extends to physicians not accepting their committee responsibilities. Some hospitals are considering making attendance at committee meetings a prerequisite for renewal of privileges. However, physicians feel that informal mechanisms and their own efforts are likely to achieve greater success with the apathetic. When the medical staff starts asking someone why he or she was not at a particular meeting, or tells the person it is too late to try and influence a decision because he should have been at the meeting involved, when doctors themselves say to their fellows "Where were you when that was discussed?" then physicians will become involved.

What form should involvement take? It is evident that circulation of information through newsletters and such merely adds to the clutter on a physician's desk and competes unsuccessfully for his attention. And given that doctors supposedly read an average of 1.8 nonmedical books per year, the struggle for their attention is uphill. The occasional large meeting in which management addresses a bored group of doctors waiting for drinks seems equally ineffective. Information must be communicated through involvement, and the only reasonable solution appears to be to involve doctors more widely in the business of the hospital. This itself is a problem for, as physicians become more involved with committees, they resent the time taken away from their income-earning private practice; this is true even of those physicians who acknowledge that this is time well spent. One doctor summed it up well:

> One must assume that [physicians] realized they cannot all be involved in everything from the beginning. The majority of medical staff business is managed by the executive committee which is only a small number. Physicians are prepared to delegate some issues, but not in all situations. The feeling is that the executive committee is not disclosing things about a specialty, which usually is not true. I do not think there is a good way of getting around this except by confining the numbers of people involved. Physicians are terrible gossips. There is a tendency to be confidential outside

> about your patients, but you let everything down when you talk to your colleagues, and there are some indiscrete conversations.

This is no small matter. In a competitive era when management may need to move fast and engage in delicate negotiations that could be jeopardized by premature disclosure, careful selection of those doctors to be involved at early stages is essential. The remaining physicians can be told later, as occurred in one major merger where the board informed management a month before execution and the doctors on the day itself. The fallout simply must be lived with. But management is more often guilty of ignoring its doctors, to the detriment of any possibility of true partnership, than of excess in the opposite direction.

THE INFLUENTIAL DOCTOR

Who, then, does management pay attention to? As one CEO put it,

> I would like to talk to the person who puts in more and therefore would like to be listened to more. I think there is a tremendous amount of back scratching that goes on among hospitals and doctors. I do not want to play doctor. I don't want [the doctor] to play [administrator], but we are all going down the same road together. There are people that thrive upon the bureaucracy of administration, medical administration, that is required in a hospital. They like it, they enjoy it, they want to do it. Some want to play tennis, some want to be on committees. Others will put up with it simply because they have to. But take Doctor A, he is excellent at all those various things, he will put in the time, and therefore, he has been chairman of the board, he has been chief of staff and chief of surgery, as well as serving on HEW committees and on the board of governors. You find someone that does those things well and you keep laying on him until he calls "uncle." But the converse is also true. When Doctor A says he needs a piece of equipment in order to do surgery here, I don't question whether or not we can justify it economically, I go get it. But we are not going to belly up to the whims of one doctor who says "Fire Nurse Jones, I don't like her." You don't do that these days. If they say we need a different staffing ratio and here's why, then I will be very reasonable with the docs if they will be reasonable with me and just explain, just go through the processes.

Management has to be careful not to be overly selective in whom it listens to, however, or it will get into the bind criticized by the physician above. As one physician put it,

> Management is only hearing a small number of physicians. They are the hospital-based docs—radiology, pathology, and perhaps ER. There's a sec-

> ond strata of surgeons and anesthesiologists. Even though the surgeons aren't hospital based, they depend on the hospital for the majority of their income, and they have a lot of time to interact with administration and the powers that be. [That is] who is heard. The office-based physicians—family practice, pediatrics, psychiatry—even though they may be greater in number, are not represented. I would like to see management make a consistent effort to tap into those people, though I am not sure it would profit them. We are not organized, we don't make waves, so from [management's] point of view, there is nothing to gain from it. They should interview the 60 of us, or come to departmental meetings and try to establish more of a liaison with the majority of physicians.

But how, with limited time, can management talk to the numerous doctors, many of whom are acknowledged as being apathetic? Or does management inevitably have to select? (That selection will be based on criteria not necessarily agreed on by the physicians themselves.)

Often those physicians who most strongly express the need for greater involvement tend to be those who do not have official positions within the hospital, i.e., are not department chairman or chairmen of committees. But, surprisingly, there is general agreement in most hospitals about what it takes for a physician to be influential.

> If you are new in town, don't say anything bad about anyone because you don't know whom they're connected to. Say thank you for your consults and contribute to the hospital.
>
> Make sure you provide service and support to your patients that even the most aggressive critic would respect you for, provide service to physicians who refer to you with 100 percent availability, and get into the community—join the church, service clubs, etc. This last is one that most doctors miss and that the inner circle requires, that the physician is willing to commit not only time to the patient and the referring physician but to the medical staff and the hospital. The quality of what the physician stands for in his care is critical.
>
> Respond to consults in a timely manner, give good patient care, and attend assigned committee meetings.
>
> Demonstrate excellence in what you do, that gains respect of staff, physicians, and administration. Do your other work, records, committee activity. Put patients in the hospital and generate revenue. And balance aggressiveness with a demonstrated willingness to work within the systems and not be a maverick. Influential doctors are not always the large-volume producers, but they usually have these characteristics. Most physicians would acknowledge that the high-volume admitter is going to get more attention, but there are also physicians who may admit a lot of patients but

> who are listened to more intensely for other reasons—notoriety, having been mentioned in the newspapers, maybe [being] more outspoken and more of a public figure.

But mostly it is in the performance of quality medicine, in the diligent performance of one's duties, and therefore in the respect of one's colleagues, that influence lies.

> Ability will show eventually, but availability shows immediately, so you have to be around. Mix socially, be active in the medical society, be available to nurses and others, give lectures and talks, give free time. That type of thing will do more than anything else. Get into one or two committees when you start, but not more, because that would be pushy.
>
> Basically, you have to be a good physician, you have to be respected in the medical community, have good rapport with nursing.

Physicians do respect the fact that those of their brethren who make an effort are more likely to be influential. The influential doctor is, in essence, somebody who has been around for some time, has the respect of his or her peers clinically, has a good reputation in the community, is willing to serve on committees, and has put time in to pay his dues. Such physicians are respected by their peers and heard and sought by management. The rare exception now is the influential doctor who is regarded as available rather than able, who is a high admitter and nothing else, and who is a good old boy.

TOWARD TRUE PARTNERSHIP

In view of the fact that physicians name influence as one of the three major factors governing their feeling of loyalty and devotion to a health organization, and because physician loyalty and devotion are crucial to the organization's well-being, so attention to influence is critical. Physicians expect to be represented on the board, expect this representation to be significant—i.e., voting—and expect it to include at-large physicians. The latter group should understand that they are not on the board to advance personal interests or the interests of friends or colleagues, but to give their informed judgment and to represent doctors at large. They are there to clarify for nonprofessionals the impact of decisions on the organization and its physicians. Representation on the board is part of a broader concept of *partnership* espoused by physicians.

Partnership means more than the nominal involvement of doctors; it means a sharing risk and benefit, and perhaps even doctors do not fully realize its true meaning. Health organizations that pursue true partnership are more likely than those that do not to do well strategically and operationally in tomorrow's health care environment. The specifics of structure are less important than carrying through partnership as a sharing of decision making at all levels. Thus, physicians should sit in on all management committees, as managers should on all physician committees. Physicians should be sufficiently informed and educated to have a good grasp of strategy, and those physicians with management responsibilities should have adequate management training. Chairmen of departments should be selected not just for their clinical or research capabilities, but for their managerial capabilities, because much of what they will do will involve management. (Selection on the basis of managerial ability is still rare even in the most sophisticated teaching hospital, let alone in community hospitals.)

Health organizations will increasingly have to put pressure on physicians to diminish organizational costs, which will diminish physician income. However, if health organizations seek to diversify to enhance revenues from activities other than patient care, it would seem reasonable to offer physicians the opportunity to participate financially in such ventures. But a caveat can be derived from a salutory example. One community hospital, seeking to prevent a competitive threat, bought a building intended for use as a surgicenter by a competing group of physicians. The chief executive officer then offered the building to his own physicians for a surgicenter, only to be turned down by them, for they had no clinical interest in it once the competitive threat had been removed. Left with the financial burden, the CEO had no recourse but to seek an outside group of doctors to rent the facility!

Doctors only tend to be interested in joint financial ventures when their income is hurting because their private practice is being cut back, when the venture is linked to their private practice, or when the physicians are essentially entrepreneurial and used to making financial investments of this order. Whether physicians should be offered an interest in joint ventures in patient care is a more complex matter. In the past, financial benefit from involvement in a clinical activity was anathema to most doctors. This is altering, however, and the issue seems to be more open. With more doctors seeking shrinking health care dollars, this will change rapidly. In fact, the same physicians who talk for hours to their brokers about tax shelters may fail to see the financial attractiveness of hospital ventures, perhaps because they believe that professional and business "hats" cannot sit on the same head at the same time. Traditionally, certainly, the doctor has kept them separate. However, the link between professional and business activities now being made by health care organizations is being made much more slowly by the physician. Architects realized the need to be both professionals and businessmen much earlier when faced with companies that both designed and built, forcing architects out of their comfortable existence as professional designers, clearly and neatly distinct from the messy world of contracting. The design/build companies combined both skills more economically and efficiently and were more competitively successful in the marketplace. The physician may face a similar situation.

On the other side of the partnership coin, hospitals, faced with the potentially ephemeral loyalties of doctors with many alternatives, should begin to wonder about the free ride that they offer their physicians. It is customary for a hospital to provide space and equipment for its doctors, who have to purchase these at great cost for their private offices. When physicians feel that they can obtain such items wherever they go, there is little to prevent them from going. Why should hospitals not require physicians to buy space and equipment, or at least to partially pay for it, offering physicians a thoroughly adequate return on their money, but linking the doctors inextricably financially to the organization? While physicians may gain a significant financial benefit (or tax advantages) from their investment, they will equally risk a significant financial loss should they choose to leave precipitously. This is consonant with the notion of sharing risk and benefit.

The basic rationale for proposing (true) partnership as a critical approach for health organizations to secure the loyalty of their doctors, is that the only ways to deal with diverging interests are to bargain about them or to harmonize them. Traditional organizational approaches have focused on providing intermediaries or mediating processes. Mediating processes involve attempts to talk through problems; intermediaries involve management-appointed physician managers who are shot at by both sides. Where interests differ, they must be brought into consonance, and true partnership does just that.

Of course, compensation mechanisms must, in general, be redesigned to reflect organizational priorities as well as physician concerns. Few health organizations, other than those which pay bonuses for volume, link compensation to performance. Yet if physicians are to pay attention to matters of managerial interest and concern, such as maintaining certain cost or quality standards, such behavior must be linked to incentives, financial or otherwise.

There are, of course, some issues to be faced. How do you offer equity in joint ventures or other arrangements? Should shares be offered free to all doctors or should doctors buy shares? Should high admitters or loyal doctors be offered shares? If doctors are supposed to buy in, how can the young physician with a family and a large debt buy as many shares as the established doctor? Whom do you want to encourage and how can you do it? One way to approach the spirit of partnership is to get doctors to suggest the criteria and to come up with a formula that must satisfy all physicians, not just a few. This is an especially thorny issue, though one that should not be allowed to bedevil, as all doctors are not equal.

Partnership, then, involves the interpenetration of management and physicians and the sharing of risk and gain. Only through true partnership can trust be enhanced and paranoia diminished.

PHYSICIAN UNIONS: BACKGROUND AND AN EXAMPLE

The professions are currently undergoing an industrial revolution similar to the one experienced a century ago by the crafts. Many professional roles are becoming bureaucratically structured. Increasingly, professionals are finding employment in large organizations; professional activities are becoming more standardized, rationalized, and mechanized; and, as new divisions of labor are established, professional work is becoming more collaborative. Professionals who typically work in organizations—nurses, teachers, engineers, social workers, and even physicians—are turning toward unions, with or without the consent of their professional associations,[18] because this is one way of ensuring adequate voice in the absence of partnership.

Unionization came late to the health team mainly because there was no one to be united *against*, nobody to bargain *with*.[19] But at the present time, three physician union-type movements appear to be developing. The first involves self-employed physicians who believe that the American Medical Association has not been responsive to their fears that government, insurance companies, and hospitals are interfering with the doctor-patient relationship. The second comprises many hospital staff officers whose Physician's National Housestaff Association was created to provide a single, powerful organization to negotiate with employers.[20] (In October 1975, the Attending Physicians Association of the City Hospital Center in Elmhurst, Long Island, which involved employees of Mount Sinai School of Medicine, became the first union recognized.) The third, the organization-based union, is exemplified by the action of doctors who worked for the Group Health Association (GHA) in Washington, D.C., a prepaid health care plan, and who voted to certify a union in 1977. The 80 doctors employed by GHA were paid salaries ranging from $32,000 to $71,000. The basic issue dividing workers and management was not money but working conditions and the right to participate in policymaking. According to Norman Lieberman, a spokesman for the union, "quality medicine" rather than "quantity medicine" was a primary concern, for example, "the question of how many patients a doctor should see in a day." Added Lieberman, "I don't think that a pulmonary specialist should be seeing kidney problems."[21]

---

[18]G. V. Engel and R. H. Hall, "The Growing Industrialization of the Professionals," in: *The Professionals and Their Prospects*, ed. E. Friedson (Beverly Hills, Calif.: Sage Publications, 1973), pp. 75–88.

[19]D. Woods, "Unions Moving into M.D. Offices and Clinics," *CMA Journal* 111 (October 19, 1974), pp. 862–74.

[20]Engel and Hall, "Growing Industrialization."

[21]N. Daniels, "On the Picket Line: Are Doctors' Strikes Ethical?" *Hastings Center Report* 8, no. 1 (February 1978), pp. 24–29.

The background was that the Group Health Association of Washington was one of the first health maintenance organizations. It was started in 1937 by federal employees of liberal bent who were concerned with creating a health organization that would not be dominated by doctors. They therefore formed GHA as a consumer cooperative, and so it has remained to this day. Members still elect the nine-member board, on which the same activist figures appear and reappear. Management and the doctors are invited by the board to its meetings, the executive director and medical director usually attending.

Prior to 1970, employed physicians made individual arrangements, of a somewhat arbitrary kind, regarding salary. As a result, the idea developed that the doctors might form a corporate entity similar to that of Kaiser, to improve their benefits and security, but according to a legal opinion, the District of Columbia lacked legislation permitting physicians to incorporate as a professional corporation. In 1975, physicians reiterated their concerns that, as GHA had grown larger, it had become more impersonal. The original alliance between consumer and physician had weakened, and instead of feeling like partners, the doctors felt they were now employees. They withdrew from involvement in the organization to focus on clinical care. The medical group, facing the alternatives of an independent organization or a union preferred the former, and therefore formalized the medical group's status, though it was not yet a corporation, together with a nine-person medical council consisting both of chiefs and at-large physicians. The group negotiated a yearly capitation rate, its own salary structure, and distribution of its surplus funds. (An interesting footnote is that Dr. Mitchell, who was president of the council and medical director, later became president of the union.) In 1976, following a complaint to the National Labor Relations Board, the physicians were told that they were not legally a corporation, and because they were behaving like a union, they should form one officially. The reason given was that the board was representing employees bargaining with management. In 1977, the board retained a consulting company to study organizational alternatives for the physicians. A short six weeks later the consultants, returning half their fee, proposed a corporate structure, much to the board's distaste.

The consulting report found common threads in the crises common to prepaid group practice. Dramatic membership increases revealed flaws in the organizational structure in that systems developed for small groups did not work for larger groups. Crises occurred because the administration or the physicians believed that the other group was not performing. Physicians are different from other providers and occupy a special role, demanding and obtaining input into decision- and policymaking by increasing their management roles. More disputes have involved policymaking, roles, and authority, than economics. Essentially, personal and professional satisfaction is more important than money. The alternatives considered by the consultants were: do nothing, work as individual employees, negotiate individual physician contracts, form a physicians' union, and form an independent medical group. The consultants concluded that muddling through, i.e., doing nothing, was irrelevant, that the proposal concerning physicians as individual employees was unacceptable, and that physician contracts entailed possible disadvantages. A physicians' union would frustrate the goals of GHA, resulting in attrition of physician leadership and of conscientious physicians. However, a contract with a medical group, the consultants felt, would result in an opportunity for GHA to retain its essential nature and goals while enhancing the medical delivery system. Consumer ownership and control would then rest with GHA, and the consultants felt moreover that this would maximize board-physician cooperation, clearly define the roles and responsibility of medical leadership, increase physician responsibility and accountability, and offer the most potential for cost effectiveness while not conflicting with NLRB regulations. The emotional fears that such a contract might evoke were, they felt, groundless. No fundamental change in the nature of GHA would result.

The board, still mistrusting the doctors and afraid of a separate for-profit entity and of losing control, passed a resolution proposing a joint doctor-board committee to study the issue further. But even this action was abruptly reversed in a five-to-four vote electing three new trustees on an anticorporation slate. The new board forbade a separate corporation.

A union lawyer was retained by the physicians and, in late April, reported on the advantages of unionization. He pointed out that unlike a corporation, a union required that the board of trustees negotiate with them. The union was the exclusive agent and the employer might not change existing benefits without negotiation. The union could negotiate matters such as compensation, work hours, assignment, transfer, promotion, travel, educational benefits, job security, grievance procedures, retirement, and insurance. Managerial and supervisory employees were excluded from the bargaining unit or coverage by the contract. It was pointed out that a union is basically certified for perpetuity and is intended to last as long as the employees it represents desire its services. It can be dissolved via vote, in much the same way it is certified. To form a union required adopting a simple constitution setting forth goals, offices, shop steward structures, negotiating procedures, means for contract ratification, financial systems, and membership requirements. Members should be solicited to sign authorization cards designating the union as their representative for collective bargaining and authorizing dues reduction. Fifty percent of those eligible were required to sign the cards for the union to be recognized. The NLRB would determine the appropriate bargaining unit—i.e., who was covered or excluded—and hold a secret ballot election. If a simple majority approved, the union would be certified and bargaining on a contract could begin.

In spite of a counter offer by the board, on October 20, a letter was sent to the board reporting that the doctors had formed a union. An NLRB-supervised union election was held, with 60 of 80 physicians voting, and two thirds of those voting in favor. Sixty doctors had been willing to join a corporation if GHA had sanctioned it.

In early 1978, contract negotiations began but broke down. A strike was voted nearly unanimously and continued for 10 days. Following mediation, a contract was finally signed that incorporated the physicians' basic demands. Later contracts improved physician work conditions, explicitly omitting productivity and efficiency goals, standards, and incentives.

In a more recent contract, the union gained for physicians the right to limited private practice and further improved benefits and salaries, while management negotiated a sharp increase in the number of physician management positions.

Today, union members are generally satisfied with what their leadership has achieved, though they easily forget and become apathetic until the next time there are problems. There are some concerns over perceived violations of the contract by management and some problems with the actions of physician managers. Because there is no viable alternative for the physicians as yet, the union will survive and is flexible about comanagement. Some union concerns have to do with the pressure for extended hours and the use of physician extenders to enhance productivity, which management favors. The union wants physicians to be able to choose. The union feels that management has sometimes harassed individual doctors and dealt with physicians bureaucratically rather than informally.

Management, in turn, while feeling a kinship with its union colleagues, feels that it has been difficult to get union members to attend to administrative details that have to be dealt with, though management understands that doctors choose HMO practice to free themselves from such details. The lead physician, the senior union position below management, faces conflict because he or she cannot really supervise fellow union members. Productivity, and the incentives associated with it, are now a priority with management because unit costs have escalated, due, in part, to the very success of the union in gaining advances in salaries and benefits for members, and in part to increases given union members who have been with the organization a long time. Management feels that some management prerogatives have been negotiated away, and that management flexibility regarding job assignments has been much restricted by the union contract. These restrictions, management feels, limit its ability to be competitive in an increasingly competitive environment. Management feels that it has tried to deal with problems on an informal basis and to avoid grievances, but that it is not always easy to do so.

GHA has grown, regionalized, and decentralized in the face of stiff competition, particularly from Kaiser, and this fragmentation is feared by the union as potentially weakening its coherence, as does the hiring of part-time physicians. But both management and the union understand the nature of the competitive environment, and both are equally concerned about GHA remaining viable.

It may be anticipated that unionization of the medical profession in the United States will increase sharply in the years ahead, especially when one considers that by the end of 1975, as many as 100,000 physicians, or close to 25 percent of all practitioners, will be working primarily as salaried employees. While it is not easy to come by exact figures, some estimate that as many as 55,000 physicians in the United States are already affiliated with medical unions. At the national level, there are two unions, the American Federation of Physicians and Dentists and the National Physicians Council, the latter affiliated with the American Federation of Labor–Congress of Industrial Organizations.[22] The Union of American Physicians, begun in California, and the American Federation of Dentists and Physicians, based in Missouri, grew from 1,000 to 10,000 members betweeen 1972 and 1975.[23]

The four-day strike, in March 1975, by the Committee on Interns and Residents (CIR) in New York City, described as "the first major strike by physicians," was over work conditions and patient care issues. The two-year contract ultimately negotiated with New York's League of Voluntary Hospitals included the creation of a committee composed of house staff and attending physicians, to develop standards and guidelines for patient care, to set up house-staff work schedules, and to act as final arbiter of grievances. Richard Knutson, M.D., then CIR president, described the contract as "incredible" and predicted that the agreement would have nationwide impact on the relationships between hospitals and physicians.[24]

PHYSICIAN UNIONS: ARGUMENTS FOR AND AGAINST

In the next generation, the great majority of physicians will find themselves in bureaucratic organizations. Such physicians ought to have the right to negotiate. Increasingly, their goals will be more like those of other trade unionists. Yet the majority of the medical profession still denies the public the right to negotiate the price of physician services. Increasingly, such prices

---

[22]S. Wolfe, "Worker Conflicts in the Health Field: An Overview," *International Journal of Health Services* 5, no. 1 (1975), pp. 5–8.

[23]Daniels, "On the Picket Line."

[24]N. Nole, "Doctors Move beyond Medicine—1975 Administrative Review," *The Hospital Medical Staff* 5, no. 4 (April 1976), pp. 20–27.

and arrangements for payment for physician services will come to be negotiated rather than unilaterally imposed, even in the United States. Under such circumstances, a greater number of conflicts are bound to arise. While compromises and concessions are necessary in such conflicts, a line must be drawn—it is an illegal and criminal act for a physician to withdraw his services from the sick or to abandon his patients. Thus, there is a need to ensure satisfactory negotiating mechanisms.[25]

Physicians are, however, professionals. Professionals have a commitment to enhancing the standards of their profession, to preserving and expanding the legacy of knowledge and experience at the heart of their professional activity, and to holding their colleagues to high standards of performance. Moreover, physicians have a special professional relationship to patients, a relationship that places unique obligations on doctors to provide patients with the best service they can provide and which involves, for physicians, a certain confidentiality, trust, and autonomy. The theory is that this relationship is threatened if patients feel that doctors are significantly motivated by pecuniary interests rather than professional duty. But, so the argument goes, trade unions are primarily instruments for advancing the self-interest of their members, and the physician who becomes a union member will undermine the doctor-patient relationship at the heart of professional performance.[26]

The contrast is overdrawn on both sides. Trade unions have historically been fairly narrow vehicles fighting for bread-and-butter issues for their members. But where is it written that unions are restricted to such concerns? Unions have seriously failed to serve the real interests of their members because they have had too narrow a view of the interests of their members and of the relationship between the interests of different groups of workers.[27]

Without vigorous representation of their rights by forces that have been conspicuously lacking in the past, physicians must certainly be reduced to the level of public functionaries, ac-

---

[25]Wolfe, "Worker Conflicts in the Health Field."

[26]Daniels, "On the Picket Line."

[27]Ibid.

corded no more respect or status than postal employees or public school teachers in their preunion days.[28] It may be, however, that whereas these physicians, in the past, had considerable control over their professional lives, they are now encountering increasing government regulations, rises in costs, consumer demands, and some loss of their former social status without the job tenure and other fringe benefits afforded their hospital-staff or academic colleagues. Thus, they see these changes as a direct threat. For example, high malpractice insurance premiums do not immediately affect hospital-employed physicians, as they are costs to the hospital. But private-practice physicians, who have no established negotiating machinery, are beginning to believe that organization and collective bargaining are their only recourses.[29]

Strikes by interns and residents have focused on wages, working conditions, and participation in decisions relating to patient care, training, and hospital priorities. Physicians in private practice were mobilized into collective action by soaring malpractice rates. The common threat in these job actions is that when substantial numbers of both groups of physicians view their interests as threatened, feel they are losing control over their professional lives, and believe they have no other resources, they make the same decision that teachers made years before—they abandon the independent outlook of the professional for the power of organized action.[30]

In a society increasingly dominated by organized power blocks, the appeal of unionization to professionals is growing largely because the independence of the professional has diminished. Some strikes have occurred not because of a dispute with hospitals but because of soaring malpractice insurance premiums. Private physicians are attempting to combat the strength of the institutional Goliaths by forming and joining associations, guilds, and even unions. But such organizational efforts face significant legal problems. If traditional legal concepts per-

---

[28]S. A. Marcus, "The Purposes of Unionization in the Medical Profession: The Unionized Profession's Perspective in the United States," *International Journal of Health Services* 51 (1975), pp. 37–42.

[29]S. Wassertheil-Smoller, L. Croen, and B. Siegel, "Physicians' Changing Attitudes about Striking," *Medical Care* 17, no. 1 (January 1979), pp. 79–85.

[30]Ibid.

taining to the status of physicians are unthinkingly and anachronistically applied to the united endeavors of all doctors, not only may the physicians be forced to forego the labor relations rights and protections available to other workers, but they also may be exposed to the risk of substantial antitrust liability.[31]

Bob Miller, personnel director at Toronto's St. Joseph's Hospital, believes unionization is alien to professional and clerical employees; unenlightened management is what usually drives such people into a union, says Miller, and if management does not like the thought, it should take appropriate preventive measures. What measures? Miller's formula is communication—managers who listen as well as talk—and sound personnel policies including a grievance procedure, mechanisms for determining seniority, vacation allotments, and so on.

Miller is convinced that, while salary always figures prominently in any labor dispute, it is often a convenient front for deeper, less-definable concerns such as recognition, security, and desire for some knowledge of the overall machine in which the individual worker may feel he is just a minor and dispensable cog.[32]

The Association of American Medical Colleges (AAMC) has gone on record as opposing withholding of medical care by physicians as a means to advance their own interests. The association felt it is basically unethical for physicians to strike to achieve what they perceive to be social goals, Dr. John A. D. Cooper, AAMC president, said.[33]

The popular image of the doctor is that of a kindly soul prepared to struggle through wind and weather to do his best to help the suffering sick. Indeed, this is the image most doctors like to have of themselves—good and determined men and women prepared to rise at any time of the day or night to use their expert abilities to serve their fellow man. (This ethos may be traced back to the medieval Christian Brothers and Sisters of Charity who gave their all to save the sick.) But the image of dedicated altruism has suffered in past years in Britain. Consultants and junior hospital doctors have shown themselves willing to neglect

---

[31] Nole, "Doctors Move Beyond Medicine."

[32] Woods, "Unions Moving."

[33] "AAMC Opposes Physician Strikes," *U.S.-MED* 14, no. 23 (December 1, 1978).

their professional commitment to care for the sick to protect their own interests, professional in the former case and financial in the latter. These doctors' actions were supported by the British Medical Association, once looked on by some of its members, at least, as a stronghold of traditional ethics.[34]

Lord Taylor of Harlow was afraid that neither moral indignation nor moral leadership had much influence on a powerful government dedicated to pragmatic expediency and believed that problems arise for professionals in a socialist state that have yet to be resolved. Of course, if conditions became intolerable, doctors could resign from the National Health Service (NHS). Some years ago, British general practitioners, who are independent contractors deriving most of their income from capitation fees, contemplated resigning and seemed confident that they would be able to maintain their service to patients on some privately arranged financial basis. For members of hospital staffs, all of whom are salaried, resignation would be more difficult, although it was thought that they might be reemployed through agencies organized by the profession. Nevertheless, because the NHS is now nearly the monopoly employer of British medical labor, it is unlikely that mass resignation will ever take place, and some means will have to be found of resolving the serious conflicts that may arise when doctors have professional responsibilities to their patients on the one hand and contractual obligations to their government employer on the other.[35]

Sir Theodore Fox, for many years the editor of the prestigious medical journal *Lancet*, believed that doctors must decide whether they are industrial workers who strike with any provocation, or whether they are members of a profession who do not strike. They could not be responsible doctors one day and industrial workers the next. Others thought that this was too simplistic a view in the context of British doctors working in a nationalized service where, inevitably, they are industrial workers in relation to the NHS machinery and at the same time professionals with a professional ethic in relation to individual patients.[36]

---

[34]"Industrial Action by Doctors," *Journal of Medical Ethics* 2 (1976), pp. 1–2.

[35]"By the London Post: Thirty Years On—Should Doctors Strike?—Sundry Clippings," *New England Journal of Medicine* 299, no. 17 (October 26, 1978), pp. 936–38.

[36]Ibid.

Perhaps the underlying problem in physicians' relationships with government is the ambivalence of those relations: for example, in the United States, doctors are partners with government in the implementation of medicare, they then become antagonists at the bargaining table with that same government over the "obscene" question of money—who gets paid for what in operating medicare?[37]

WHEN CAN THE DOCTOR ORGANIZE?

"Professional" means someone engaged in work (1) predominantly intellectual and varied as opposed to routine mental, manual, mechanical, or physical work; (2) involving the consistent exercise of discretion and judgment in its performance; (3) the result of which cannot be standardized; and (4) requiring knowledge of an advanced type that is customarily acquired by a prolonged course of specialized study.[38]

A union is an organization of employees formed for the purpose of regulating relations between employers and employees. It has a written constitution, rules, and bylaws that set forth objectives and purposes and define the conditions under which persons may be admitted as members.[39] However, until recently, physicians were not, strictly speaking, regarded as employees. This could be remedied by amending legislation allowing certain professional groups to be deemed "units of employees appropriate for collective bargaining."[40]

Physicians may be associated with hospitals in three distinct ways: as independent contractors with access to hospital services and facilities; as staff physicians employed full-time; and as interns and residents completing their medical education. In the first two capacities, questions of labor law are clearly likely to arise.[41] What about the last?

---

[37]Woods, "Unions Moving."

[38]P. M. Swiercz and J. K. Skipper, "Labor Law and Physicians' Privileged Position: An Example of Structural Interest Influence," *International Journal of Health Services* 12, no. 2 (1982), pp. 249–60.

[39]Woods, "Unions Moving."

[40]Ibid.

[41]Swiercz and Skipper, "Labor Law and Physicians."

In a precedent-setting case involving the Ohio Valley Hospital Association, the NLRB board voted to exclude house staff from a bargaining unit that had an all-professional membership. A number of reasons were cited for this exclusion: (*a*) essential functions of physicians cannot be performed by other employees; (*b*) limited supervisory authority over physicians is confined to other physicians; (*c*) responsibility to direct all other professionals is inherent in the physician's role; (*d*) physicians are paid more than most other professional employees; (*e*) physicians have unique and extensive education, training, and skills; and (*f*) the NLRB has excluded registered nurses from bargaining units of professional employees, and physicians are entitled to the same treatment. The Board in denying the request to include doctors, held that house staff are not employees in labor law because they are engaged primarily in receiving graduate training and are primarily students having an educational rather than employment relationship with the hospital. Because physicians would consistently be a minority group within a bargaining unit made up of a complete health care team, they would run the risk of having their dominance of the whole health system undermined. A broad-based bargaining unit would result in a direct challenge to the dual hierarchy which has long been a recognized feature of a hospital organization structure.[42]

In a recent *New England Journal of Medicine* article, the rhetorical question was asked:

> Can doctors who still offer their skills on a fee-for-service basis—and who consider themselves to be in "private practice" or to be "independent contractors"—really avail themselves of this union mechanism, which was developed primarily after all, to represent the interests of salaried workers?
>
> The answer is a resounding yes, especially when one accepts the government's own definition of what establishes an employer-employee relationship, then examines how completely physicians now fit that definition of "employee" in their new relationships with HMOs, PPOs, and medicare, and in virtually all areas of their emerging interactions with the hospital industry.
>
> Internal Revenue Service ruling 66-274 establishes a set of four criteria to be used in determining whether sufficient control exists to deem a given employment relationship one of employer and employee:

[42]Ibid.

> The degree to which such individuals have become integrated into the organization or firm for which the services are performed.
>
> The substantial nature, regularity, and continuity of his work for such a person or firm.
>
> The authority vested in or reserved by such a person or firm to require compliance with its general policies.
>
> The degree to which the individual under consideration has been accorded the rights and privileges which such a person or firm has treated or established for its employees generally.
>
> That we have now become employees is established with certainty by the application of the "right of control" test under the National Labor Relations Act and ultimately by the power of those we work for to hire and fire—a right clearly claimed for itself by management in all existing HMOs and PPOs, by medicaid and medicare, and increasingly by hospital administrators as they also assert their right to base the granting of medical staff privileges on the physician's conformity with their own economic goals.
>
> It becomes evident, then, that it is not simply the offer and acceptance of a salary paycheck but the degree of control that one party can exert over another that determines the existence of an employer-employee relationship. Doctors have lost the ability to set their own fees, to determine freely the nature and number of units of service they can render, and even to decide where the service must be rendered; they have thereby become employees, no less so simply because they are paid for piecework rather than on an hourly or straight salaried basis.

The author concluded:

> The medical profession is confronted with a new set of problems to which the assumptions and solutions of the past are no longer applicable. Because this is in every respect a classic case of the sociologic reallocation of power, we are obliged to become adaptable enough to embrace mechanisms that will, we hope, preserve some of our strengths as a profession and that—although they are perhaps not the ones we might have employed under less trying circumstances—have worked well for others who have already been confronted by problems like ours.
>
> Throughout the history of our own union we have had to respond to the charge that it is "unprofessional" for doctors to belong to a union. We become more convinced with each passing day that only by standing together as a determined and ethical trade union of doctors can we protect and preserve at least the best features of that legacy of "professionalism" of which we are so properly proud and which seems to be slipping away from us in the absence of any other effective agency to represent us.[43]

---

[43]S. A. Marcus, "Trade Unionism for Doctors: An Idea Whose Time Has Come," *The New England Journal of Medicine* 311 (December 6, 1984), pp. 1508–11. © 1984 Massachusetts Medical Society. Reprinted by permission of *The New England Journal of Medicine.*

CHAPTER FIVE

Managing Loyalty and Devotion

Physicians of the utmost fame
Were called at once; but when they came
They answered, as they took their fees
"There is no cure for this disease."

Hilaire Belloc

LOYALTY AND DEVOTION—THE BASIC ISSUES

One key to success in health care markets is attracting and keeping physicians and the patients they control, i.e., managing loyalty and devotion. Loyalty is defined here as the volume of admissions and/or the share of practice brought by a physician to a hospital. Devotion is defined as the diligence with which the physician fulfills his or her responsibilities toward the institution, i.e., the number of committees they sit on, their attendance, and the hours that they give to activities such as fund raising. Loyalty and devotion are not simply given, they are earned. This chapter deals with the importance of managing loyalty and devotion and how this may be accomplished.

Even in an era in which many doctors are salaried, many patients attend clinics, and more patients each year subscribe to health care organizations such as HMOs in which they may not have a designated physician, the fee-for-service attending physician still controls the bulk of private patients. It is this group of private patients that can make the critical financial difference for many community or teaching hospitals. In the practice pattern impact study (see Preface and Chapter 7), 85 percent of 250 city patients interviewed at one teaching hospital said that the most important factor in deciding which hospital they should go to was the doctor's recommendation. Beyond this, good care, location, and friends' recommendations were also important. Clinic patients valued the doctor's advice less, only 62 percent (of 250) ranking it as very important, and it was ranked closer to the other

TABLE 5-1 Physician Choice of Hospital

Availability of technical/subspecialty resources
Geography—accessible from patient's home or physician's office
Quality of medical care
Quality of nonmedical care, i.e., hotel characteristics
Referring physician location or preference
Teaching availability
Loyalty, i.e., trained at institution
Patient choice/aversion
Coverage for cases

factors. Suburban patients rated the importance of their physician's recommendation even higher (95 percent of 250), than did those in the city. Moreover, 76 percent of all patients indicated that they chose a doctor first, and only 12 percent chose the hospital first. (More private patients than clinic patients chose a doctor first, 83 versus 62 percent.)

In the same study, 63 doctors were interviewed personally and a further 100 answered a self-administered questionnaire. Asked about their patients' loyalty, a majority (56 percent) felt that over three fourths of their patients were loyal to them, and this figure went up to 71.4 percent for high admitters. In other words, doctors and patients say much the same thing; doctors decide for patients which hospital they should attend.

Physicians were also asked about the extent to which they had multiple affiliations and would transfer patients from the hospital under study to some other hospital if the hospital took actions the doctors felt would harm their practice. Of physicians surveyed, 83.7 percent had multiple affiliations, with 63.5 percent actively admitting to hospitals other than the one in the study. Doctors could easily specify the hospitals they would use if they had to shift, and only 10.7 percent of those physicians interviewed felt that the transition would be very difficult. The potential impact of untoward action by the hospital, in this instance rebuilding on a site unattractive to the physicians, could well be catastrophic. Physicians estimated that they would shift as many as 59.9 percent of admissions (over 6,000 patients) to other hospitals. Even if exaggerated, these are compelling figures. The bases of physician choice of hospital are given in Table 5-1.

Physicians estimate their switchable share of practice at anything from 15 to 85 percent, even though location is of considerable importance. In the 10-hospital study, according to at least one chief executive officer

> the only loyalty from a physician that you can count on is geographic. If it is easier for him to practice at your hospital than it is at the other hospital then he will do that unless you give him some practice-related reason not to. In other words, if you mess up his patients, if you cannot do well, then he will override his dislike of travel and he will go to a more distant hospital.

Admissions seem to be all-important to managers. It is tempting for managers to believe that admissions are as important to physicians. Not so. In fact, when physicians are asked about the sources of their income, they obtain roughly 30 percent each from admissions, procedures, and office practice, and a further 10 percent from consults. While this last seems small, it is from consults that admissions and procedures derive. Therefore, any action on the part of a hospital that helps or hurts consults, office practice, or procedures is as important to the physician as actions affecting admissions. Since most physician conflicts are over either "turf" or resource availability, each of which directly affects procedures, management tact becomes important in facilitating the resolution of such conflicts (see Chapter 7).

The impact of hospital actions on individual physicians is amplified by what physicians believe will be the effect on their referral network. There is a marked domino effect, as many physicians rely heavily on their fellow physicians for referrals, and in turn refer patients to them. If doctors believe that their referral physicians will leave as a result of hospital actions, regardless of their own attitude, they will take defensive measures and leave themselves. In the practice pattern impact study, well over three quarters of doctors surveyed referred patients primarily to their fellow physicians at the hospital (rather than elsewhere), while about half received at least 10 percent of referrals from their fellow physicians at the hospital.

The concerns of physicians are expressed cogently below in a brief case study of a 210-bed community hospital. Some 20 physicians were asked about their feelings regarding the hospital and what it had done and might do to enhance their loyalty and devotion.

A Case Study

Saint Mary's is a small, 210-bed acute general Catholic hospital in East Orange, New Jersey. Surrounded by institutions, some of which are teaching hospitals and many of which are larger, that compete both for its patients and physicians, Saint Mary's, a few years ago, became part of a three-hospital Catholic hospital group, HCAN (Health Corporation of the Archdiocese of Newark), run by secular and highly competent managers.

Saint Mary's has faced and is facing a number of problems. From a small, cozy, closed-staff hospital dominated on the one hand by nuns, and on the other by a left-alone medical staff, it has struggled to maintain its warm positive patient and physician-oriented climate while adjusting to the rigors of competition and efficient corporate management. It has also had to face the impact of DRGs, of an aging physician population with high admitters leaving, and of playing technological catch up. The result of these last three factors was that from being in the black, for a period Saint Mary's went into the red.

Recent improvements have included bringing in modern technologies in a number of areas, adding a significant number of new, younger physicians to the staff by opening up the applications process, and prevailing on long-time physicians with multiple affiliations but with primary loyalty to Saint Mary's. The results have been positive—once again, Saint Mary's is in the black. But it still faces competition from surrounding hospitals, though at least one of these may close and another may move. The younger physicians are not yet admitting significantly, and the issue is how to compete effectively, particularly how to maintain and enhance the volume of admissions from existing and new physicians. In other words, how to maintain and enhance the loyalty and devotion of new physicians to this small, attractive hospital.

What can the hospital do? What can the corporation do to reduce its somewhat negative image among physicians and to use its resources effectively to the hospital's and physicians' advantage? Most particularly, how can the corporation and the hospital counter the prevailing paranoia of physicians, a paranoia common across the country, but one exacerbated here by particular fears? These fears have been fed by a consulting report examining options for Saint Mary's that included the possibility of closing it. Physicians perceive that their fate is in the hands of a corporation whose decisions they feel they know little about and over which they feel they have little influence, a not uncommon state of affairs today.

Physicians feel that Saint Mary's is an attractive, warm, comfortable, and kind place that their patients like and that they find easy to get patients in and out of. It is attractive; the food is good; it is clean. It is easier to have your patients in one place. The nurses and ancillary services are good, and the atmosphere and ambience are pleasant. It is like an excellent country hospital. Physician-patient and physician-management relations are good. Things are done personally, with special attention paid to the physician. The nuns add something to the atmosphere. Histories and physicals are dictated and on the chart in 24 hours, labs and X rays are on time, so it is easy and simple to do a rapid workup.

Basic physician concerns have to do with the hospital's competitive future. Some concerns are the result of the distance of the parent corporation and of the poor quality of information physicians feel they receive from HCAN. Information is slow or late, or takes the form of gossip or rumors from patients, colleagues, or other health organizations.

Physicians are also deeply concerned about influence. They feel they have little or no opportunity to influence the future of Saint Mary's, i.e., their fate. They feel powerless unless (and this applies to a few) they end-run management to pressure the HCAN board. As physician users, they have little or no input into HCAN purchasing decisions, yet have to occasionally put up with low-quality equipment that creates problems. A specific example given was the purchase of poor quality catheters, 10 to 15 percent of which burst in use.

Physicians probably correctly perceive that the major decisions affecting Saint Mary's are no longer made there by someone to whom they can go, but are made at a distant corporation over which they have little influence. Physicians feel, moreover, that while the past management had values and interests similar to their own, HCAN is a business and is not necessarily going to look out for the physicians' interest.

With regard to specifics, new physicians seem little involved and do not always come to meetings. The consequence is that the few doctors who are diligent and responsible are, ironically, "punished" by being put on more committees. It is not clear whether the emergency room is an emergency room or a walk-in clinic; if it is the former, it must be upgraded. The hospital not only needs new primary care practitioners, but also new subspecialists in at least a few focused areas, if it is to be competitive. The physician-education program is poor and needs distinct improvement. The radiology department is archaic and needs more diagnostic equipment. The lab also needs additional equipment. Doctors are playing "musical staff" to protect themselves, joining other local hospitals, obviously as a result of fears of Saint Mary's closing. New doctors are not yet adding their fair share of admissions, but it is not clear whether this is because it is too early, because they joined Saint Mary's defensively, or because of their particular specialties. Primary care physicians are not consulting subspecialists as much as they used to, perhaps because they are keeping the patients themselves at a time when physician income is plateauing or dropping.

The general conclusion is that physicians would like to see Saint Mary's continue to improve both its physical plant and equipment and its staff so that the hospital can remain competitive.

A tentative conclusion is that most physicians are generally happy with the hospital, with its management, and with the changes made to date, but approach the future with great gloom, feeling that this future is intimately connected with HCAN's decisions and that they must deal with HCAN.

Physicians made three kinds of suggestions: improve information, improve influence, and improve the hospital. Suggestions regarding the hospital essentially fall into three areas: expansion of admissions, upgrading of facilities and staff, and suggestions relating to physicans. Existing advantages should be maintained or enhanced by reducing the time lag regarding state-of-the-art technology, at least for routine patient care. Physician privileges should be a function of the extent to which physicians engage in required committee work, for committee work cements the relationship of the physician to the hospital. Committees could meet at times suitable to members, rather than at the whim of a chair concerned with his or her own convenience. The staff has toyed with the idea of having a minimum number of admissions as a prerequisite for privileges.

While new physicians are generally happy with the hospital and what is being done for them, additional public relations would be helpful. New physicians are diffident about requesting new equipment because this may reflect on the standards of older physicians, even if such equipment is desirable and necessary. New physicians would also appreciate the intervention of the hospital in recommending them as potential replacements when older physicians retire.

Finally, physicians are extremely interested in the possibility of financial joint ventures. They would like regular information from HCAN about its plans and developments, not only those affecting Saint Mary's directly. They would like more open lines of communication. If confidential issues arise, then select physicians should be involved. Doctors would like the opportunity to give feedback and have some influence. They would like to have voting physician representation from Saint Mary's on both the hospital and the HCAN board.

What implications does this case have for the general issue of enhancing loyalty and devotion? Most Saint Mary's physicians will only admit to discretion over 10 to 15 percent of their admissions. The most important factors are patient preference and geographic proximity, followed by the availability of procedures, technologies, and subspecialties. So physicians may admit "easy" patients to one hospital and "hard" ones to another. However, at least one physician acknowledges that many of his patients have little preference and he can influence them. He was able to shift some 35 percent of his admission volume from one hospital to another within an 18-month period. Whether this is a function of his particular specialty is not clear. In view of the discrepancy between most physicians' stated views and this physician's acknowledgement, this would seem to be an area worthy of further specific research.

The implications are that a hospital must intervene at a very early point to influence admission volume. In other words, it is important to offer physicians offices close to a hospital or place care facilities close to patients. It is also important to maintain state-of-the-art technological procedures for the "hard" patient and to maintain coverage. However, a significant factor may also be the availability of beds for, and attitudes toward, certain categories of patients whose attractiveness may increase inversely with a dropping occupancy rate! For example, geriatric nursing-home patients, when the census was high, were difficult to admit, because resident and nursing attitudes were unfavorable. Dropping occupancy resulted in easy admission of and changed attitudes toward these patients.

The strategic and cost implications are obvious, but it is difficult to arrive at definitive conclusions. Additional research is needed to clarify the dynamics of admission and referral. What is the relative importance of physicians as referral sources, as opposed to alternative sources of referrals such as the emergency room or other forms of health care delivery such as urgicenters and surgicenters? What are the relative contributions of new and old physicians, and how quickly does a new physician's practice grow? Are there clear distinctions between primary and secondary admitters where physicians have multiple affiliations, and can physicians be shifted from secondary to primary? In the one case of a major shift in a physician's referrals, Saint Mary's was still the physician's primary affiliation, though the hospital's proportion of his patients had dropped to around 60 percent. This was pushed up to 95 percent on the urging of Saint Mary's management. Another prominent physician admits less than 5 percent of his cases to Saint Mary's, but asserts that he could not do much about this without a major change in the technology available at Saint Mary's, because his cases, with few exceptions, are totally technology dependent. It would seem, therefore, that in a number of instances there are relatively small shifts that might be made with relatively small additions of technology or some management pressure. There may be larger shifts possible as a result of major investment, but this is not clear.

THE 10-HOSPITAL STUDY—WHAT DOCTORS SAY, WHAT CEOS DO

The situations described above were echoed in the 10-hospital study. Physicians in the study stressed that what they valued

TABLE 5-2 Physician Expectations Leading to Hospital Loyalty

Positive Factors	*Negative Factors*
Nursing care quality and responsiveness	Insensitive and selective recruiting
Support services, e.g., secretarial/ administrative	Supplying space and equipment to potentially competing physicians
Hotel functions, e.g., attractiveness, cleanliness, diet, security, and parking	
Equipment up to date maintained, state of the art	
Favorable schedule with regard to admissions, operating room	
Medical support services, e.g., residents, interns, high-reputation consultants, and teaching	
Minimal hassle, e.g., fast admission routine, good to work in	
Access to economically desirable technologies and rosters	
Consultation privileges	
The awarding of service patients to attendings	
Access to resources on an individual or departmental basis	
Influence over staffing	
Private room space	
Quick, accurate reporting on use of ancillaries	

was an adequate voice, that the hospital should make doctors' private practices easy and efficient for themselves and their patients, and that they wanted the opportunity for partnership and joint ventures. Physicians expected their hospital to provide the items listed in Table 5-2.

While voice is important, physicians are realistic about what it means. What they want is an opportunity to be involved and have their voice heard—they do not expect "yes" all the time. What they do expect when they get "no" for an answer, is for the response to be prompt and rational. They want fast and reasonable responses to their concerns, and they want to know what is going on. Paranoid in general, now paranoid in particular given developments in health care that encourage hospitals to act in ways inimical to their physicians, doctors want their institutions to behave in a way that fosters trust.

It is important to understand the unit with which the physician identifies if effective programs to enhance loyalty are to be developed. Corporations and hospital systems would like to believe in, and indeed mount programs to secure, physician loyalty, but evidence suggests that physicians tend to identify most strongly with the smallest unit with which they work.

One Health Corporation of America (HCA) hospital CEO felt that loyalty to the corporation could be enhanced. HCA can provide support to the physician in his or her office for transcription, accounting, and data systems, and even underwrite the cost of some services. Doctors can be given an opportunity to integrate practices in their offices and in the hospital. They can be a help in starting things the physicians want, such as Independent Practice Associations (IPAs). Through such efforts, loyalty to the corporation, the CEO believed, could develop over time. What HCA is doing is understanding the value chain of the physician—the set of activities that the physician engages in in the course of practice—and influencing that value chain favorably by reducing cost and improving quality for the physician.

Most doctors would disagree with the CEO. If anything, physicians feel that there has been a shift away from identification with hospitals to identification with their private offices. Certainly loyalty and identification with a single institution is hurt by the current defensive trend toward multiple affiliations as a hedge against future problems. Identification is more complex in academic medical centers because physicians in such centers are more likely to identify with a department than with an institution, and loyalty is less the result of practice support than of the department chiefs' support of doctors' research and academic careers.

Toward whom should management direct its efforts to secure loyalty? The high-volume admitters? The high share of practice physicians? The young doctors who will become the future high admitters? Those who are loyal to the institution in the sense of taking risks and throwing in their lot even if they are not high admitters? These are not trivial issues, for a chief executive officer's time is limited and cannot be devoted to each of perhaps several hundred doctors. Less than half of a medical staff actively admits, and high admitters (50 to 100 cases minimum) are but a handful. To some degree, the answer has to be those doctors on whom the hospital seems dependent in the near future. It is, however, obvious that it will take different actions on the part of management to secure the loyalty of an extremely successful and established mature practitioner and of a young beginner. The strategy of management must be thought through, and the future physician profile should determine where the hospital chooses to put its efforts.

In the 10-hospital study, hospitals varied markedly from a low loyalty rating of 2.5 to a high of 4.3 on a 1 to 5 scale, the loyalty rating being physicians' evaluations of the extent to which they perceive the hospital as having made an effort to win their adherence. Since the hospitals rated at either extreme happened to share doctors (they were in the same town), they provide a useful example for analysis. The hospitals differed in that one was a small, for-profit community institution and the other a large teaching hospital. Doctors saw the smaller hospital as being much more responsive to the growth of and changes in the community, as well as to their needs. The smaller hospital had tried to treat patients better and communicate more with physicians. The larger hospital seemed not to care whether the food tasted like rubber, and it did. Yet the CEOs in the study agreed that what the physician really wanted was to feel comfortable about his patients, to have his orders carried out promptly, to have prompt and accurate lab reports, to have nursing service care for his patient without calling the physician, and essentially to have a feeling of comfort and satisfaction for himself and the patients.

The CEOs further concluded that all patients really want is hot food, courteous and friendly staff, and cleanliness. Yet, in spite of the teaching hospital's good equipment, facilities, staff, and doctors, the physical structure left something to be desired, maintenance was poor, and doctors felt the organization was cold and bureaucratic. The smaller hospital had also done a better job on working at relationships with the community, opening the hospital to public functions and health fairs.

Doctors and CEOs obviously often do not see eye to eye or share the same values. Perhaps the CEO is out in front with regard to financial incentives and joint ventures, perhaps the physician is. But some degree of consonance is important if conflicts are to be avoided. This can be hard to manage, for shifts in mix that benefit the hospital may leave a nidus of doctors snarling. Many hospitals are evolving from high-quality cottage industries to larger institutions with new physicians seen by their fellows as different, less loyal, and more selfish. In such hospitals, there are not only shifts of resource allocation, but also more committees and bureaucracy, and thus greater difficulty in getting things done, which also adversely affects the sense of loyalty. With prospective reimbursement systems, there is an advantage to developing a richer patient mix and therefore more specialized cases. In turn, this means the recruitment of more subspecialists and the allocation of resources such as the operating room more to specialists than to generalists. The general physician and surgeon feel aggrieved because they regard themselves as providing the institution's bread and butter.

At a small, rural community hospital, this evolution resulted in a medical staff plagued by distrust, with doctors feeling that the hospital had not done much for them and had taken them for granted, even though patients had been well taken care of. Physicians did not feel involved, and decisions had been made without their input. While new management at the hospital was far more aggressive than it had been in the past, and this was welcomed by the doctors, physicians were ambivalent about much of what had been done. In the effort to recruit physicians and services, space and equipment had been given to the new arrivals and this was resented by the old guard. What was necessary from the hospital's standpoint had made the older family physicians unhappy. A new cardiopulmonary director, for example, was given a desirable office, and this was resented by other doctors. A new ophthalmic surgeon was given a large amount of new equipment, without going through regular channels, then the old ophthalmologists were told the new hire would monitor their use of this equipment.

> They have provided facilities and equipment for certain specialties which has encouraged those specialties but not the rest of us. It was probably not a very bright step to have taken.
>
> If you provide office facilities within the hospital at a competitive rent for some people, you alienate the rest of us who have to pay rent for our own premises.

But this doctor goes on to point out

> You would have to put up a physician office building, which is one thing, but is indeed being talked about. But even then you will alienate the people who own their own medical premises. I do not have an answer for that one.

You obviously cannot keep everyone happy if you are to be strategically successful, but insensitively implemented actions result in incidents that are remembered, repeated, and become part of an unhappy folklore.

Again and again the importance of good "hotel" services is stressed by both physicians and chief executive officers. One CEO says that, in return, he expects his physicians to use the hospital exclusively if possible, and that doctors, when necessary, should use an affiliate if his own hospital is not appropriate.

> [Doctors] should give the hospital all their patients when it is medically indicated unless it is the preference of the patient to go elsewhere. And even when the patient wants to go somewhere else, the doctor should explain why they should go here.

This senior manager expects his doctors not only to bring their patients in more or less exclusively, but also to participate actively in governance and to bring up and help solve problems, as well as to help market the institution. In turn, doctors expect management to listen and react to their concerns when expressed clearly. As one CEO defined it,

> For a physician to be loyal what does the hospital have to offer? The hospital is a hotel staffed with a cadre of people and has written certain protocols to handle a number of given situations. What you have to look at are your services of that hotel, be it the cleanliness, the dietary services, security, and/or efficiency. The facility has to be relatively attractive, has to maintain equipment (the only difference between men and boys is the price of their toys) which is up to date. When you have those things in place, you can start attracting physicians. The other pieces are money for new programmatic activities and an administration which is responsive to the needs of the physician as well as the needs of their clients.

Another was more cynical:

> I'm not sure anybody has any loyalty anymore. I think the way that most hospitals "secure" the loyalty of their physicians is based entirely on their ability to provide for those physicians patients with the least amount of input required from the physicians. If the physician is totally comfortable with his patients, his orders are carried out promptly, the nursing service has the ability to care for his patient without calling him two times a night

> and so forth, he is going to take the line of least resistance. If he feels comfortable with his patients in the [intensive care unit], if he feels that the patient is going to do well, that his orders are going to be carried out, if he feels comfortable, then he will be loyal. Obviously, the patient has to be satisfied with the degree of nursing care received, though I am still of the opinion that the consumer really doesn't know anything about anything other than whether the food is hot and whether people are courteous and friendly and . . . the hospital is clean. Beyond that, the consumer has little knowledge of what is occurring and what's happening. But the physician has a great deal of knowledge, and he knows when he makes his rounds at 7:30 if all his lab reports are there, everything is accurate and complete, and that the patient is well.

The CEO's skepticism about loyalty is shared by another:

> Physicians are loyal to physicians. They are not loyal to a hospital. There are some that identify with a facility and their ability to have input, but mostly they are loyal to their practices and secondarily to their peer group and third to the institution. The reason they support the institution is because the institution provides those aspects to their patients that makes them look good.

This CEO believes it is meaningless for a corporation to attempt to secure loyalty. He is moreover skeptical about wide involvement of physicians for, as he says, "We have an extremely important project going on right now, and we have had to be very careful in only involving physicians in the planning process that we knew could handle confidential material and that comes through experience."

Physicians like to share information and never see themselves as being violators of confidentiality. Voice is important, CEOs acknowledge, even if it has to be selective.

> We've given physicians a voice in the running of the hospital through committees. Administration listens to the executive committee and does things, not for profit, but because they are correct. The governing board is very receptive to what the doctors say. There are two doctors who are members of that board. The size of our hospital and its commitment to state-of-the-art equipment has always been there and attracts doctors. The board wants the best for its doctors, and it is important to them that equipment be maintained and up to date. There is a big demand in this city for private beds, and this hospital is trying to get three additional floors of private rooms. On the negative side, some physicians feel there is not [as much] individual attention given them as at the other two hospitals with which we compete, both of [which] are for profit. We need the same number of private patients, but we are larger and we have salaried physicians

whom some of the attendings feel compete with them, and that does cause some problems. Also we have residents and medical students, which are both plusses and minuses.

The larger high-technology hospitals emphasize what they can offer, high-technology equipment.

About 60 percent of our patients are admitted by tertiary physicians, the majority of whom are surgical subspecialists. These physicians are interested in buildings and rooms and equipment, that is being pretty frank about it, and the way we maintain loyalty is to provide an atmosphere where they can do tertiary care, not only with the best equipment locally, but as good as there is available in the country. We have to insure a good profit margin to provide that equipment, with private room space, or space and gadgets and lasers. That's what they're looking for.

This contrasts with HCA's approach which is "to do what we can to maintain the physician's private practice. The great fear is that [the physicians] will lose that opportunity. As a company, our fear is we will lose the private practice. Our whole system is built on free enterprise. Quality drops when physicians are salaried." Hospitals are getting more ingenious in what they offer in this desperately competitive situation.

Hospitals are opening up their staffs and making the packages sweeter. In California they are giving stipends and bonuses, and Humana is willing to buy out practices and hire physicians to run their own practices. There are all kinds of nuances being tried experimentally around here. One case in point is a hospital which bought a CAT scanner and instead of purchasing it themselves, they formed a limited partnership of members of the staff, giving them investment tax write-offs for which they had to put up very little money which they got back anyway at the end of the year. That took four of our physicians away from this hospital. Other hospitals are trying new marketing approaches. Medical schools are making deals. If physicians bring their cases to them, they will become faculty members with tenure and salary.

Do managers distinguish between physicians in attempting to attract them?

I go more on volume. The larger the practice, the more successful the physician, the more you tend to isolate that physician as the one you want to work with because he has a larger base. We want the supporting physicians. Even if they're not active admitters, they're consultants and seen as being qualified.

You want to keep the loyalty of certain key people who are valuable, whose loss would hurt the institution. For each of them administration would say "What do we have to do to attract and keep you?" We give consideration to individual input when building physician plants and structures and organizing services. The individuals who have cast in their lot with us are brought into the decision-making process. We handle their requests for admissions and equipment differently, though it is hard to do this in a way that doesn't antagonize other physicians. We're rewriting our bylaws to reward the loyal, with selective giving of consultation privileges and privileges to do certain kinds of procedures, as well as the awarding of service patients or being put on the roster to do certain procedures. All these are determined on the basis of loyalty. You give good things to the loyal. Once the loyal would show their loyalty by taking care of service patients free of charge. Now with the glut of physicians, most service cases have some kind of insurance, so these cases are good and apportioned to our friends rather than looked upon as a scourge.

Managers do not necessarily expect that all physicians will admit all patients to their hospital. What they do expect is for physicians to admit those patients for which the hospital is appropriate. In a high-technology hospital, for example, managers do not expect the easy cases that can be admitted to a community hospital. "So an individual who is not necessarily active in all regards but always sends his open heart surgery here, he is loyal at least to our open heart surgery program."

One astute physician manager described what he has tried to do to enhance loyalty and devotion:

It is an expansion of the time and effort concept. There is a real palpable difference between the hospital staff member who really cares about the hospital and spontaneously generates solutions to problems in contrast to the physician who is constantly criticizing and complaining but rarely couples that with a suggestion or a concrete solution.

Doctors need to get feedback, recognition. They need a sense that when they have a concern and express it clearly that it is listened to and reacted to. It is the same dynamic of any human relationship. Whether it is done by the administrator or the department head depends on the issue at hand. Some of the little tangible things that are not seen frequently at this place but may be too much at the hospital—the 5-year pins in the lapels, the 10-year pins. One of the things that has struck me is that physicians have a high need for autonomy and power, neither of which works well when you're trying to build a team in an institutional setting. That is one of the conflicts that comes up. It may be insoluble, but I have tried to make all the physicians in my department chiefs and not Indians for that very reason. They are much more engaged in the department and sacrifice autonomy to gain allegiances and form coalitions to achieve some other goal. The person who is assigned the responsibility to run the medical side of the joint medicine-psychiatry alcohol unit really has the sense that he is in charge of that. At the same time, when he has to function as a member of

> the department, he has a better understanding of what that director has to contend with. That creates a mutuality; each has autonomy and power in one area and can yield in other areas. Where they do not work well in my department reflects the fact that I have not been able to implement that policy as well as I should have been able to.

But even this doctor regretfully recognizes that loyalty can also be bought. Another thoughtful doctor commented on loyalty:

> This one is difficult. Since I've had lots of positions in the hospital and am now on the board of trustees, I've been one who has been involved up to my eyeballs and one who feels a great loyalty to the hospital and has been working for it. There are lots of physicians who don't, and there are more and more physicians who have more than one hospital affiliation. I think that's a great danger to any medical staff because those physicians, and I can see it here, are the ones who regard the hospital as something that's there for their convenience and their use, and if it doesn't shape up, they start to bitch. These people are of no value to the hospital except they bring patients in. We have some specialists of an ilk that is not sufficient to warrant a practice in this community alone—the ENT [ear, nose, and throat] people, neurosurgeons, etc., and I have seen this as a threat to the hospital. In the past, and during my career, this has evolved colossally from a cottage hospital with high-quality service and physicians to a much larger one with many newer physicians who are qualitatively and quantitatively different than I in the atmosphere in which they were trained. They have, built in, less loyalty, more selfishness than we did. They're a different animal, not across the board, but you realize what I'm trying to say. In times gone by, the medical staff ran the hospital. We did what we wanted to do. If I wanted to introduce a new procedure, I introduced it. I went out and got the gear and told the operating supervisor tomorrow I'm going to do such and so, and it got done. That's no longer possible. There has been a gradual increase in the difficulty of getting things done, through no one's fault. Now we've got to go through committees, and it becomes more difficult, and this tends to put people off. It's inevitable, it's difficult for the hospital to deal with. Sometimes I feel it would be nice to have a dictator who dictated and said this is the way it's going to be, and that probably is the advantage the physician sees in Health Corporation of America (HCA) hospitals. The physician goes to the administration, says he wants to do such and so procedure, they say how many are you going to do? Eight to ten a year. How much will it cost? *X* dollars. It's either good or bad, it gets done or not. This generates physician loyalty, the ability of the hospital to respond promptly to needs. Or, conversely, they say there's no way they're going to do that.
>
> What has the hospital done to attract the loyalty of physicians? It has provided an extremely pleasant place to work. The nursing is good, the quality of the medical staff is excellent across the board. We do not have a confrontational attitude toward the administration. They respect us. The board has never been heavy handed. It's comfortable.

What else is needed?

The feeling that the board and administration are more alert and conscious of what the physician's needs and problems are on a timely basis. I don't know how they can demonstrate that other than by increased interchange of ideas. Board involvement in medical staff affairs, medical staff involvement in board affairs, more one-on-one contact would be positive. And more prompt reactions to things like medical office buildings, new CAT scans. This hospital hasn't done very well in that regard. I don't think it can be bought.

Another doctor pointed out the management deficiencies that create problems for him.

There has been a good relationship between administration and physicians. The biggest problem is there is a lack of expertise and top-notch people in administrative places. This makes it difficult for the medical staff to progress because you're not talking to intellectual peers, and the management abilities of these people are minimal. I realize that allows someone who's been part of the system for a long time to be manipulative. I can get anything I want done in this hospital. I know more about the departments than management has any concept of. It's partly because I've taken time to do that. The biggest danger is that physicians don't have the time or the managerial ability themselves to fill that gap. I'm going to lots of meetings which are dealing with petty approaches to massive problems. That's why I was late today. We were talking about a recall that was done unilaterally by a supervisor on a Friday afternoon. There are hospital policies which prevent that, such as a special type of IV solution.

My philosophy is that a group which develops something shouldn't be the group that gives the final approval to it. We've been careful on the executive committee not to develop policies, but to have them developed elsewhere and come up to us for approval. Unilateral action happens between a riled-up nurse or a low-level administrator or physician and results in disastrous consequences at times. The implications are not usually appreciated by administration. They don't see the big picture. They spend all their time putting out fires. This promotes immature relationships. I have documented how things are done. Another example is the capital equipment process. We got a review group going. One hundred eighty thousand dollars is going to go through the group, but $160,000 is going to be doled out through the old channels—who you know. It makes a farce out of the whole planning system. This hospital does thousands of studies, but no one can implement them. People shouldn't have to spend as much time as I do. But there isn't internal expertise, and I don't see any alternative except a professional group running a hospital, which would make my job a lot harder. There also needs to be a strong group of trustees which would have strong physician representation. Amateurism is gone, and that's too bad. Many programs have failed.

These are final comments:

> It's the personal attention I get. The personnel from attendants through the nursing staff, cater to me. My patients get special attention because they're my patients. It doesn't happen in the other hospitals.
>
> I know that 85 to 90 percent of my practice is discretionary. I have judged that my reputation would not be hurt here. This hospital is going to work out a joint venture with physicians, the office building.

And a note on equity: "There has been some discussion on what constitutes adequate usage. A person should admit 10 to 12 patients a year to be on the active staff; they should attend staff meetings to demonstrate interest. People who have not met requirements go on courtesy staff."

Some physicians demonstrate their loyalty by helping to raise funds, through direct personal and professional relationships, through a sense of community, or by sitting on a board. Such physicians become bitter when they see management devoting itself to high admitters.

> The problem is the assumption that the hospital knows who its physicians are. It becomes self-serving—those who admit to the hospital are its physicians and those who do not admit, when they start doing, become [the hospital's] physicians. So simply getting physicians to admit is not really a sign of developing loyalty. There's a decreasing number of hospital beds and an increasing number of physicians, and where there is turmoil at nearby hospitals, it forces physicians into admitting here. One of my major concerns is that the hospital knows which are its physicians. To me, it is those who have cast their lot with the hospital. What that means is an individual who devotes so much time to his activities at this hospital that were something disastrous to happen to it, something disastrous would happen to him. In other words, he is willing to take personal risks to keep the hospital going, and I put myself in that category. Personal risk means economic risk and professional esteem and not being afraid to lose a patient. What I expect is attention to my needs, my patients, and my practice. What I find is that it is difficult to schedule cases, to find the instruments I need, or for the hospital to seem willing to obtain instruments which are state of the art for me while they are getting them for other specialties. The operating room is geared to specialists, and not to general surgeons like myself.

Focusing on the high admitters is a common gambit of CEOs. At one large urban community hospital, the CEO has a top 40 group. Each represents 1 percent of hospital revenues annually, so the group admits 40 percent of the hospital's revenues. Many of these doctors sit on the general executive committee and are chiefs of departments. In addition to meeting them in those settings, the CEO spends a great deal of time with them personally, keeping them informed and providing them with facts. But he also values those older physicians who are winding down their practices and have been on the staff for years. He believes that in telling the same story over and over doctors, being data-oriented people, will begin to trust the credibility of his administration as he demonstrates its openness.

Doctors do understand, even if they do not like it, that management must begin seeing doctors as businesses and that there will be winners and losers and sometimes loss leaders. But for some physicians, nothing the hospital can do will make a difference, for location is, as pointed out earlier, the first issue when it comes to choice of institution.

Over and over, much of what hospital managements do to win the trust of their doctors is undone by one insensitive maneuver. One CEO tried to open an outpatient department for extended hours, hoping thereby to increase his share of market. The doctors that he had hoped would staff it were in their private offices at the time they were expected to be at the outpatient clinic. So he was forced to staff the department with full-time in-house physicians, which inevitably exaggerated the fears of those doctors suspicious that the hospital might indeed engage more full-timers in direct competition with them.

Earlier it was pointed out that academic medical centers and community hospitals may define loyalty and devotion differently. One department chairman in an academic center says that his doctors will take calls every night of the year and sleep in the hospital when on call, but only when he asks them to. Devotion is the extent to which such doctors will give free service over and beyond duty. To obtain such behavior, department chiefs give strong support to their doctors in those things that will enhance the physicians' careers, such as helping them get grants, write the right papers, or go to the right meetings and get into the right societies. The hospital obviously cannot do much about such things other than supporting the chiefs in their efforts.

One final contrast, again between an academic medical center and a community hospital. In the 10-hospital study, both types had high ratings for loyalty but through very different kinds of efforts. The teaching hospital had many high-technology units, had given many physicians offices and space, and paid a lot of attention to the 10 top admitters who were personally given a gift each year. They provided early operating time for private surgeons and flexible operating room schedules. (The full-timers were guaranteed the times they wanted and a minimum number of hours, much to the resentment of the private doctors.) What was missing, however, was the private touch, which the smaller community hospital provided. As one doctor said, "The teaching hospital has the best intensive care in the world, 24-hour emergency room, 24-hour operating room, everything you want, dedicated people and doing a good job, but when the patient comes out of that high-tech unit and goes on the ward, it is like putting them in a parking lot."

At the smaller hospital, dinner was brought to the surgeons; at the teaching hospital, sterile technique was valued.

One pediatrician sums it up quite nicely.

> In pediatrics, there are active departments that support attending staffs. A lot of it is geographical. To a lesser extent, you admit because maybe you like grand rounds, the school affiliation, there may not be problems with utilization, committee requirements. There is a multifactorial interplay. Patients do not like to go all the way across town for emergency care. They like the local scenery. So physicians in pediatrics will admit their patients because of locality. For malpractice purposes, you should send your patients to the closest hospital. The closer your practice is to the hospital, the better. The second point is how the physician is handled in the inpatient setting. The most important is how the patients are handled. The fewer the complications he has to deal with, the better. If there is a problem with nursing care that develops, he will pack up his bag and move down the street. A residency or an intern plays a minor role in this setting. Sometimes it works against you. Some physicians want the responsibility. But mainly it's patient care. In pediatrics, make sure that the baby has the right pajamas and that the milk and food are given properly. The fewer complaints the physician hears from the mother, the happier he is. When the mother is happy, the physician is too. Medical care is apart from that issue. The mother may not understand treatment or the seriousness of situations, but if that bottle isn't delivered every four hours, that is an important aspect. Hospitals are competitive, and you have to size up your competition. Basic inpatient care. For tertiary facilities, physicians are attracted to active consultants. Delay in consult and utilization goes around, and they find out their patient has been terminated benefits because of delay of management, that presents complications. Nursing care is very important, especially in pediatrics. Smiling, being pleasant, going out of your way to help, more important than the physician who gets a feedback from that. Resident and intern coverage play a minor role depending on where you are. In pediatrics, half the physicians handle their own cases.

In conclusion, it is important for management to identify the physicians it wishes to attract and keep. These physicians should be a mixture of those who will admit heavily and those who will throw in their lot with the hospital. The latter individuals should be brought more into the decision-making process; they should receive priority for admissions (being careful not to antagonize the others!); and bylaws should reward the loyal. In other words, consultation privileges, access to technologies, the awarding of service patients, procedures, and operating room rosters should be determined on the basis of loyalty. Give good things to the loyal. Once the loyal showed their loyalty by taking care of the service patients free of charge. Now such patients have insurance, so they become a "good" that can be awarded. But a judicious hand is important, for it is exactly in this area that some of the most difficult and rancorous conflicts can arise. Whether access to economically remunerative procedures and technologies should be given to those who are loyal, whatever that means and however it is defined, or to those who are qualified to perform procedures, is a major bone of contention, where the two are not synonymous.

While much of the foregoing discussion applies to IPAs as well as hospitals or HMOs, it may well be necessary for IPA managements to consider some additional measures to secure the loyalty of their physicians and to increase their share of practice with them. Indeed it is probably useful for IPA managements to consider the kinds of practice profile they want among the physicians with whom they contract. Many large IPAs average somewhere between 2 and 5 percent share of practice among their physician members. At this level the IPA is of marginal value to the physician, and management has relatively little influence over the physician. Only when share of practice reaches upward of 20 percent does the IPA's role become significant. Management should consider what kinds of physicians it wants to retain or lose as contractors.

VALUE CHAIN ANALYSIS

A good way to analyze the actions which management might take to secure physician loyalty is the technique of value chain analysis.[1] As health organizations seek competitive advantage in an increasingly stringent and competitive marketplace, they must either develop strategies based on being the low-cost provider or must differentiate themselves from their competitors by offering products or services of a distinctive nature providing value to the buyer, whether employer or employee, for which he is willing to pay a premium.

To arrive at a choice of strategy requires understanding the health organization's own value chain as well as that of the buyer, and matching them. The value chain is the set of strategically relevant activities to which value—whether financial or intangible—may be attached. Thus a staff model HMO whose value chain includes keeping hospital and ancillary costs to a minimum may restrict the free choice of services and physician, and this will match employers/employees value chains who are also concerned about cost. But there will not be a match with potential members who have a high value for free choice of service and/or physician and are willing to pay more for it; these will probably select an IPA that offers greater choice—and a higher premium.

Organizations seeking to differentiate themselves must have a true basis for doing so; they must deliver as well as communicate the nature of their difference. Failure to do both leads to disenchanted buyers, as occurs for example, when eager IPA marketers exaggerate to prospective members benefits which subsequently have to be denied by the individual physician seeing the individual member. A true basis for differentiation lies in being able to reduce cost or improve quality for the buyer. There must obviously also be a viable market for the differentiated product or service.

Hospitals and IPAs both seek to secure physician loyalty as one set of buyers, although in different ways. Hospitals want their services to be used, and IPAs want doctors to see their members or refer members to them. Success in securing physician loyalty requires understanding the physician's value chain. It should be noted that in this, as in other respects, doctors are not alike for they have different practice patterns and different practices, which reflect differences in their value chains.

---

[1]Porter, M. E., *Competitive Advantage* (New York: Free Press, 1985).

The private practice physician's value chain encompasses all of the activities involved in setting up and engaging in the practice of medicine and includes, for example, such activities as:

Setting up

Choice of practice site (market research).

Leasing, purchasing an office.

Acquiring, maintaining equipment.

Securing, organizing a staff.

Establishing a referral system.

Establishing a record system.

Running a practice

Appointment system.

Selection of patients.

The patient encounter.

Follow up.

Referral to hospital, laboratory, or specialist.

While tangible value is easily attached to each of these, intangible values are also important because they reflect the doctor's preferences and choices, although they may be harder to assess. Each doctor may make a different tradeoff between quality (however that is interpreted by him) and cost. Some inner city physicians establish practices with a high proportion of medicaid patients who, although sicker than average (and thus hospitalized more), may be less choosy about their hospital. A suburban practice with less severely ill patients may stress quality more, with patients more demanding of free choice of hospital. An IPA seeking to attract and retain doctors would find that a physician incentive system that stresses low hospital utilization would be more appealing to the value chain of the latter type of practice than the former, which would make more money on an incentive system that pays a higher capitation rate. Similarly, the offering of discounted arrangements for laboratory services such as a PPO or PPA would appeal more to doctors belonging to a capitated system such as an IPA than to those in private practice with lower cost constraints.

The Hospital Corporation of America, as one example, has been quite successful in offering support to the value chain of the private practice physician by making available market research, financing, site evaluation, office systems, and office space, all of which reduces cost to the doctor and improves the quality of the physician's operation.

Since the health care delivery system has become enormously complex, with many different kinds of buyers (including doctors), any attempt to attract different physicians with a single approach, as often appears to be the case, is bound to fail. This technique of value chain analysis provides a useful way to determine strategies and activities that will be responsive to physician variety.

CHAPTER SIX

Management's Role in Medical Matters: Managing Quality, Cost, and Recruitment

There might be medical doctors . . . cocking their medical eyes.

Charles Dickens

QUALITY AND COST AS COMPETITIVE ISSUES

Competition in health markets involves not only cost or quality, but cost *and* quality as well. In other words, health organizations are seeking niches where they will supply a particular quality for a given cost, or be the low-cost provider at a particular level of quality. Managing cost and quality then has a different connotation than simple erasure of abuse. The considerable literature on cost management, however, focuses on the excesses committed by physicians in their use of laboratory tests, diagnostic radiology, therapeutic regimes, length of stay, and regional variations in practice patterns. The equally extensive literature on quality also stresses excesses, and systems are designed to identify and deal with erring physicians who practice bad medicine.

In this era of stringent reimbursement, it is relatively easy for physicians to go along with practicing cost-effective medicine, for all physicians and all health organizations face the same restraints. As one CEO in the 10-Hospital Study put it, "I was surprised at how doctors went right along with DRG system without any pressure from us. They have knocked a day and a half off our average length of stay for medicare patients."

Doctors can also agree on eradicating bad medicine. If designated systems do not deal with abuse (and physicians acknowledge that the system works better in gross cases, for it is difficult to face each other), then

> the marketplace does a beautiful job on consultants and surgeons. There is nothing that gives me greater pleasure in dealing with a patient's family

than being able to talk confidently that I am referring their relative to a superb consultant, to find a surgeon, and vicariously to bask in the result of doing that. We have had some terrible surgeons on our staff, and the marketplace has handled it magnificently.

But the issue now is not just how to function reasonably under prospective reimbursement, or how to reduce litigation, but how to compete successfully with other institutions. This means selecting critical quality attributes that are valued by a segment of the marketplace, ensuring that this quality is delivered to consumers and that they know about it. It, therefore, involves both operating effectively and communicating well. Moreover, cost competition means being able to consistently provide a particular level of cost and being able to advertise that fact, so that the hospital may become a consistent low-cost provider to potential buyers, whether these are HMOs or patients. Both involve something more than the traditional meanings of cost and quality, because discretionary choices are entailed. Each hospital will select particular quality attributes or a particular level of cost. These choices are more easily questioned by physicians, so the implementation of a strategy based on cost and quality goals is more vulnerable to and dependent on physicians' support. All the more reason, therefore, to involve physicians in the choice of strategy and in its implementation.

While the traditional literature does not directly address this new twist, it does have something useful to say about what seems to work, and what does not. Reference will therefore be made to selected aspects of the literature that are relevant to the strategic issue of cost and quality.

The kind of dilemma facing management, with its new responsibility for ensuring quality, is exemplified by a situation confronting the chief executive officer of Midway Hospital.

Midway Hospital, like many community hospitals, has for years had its needs for radiologists served by an arrangement with an independent group. It does not have any contract or any formal arrangements with this group. The group consists of two radiologists, one of whom is the chairman of the Radiology Department, who make their own arrangements with more junior radiologists and three technicians.

There was a previous attempt, some years ago, to negotiate a contract, but negotiations broke down and one was never signed. Over the years, it became apparent to the administration of the hospital that there were concerns about whether or not the group was able to staff the hospital's needs consistently because of what seemed to be an unusually high turnover within the group. This is not only a matter of concern to the administration. Fellow doctors expressed concern that while the employees of the group are of high quality, they do not stay long with the hospital. This turnover they attribute to the terms of employment offered by the group to its junior employees. No contracts are signed between the group and these employees, and the starting salary of $40,000 is increased by $4,000 at six-month intervals to a maximum of $60,000.

Matters came to a head recently when three employees of the group approached first the vice president for medical affairs and then the administrator of the hospital, to complain about their employment situation. Each had somewhat different concerns; one had reached the maximum salary and wondered when he was going to get an increase; one was concerned with benefits; the third was concerned about what was going to happen to him given the treatment of the other two.

This was of particular interest to the administration as they had just begun an attempt to negotiate an across-the-board contract with the radiology group. This had been precipitated by a request by the group for an increase in their billing rates. The goal of the administration was to secure quality of care assurance from the group, as it is attempting to do with all medical groups in the hospital. They were concerned that the employee turnover was indirectly a responsibility of the administration of the hospital, since it reflected upon the hospital's ability to guarantee quality of care. As the contract negotiating process proceeded, the immediate concerns of two of the junior radiologists resolved themselves. One left for a more secure and better job elsewhere, while the second went on educational leave. The problem of the third remained unresolved.

For the hospital, the delicate issue was how to secure its quality of care responsibilities without interfering directly with medical practice. It attempted to place in the contract two provisions of particular note. One was to give it the right to bring in outside experts to evaluate the department of radiology's performance. The second was a provision giving the hospital the right to review any change in the radiology group's membership from existing levels which might reflect on the quality of care of the hospital. However, the central issue, turnover at existing staff levels, was not dealt with in the draft of the contract provisions.

The chief executive officer of the hospital wondered what he might put in the contract to get control over the turnover/quality problem. But he feared the sort of fight about interference with medical practice he would have on his hands if he put in anything significant.

The cost management problem is crystallized in the case of Doctor's Health Services, an initially successful IPA.

In 1975, in the James area of Idaho, Doctor's Health Services (DHS) had arisen as an Individual Practice Association (IPA) in competition with a more traditional staff-model health maintenance organization, the Idaho

Health Plan (IHP). Almost immediately, [DHS became] successful, in sharp contrast with the more checkered progress of IHP, but now it faced increased competition and the growth problems of a big business. It also faced some problems arising out of its own success. The very physicians who formed it, responding to an outside threat, no longer felt so threatened and therefore wanted to water down their own organization. Specialty groups had begun to demand unreasonable fees, and some doctors were beginning to regard DHS as "them" rather than "us." Some member physicians were over-utilizers, some were openly critical in a damaging fashion, and some were too easy with the hospitals when it came to cutting out days of unnecessary hospitalization. As a result, bed days per thousand enrollees had risen from 450 to 520, in contrast to IHP's figure of 300. While DHS was hurting financially, it was still just surviving, and this in spite of the federal cutbacks in HMO funding.

Additional competition had emerged, first from the improved management of IHP, and then incursion into Idaho of the Kaiser Foundation Health Plan with its considerable financial support and management of IHP; looming on the horizon was the possible incursion of HIP, another large New York-based plan. Blue Cross/Blue Shield had approached DHS, in fact, to take over the IPA network.

Peter Miles, Manager of DHS, was faced with some key competitive strategic issues. To remain independent, he had to persuade his own physicians to be even more tough minded with themselves and their colleagues than in previous years. While DHS allowed physicians to practice the traditional values of independent medicine (namely the preservation of fee for service, the maintenance of health care delivery within the private sector, and the capacity to provide comprehensive HMO benefits without change of community physicians), it simply could not afford what some doctors were demanding: an absence of peer review or utilization controls, a relaxation of payment levels, no attempt to control costs except hospital costs, and no modification of referral patterns. The board had supported Peter in instituting stronger controls on excess hospital utilization and installing incentives to reduce it as well as strengthening the cadre of review physicians. It had also agreed to terminate physicians with inappropriate practice patterns who were unwilling to modify them. Their board had, in fact, actually terminated an over-utilizing physician.

While DHS now had 20,000 members, double the previous year's membership and double its immediate competition, it had to accept the fact that patients joined DHS for its comprehensive coverage and service, and if these were not provided, they would leave. This meant that the premium, and in turn, expenses, must be controlled. The premium for 1982 was up 30 percent from 1981; in turn, up 15 percent from 1980. While there had been excess utilization of some services, the major area of overuse was hospital services. Unless this could be brought under control—the control was entirely in the hands of participating physicians—the projected profit of the future would be yet another DHS loss.

Peter Miles recognized that good management had been a major factor in past success, but his capacity to manage the doctors would determine the future. Doctors set policies and gave them a competitive edge; at the same time, it made DHS vulnerable when the physicians would not bite the bullet.

In this case, the physician leadership, with Miles' prodding, undertook the following steps:

1. Required prior authorization for elective admissions.
2. Placed a DHS claims analyst in each hospital to monitor admissions and help with discharge planning.
3. Reaffirmed and applied financial sanctions for physicians who did not comply with DHS rules.
4. Developed special financial education programs aimed at M.D.s.
5. Required certain surgical procedures to be done on an outpatient basis.

These actions, together with premium increases, were reportedly successful in both dramatically improving the financial health of DHS (it had accumulated a cash reserve of $3 million by 1983), and in forging bonds between the physicians and the health plan.

The problems facing traditional HMOs are both similar and different. HMO profitability is also driven by the HMO operator's ability to control medical costs. Medical costs as a percentage of premiums are high, averaging between 75 and 85 percent for all HMOs.[1] The methods HMOs use to achieve more cost-efficient, quality health care delivery can be summarized in three categories.[2] First, economic incentives involve a capitation payment, which makes the primary care physician responsible for providing services. Cost-sharing pools and splitting budget variances for cost-efficient performance reward the physician for cost-efficient hospitalization and specialty-care referral practices.

Second, patient care review procedures ensure that prescribed services are appropriate and administered according to acceptable quality standards. Procedures include:

---

[1] *The Health Maintenance Organization Industry,* Basic Report 84-67A (W. Blair and Company, 1984).

[2] Ibid.

Preauthorization of hospitalization or specialty referral.

Concurrent review of expected and actual hospital length of stay.

Daily review of all hospitalized patients who exceed expected length of stay.

Retrospective chart review by medical peers.

The third method is to substitute alternative services for hospital treatment. Home care, ambulatory or day surgery, and skilled nursing facilities are lower-cost alternatives that are often appropriate for HMO members' health care requirements.

HMOs use organizational incentives, physician incentives, and patient incentives.[3] The principal *organizational incentive* is the capitation system of reimbursement. Because the HMO receives a fixed premium in return for providing all the health care a member may need, it may stress the increased use of ambulatory or outpatient care to decrease hospitalization rates, and may try to reduce discretionary hospitalization by having all potential hospitalizations recommended by any individual physician reviewed by a panel of other physicians or by restricting the supply of hospital beds.

Where physicians are on salary, because they receive the same income regardless of the treatment they give a patient, there is no incentive for them to increase treatments and therefore treatment costs. Two types of *physician incentives* therefore are to reimburse on a salary system rather than on a fee-for-service basis, or to put the physicians "at risk". Physicians may, as a result, increase the use of preventive care through the use of early detection and treatment, or may substitute outpatient care and procedures for inpatient care, choosing to reduce the discretionary use of hospital services.

The major *patient incentive* is the elimination of out-of-pocket costs associated with the consumption of health services.[4] HMO hospitalization rates seem to decline as the HMO grows. While it is unclear why this should be so, the phenomenon seems to be in-

[3]F. D. Wolinsky, "The Performance of Health Maintenance Organizations: An Analytic Review," *Milbank Memorial Fund Quarterly* 58, no. 4 (1980), pp. 537–80.

[4]*Health Maintenance Organization Industry.*

fluenced primarily by technology and changing practice patterns.

To ensure quality services, HMOs also rely heavily on quality assurance procedures which are relatively uncommon in the fee-for-service physician's office. Retrospective peer review and regular studies of specific procedures or diagnostic categories are an integral part of the HMO's checks and balances, guaranteeing appropriate services for members. Regular satisfaction surveys also keep track of members' perceptions of the quality of services rendered.[5]

Growth of HMO membership depends on the development of a strong market franchise. In a competitive HMO market, employer groups will select HMOs based on the quality, reputation, and accessibility of the delivery system; the effectiveness of cost controls; and the organization's financial stability. Once an employer group offers an HMO as part of its fringe benefit package, it is unlikely that the employer will discontinue the benefit option unless employees express extreme dissatisfaction with the quality of the HMO services. Otherwise, the employer would be forcing employees to change their relationship with their family physician. As a result, building a quality image is critical to a strong market franchise. To achieve this, the HMO must be strong in functional areas of the business: health services delivery, marketing, finance, and managing its physicians.[6]

When dealing with cost/quality trade-offs, not only strategic but also ethical and value considerations are obviously involved.[7] It is difficult to make a valid judgment concerning reducing length of stay and at what point it becomes hurtful if patients leave early only to reappear. It is even harder to make good judgments about what constitutes ethical competitive behavior. Already medicaid patients complain that in some physician offices there are two windows and two lines, one of which moves much faster than the other and is devoted to private patients. Given the payment schedule for medicaid and medicare

---

[5]Ibid.

[6]Ibid.

[7]W. R. Fifer, "Cost/Quality Trade-Offs—The Next Crisis," *The Hospital Medical Staff*, June 1981, pp. 12–18.

patients, physicians complain that they cannot treat such patients without losing money. As hospitals recognize that the difference between a loss and profit may be private-patient revenue, they offer high-quality facilities to this segment of the market (which can pay for it) that are not available to the indigent. Inevitably the already extant two-tier system will spread. This raises ethical issues that must be dealt with by board management and the physician. Under cost reimbursement, hospitals did not have to confront these decisions, for they did what they wished and got paid for it. Under prospective reimbursement and in a competitive environment, it is the health organization that must make choices and must make them not only on economic but also on ethical grounds.

An even more complex ethical/economic issue is the fact that many technologies cannot be evaluated simplistically as cost effective or not, but may provide some, though limited, utility for a high cost.[8] If society does not come to grips with this issue, then health organizations, as they face competition, must. They will have to decide whether they can only afford technologies with a high utility and low cost, or are willing to provide marginal technologies where there is the prospect of patients paying for them.

Henry Ford Hospital in Detroit is a leader in competing effectively with regard to cost and quality. As mentioned earlier, they have diversified rapidly and extensively into ambulatory care, including not only freestanding centers but also several HMOs that will enable them to be the moderate-cost/high-quality provider in a totally owned system. Questions may be raised about this strategy. The literature seems to indicate that sufficient data are rarely available to justify the assertion that ambulatory care is cheaper and better than inpatient care.[9] Indeed, two studies seem to indicate that potential savings would be accompanied by a slightly poorer clinical outcome, and only two of many studies suggest ambulatory care would be as effective and less

[8]W. B. Schwartz and P. L. Joskow, "Sounding Boards: Medical Efficacy versus Economic Efficiency: A Conflict in Values," *New England Journal of Medicine*, December 28, 1978.

[9]A. A. Berk and T. C. Chalmers, "Cost and Efficacy of the Substitution of Ambulatory for Inpatient Care," *New England Journal of Medicine*, 304, no. 7 (February 12, 1981), pp. 393–97.

costly. Improved studies might show that savings could be achieved in the ambulatory setting, but with an inferior clinical outcome, or that a better clinical outcome would cost more and therefore pose some difficult ethical dilemmas. Few studies take into account, for example, indirect cost. It is certainly true that at the height of the community mental health movement, in the 1960s, patients were released from psychiatric hospitals both in Great Britain and in the United States for moral and economic reasons without the psychic and economic burden to the family being taken into account. The few studies that were done hinted that it might well be more costly to maintain some kinds of patients, for example chronic psychotics, in the community than in hospital. (Certainly the long-term residue of the community mental health movement has resulted in the current preoccupation with bag ladies and the homeless.)

Concerned with the market perception of their quality, Ford has engaged in a series of programs intended both to upgrade quality and to communicate that enhanced level to the decision makers in the marketplace. In particular, they have identified their relationship with referring physicians as critical to them, and have engaged in an intensive campaign to improve the quality of their service to those referring physicians. Following surveys of patient and referring-physician satisfaction, Ford engaged in an extensive process of determining quality goals, with wide involvement of physicians. These goals included achieving a patient satisfaction rate of 85 percent overall, and a physician satisfaction rate of 85 percent with specified facets of service. Ford set a series of quality standards, including a 15-minute waiting time, a one-week waiting time for appointments, parking within 10 minutes, and patient calls returned the same day. For referring physicians, there is a 24-hour hotline, written reports are sent within three days, and appointments are scheduled within a week, among other improvements. Included is a guarantee that if the patient does not receive his or her X ray within a specified time, it is free!

It is obvious that the implementation of such an extensive program can only be carried out with the full and broad participation of physicians. It is also noteworthy that, in spite of an extraordinary effort to take the design and approval of this program through many, many committees and all physician levels at Henry Ford Hospital, when it came to implementation, there was still a group of physicians that expressed reservations and resented the program because they felt that it imposed standards that represented problems for them. For this group, the program was seen as something the hospital was initiating, not something the physicians identified as needed competitively. This emphasizes a critical point: when a hospital has to engage in competitive actions, it must involve the physicians in recognizing and defining the problem in the first place (so that physicians buy into it) and in implementation of the solution because physician acquiescence may be needed for that implementation to be effective.

In this competitive era, health delivery organizations must influence quality and cost, and therefore the practice styles of their physicians. This is true whether those physicians are full-time salaried employees of an HMO or hospital, fee-for-service attendings, or contractors to an IPA. Effective strategies will be flexible and include a range from improved selection of physicians through direct impact on their practice behavior.

MANAGING QUALITY

Results of the 10-hospital study discussed in earlier chapters can be summed up in the predictable conclusion of physicians that reasonable quality assurance systems, which work marginally and some better than others, existed in most hospitals. Working marginally means that they pick up the gross abusers, but all acknowledge that minor variations are less easily eradicated. Physicians felt that quality and cost essentially concerned physicians, and that management should provide the information and the systems for physicians to work with, and should prod the doctors when the systems did not work. Acknowledging that the responsibility for failure of quality or cost systems might ultimately be management's, physicians nevertheless had very strong feelings about management's proper role. On the whole, managers in most of the hospitals surveyed were felt to behave appropriately and only moved in where it was required, and then largely in a tactful and nonintrusive fashion.

Doctors saw that managing quality presented a difficult problem:

> The major problem is reluctance of designated groups to enforce policies and rules. The problem is one of our natural reluctance to get involved. Documenting and catching someone doing something that will stand up in a court of law is hard to do. You hear things, but a lot of that through the grapevine, and maybe they're right, but it has to be documented. In today's legal climate it is hard to do anything.

Even when you knew about a problem it was tough to deal with.

> There is a person here who gives anesthesia who is not competent, and he may be assigned to your room and you are concerned about your patient. When you want to discuss that with someone they say they're sorry, they can't change it. The person who does a lot of surgery cancels those cases.

What do you do about problems then?

> One substandard surgeon had a senior resident assigned to him, and when he had a case, the senior resident did the surgery. When he tried to do surgery at a different hospital, he might have another surgeon or a physician's assistant helping him. When the physician's assistant realized he was expected to do the case and knew he wasn't qualified, he refused to scrub with the surgeon. Then the surgeon loses his privileges.

Or alternatively

> I go to that section chief and the chief of staff and the chairman of the board. We discuss what is the best way of handling it. It may be having a couple of others or a partner talk to him or whatever it might be. Those meetings are recorded and go into credential files.

Handling credential files is an extraordinarily delicate matter. At one hospital there was a major crisis when the department chief wished to have his evaluations, even when adverse, of physicians placed in the physicians' files so that the evaluations would have some future impact on the physicians' careers. The department chief's mistake in this instance was in not having fully discussed his conclusions with the physicians concerned. The physicians were successful in having his evaluations removed.

The problem is even more difficult when it is a matter of turning a hospital around.

> If people with poor quality are challenged by a small group of people providing good quality, the tables may be turned. It is very difficult to turn a

> hospital around staffwise if it has a poor staff to begin with. It takes time. If good people are there, they will expand their practices, the other people won't be able to build, and eventually the hospital will become strong.

But, "You are limited in what you can do unless somebody is doing ridiculous things. The expense and time involved for the hospital and the physicians is incredible to get rid of somebody."

Many hospitals still have less than adequate systems. "Until this year systems were nonexistent. We know who was not practicing standard medicine but could do nothing about it."

What is the role of management when doctors have difficulty or neglect their responsibility? One CEO said, "If it comes to my attention that a physician is not rendering appropriate care, I immediately contact the medical director. If it is something serious, the medical director and the chief of staff and I sit down and plan what we will do but I am proactive."

For the most part, physicians felt that management's role was to provide information, to monitor, and to observe physician behavior. Eventually, however, management had to become part of the enforcement mechanism because "it is hard to 'tell on' colleagues. You depend on them for referrals, and it is a small community."

But management must act in concert with the medical staff's wishes or there will be a major conflict. Management must prod the system rather than take it over. Physicians agreed that management should flag problems but not get involved in the doing.

> The chairman is the first person who should grab the guy. He needs documentation to support saying "Hey buddy, this has to be corrected, or else." The "or else" is that he will eventually lose his privileges. The first step is confrontation and education. Then you can say you can only see people with somebody else with you. Then if you can't work in the system, you are going to have to lose out. Are doctors any good at doing this? If the chairman is a genuine dictator, you can get a lot done. But documentation will also help, adding pressure. Management's role is to point out that there have been repetitive cases and to push the doctors with the question "What are you going to do about it?" and "Do it."

With the development of a more businesslike attitude, doctors may be more ready to deal with each other when one of them is out of line, because otherwise they will be out of business. One physician said, "We must go to a real business model and talk about a contract. If someone is working for me and he is screwing up, and I'm an influential agent of that contract, and the manager says 'you boys are screwing up,' we've got to take care of them."

But others feel that it is difficult, if not impossible, to handle quality in the current medical-legal climate. Often the courts will reverse a case, if a physician brings it. One physician said: "you're stuck with them and the only way to get rid of them is not to let them on the staff in the first place."

He felt that the most important way to handle quality was to have a better selection process rather than an approval process.

> The only thing that will stand up in court is financial irresponsibility so that you're abusing the hospital's resources. Even not keeping up with what is current will not get you off the staff. If you're going to say, "You can't do that because it is not the proper practice of medicine," and try to stop him from doing it, he will go to the court. He will get an injunction, he will parade 30 women who have had radical mastectomies in front of the judge saying, "He saved my life." He will point to the literature that will say what will be invoked tomorrow. Who is going to say we won't swing back to radical mastectomies as the new statistics come around?
>
> So you have to prove that what he is doing is harmful or costly. If you can only say, "It's different," it won't work. A weak person will back up, a person who recognizes he's wrong will back off, but if you have a strong-willed individual who says, "This is the way I practice because this is the way I believe, and it is right, and even though I am not in tune with the rest of you, this is my practice of medicine"—you cannot beat them, not with the courts as they are.

To an extent, because a hospital is in a community, and because each doctor's livelihood depends on referrals from his fellows, a physician is not going to do anything unless there is an outstanding reason. So quality assurance mainly involves information and education. For the most part, peer pressure works, doctors felt, and if errors were documented adequately, doctors responded. Management should support the physician structure and ensure a fair review process, and that is all. But doctors acknowledged that the hospitals they worked in differed markedly in the extent to which the process worked and in the extent to which doctors were willing to take on problems. In hospitals where the staff was trying to build, where there were younger, more idealistic physicians, the system worked better, as it did also where there was an admixture of management and staff, though staff must always predominate. If the doctors overly dominate, there tends to be stagnation.

The basic quality assurance system in most hospitals starts with information and education, and then moves to a confrontation first with the chief of a department, and then with either the quality assurance committee or, eventually, the executive committee. At some point, in some hospitals, mandatory consultation is required for repeat offenders. In teaching hospitals, the use of grand rounds as a way of exposing poor practice can be salutary.

> During my internship, an attending took terrible care of patients. So we had a mortality conference, and we pretended that I was responsible for every mistake that was made in the case. The attending sat there and watched the intern [the physician speaking] be crucified for all his judgment calls. The corrective action was not lost on those in attendance, and peer pressure was effective. Most doctors are good guys and want to do right by their patients.

Ultimately, repeat offenders lose privileges. The role of management is, as stated, to prod the system if the individuals or committees responsible fail to take action where it is required. It is useful, therefore, for managers to regularly sit in on medical committee meetings, such as those of the executive or quality assurance committees. But managers must remember that these are medical forums and that they are there as guests of the doctors. One CEO who sat in regularly on his quality assurance committee was resented by committee members for the excessive "air time" he took up.

Another source of conflict can be found in those teaching institutions that have town-gown mixes (which is true of most), where the academic chief might be responsible for a department consisting largely of fee-for-service attendings. A chief accustomed to the critical give-and-take of academic debate can easily offend voluntary staff and bruise sensibilities. In one teaching hospital, this led to a request by department physicians for the resignation of their chief, thus jeopardizing the hospital's strategy of upgrading the quality of care in this flagship teaching institution. (See Chapter 7.)

Given the desirability of supporting an open and confronting process for dealing with quality variations, systems such as that of the Hospital Corporation of America, which can provide legal backup to doctors taking an appropriate position, can be very effective. But it should be noted, in conclusion, that most efforts with regard to quality still emphasize eradication of bad medicine, or the bad doctor, and not the positive support of designed quality goals, as in the Henry Ford example.

MANAGING COST

Doctors have similar attitudes concerning cost management systems, which have been implemented recently and are still rudimentary.

> Since DRGs came, and I hate to admit it, we are more conscious of ordering tests or unnecessary therapies. With that, you can affect your practice. The younger physicians do not really care or understand the financial part of the hospital and tend to overuse tests and materials, while the older physicians are most cost conscious. Management should not directly settle [the issue]. They can act as advisers or give comments, but it should be left up to the physicians and departments in question.

Another physician said

> It has to be prodding. There is no exact mechanism to deal with this [when the system does not work]. There is the physician who spends too much money and the physician who does not spend enough. This still rests with quality assurance who have a horrendous job and responsibility. If that is not being addressed, administration has to go to them. If management attempted to act out of concert with medical staff wishes, there would be a major conflict.

The ideal is "to identify people who are dysfunctional and take action, but that has never been done very well [here] and I do not know the answer to that problem. Physicians would be suspicious . . . of hospital administrations in policing medical problems."

Chief executive officers tended to agree and to believe, with doctors, that providing appropriate information and then confronting, where necessary and required, seem to be the way to deal with deviations.

> Administration needs to realize that doctors are not ordering for the sake of ordering. It is just the way they think, the way they have been trained, or their own security as far as attending the patient. What needs to be done, if there is a standard for a given diagnosis, if every patient of a certain physician costs two or three times more than the average, is that that physician needs to be informed of those statistics by his own colleagues as well as by management.

The CEO quoted above felt that "it needs to be purely an informative kind of thing. I personally can not see any punishment involved, removal of privileges, that would serve nobody's purpose."

Hospital cost systems are largely designed to identify and eradicate cost deviations. They tend to emphasize appropriate admission, or excessive length of stay or ancillary use, rather than improving the cost picture or encouraging productivity. Productivity has become a matter of considerable concern to health maintenance organizations faced with rising costs and competitive downward pressures on premiums.

The management system for costs tends to be similar to that involved in quality management, starting with information and education and moving to peer review. It is important that managers who want their doctors to be cost conscious be consistent themselves. Doctors do not like unpredictable variations in charges, for example, laboratory items such as urine cultures, without explanation. How can physicians defend such variations to their patients? And doctors do not appreciate management stressing a stringent budget early in the year only to discover unexpended largesse later in the year. This is especially resented by full-time physicians who may find their bonuses affected by these mystifying maneuvers. Even though the cause may be accounting tactics, malfunctioning technical systems, or managerial inadequacy, in today's paranoid climate, physicians will unkindly assume that management's manipulation is at the root.

Generally speaking, physicians seemed to prefer peer review rather than financial incentives as a basis of managing costs. However they might change their minds if they were encouraged to share risk, for then it would only be fair to also share in potential gain. It is curious that joint ventures seem far more acceptable to doctors than financial benefits gained by saving money on patient care. Again, perhaps physician attitudes will alter as physician incomes plateau or drop. The literature on pattern of practice variation is almost unknown to staff in the hospitals surveyed. Doctors and managers alike seem barely aware of its existence, and therefore do not see it as a potentially fruitful source of information for improving health organization and physician cost performance.

Efforts toward managing costs inevitably involve physician attitudes about cost containment. One survey found that the attitudes concerning cost containment of a representative cross section of 500 physicians differed both from those of the public at large and of their own physician leaders.[10] Fewer than one half of the physicians surveyed believed that the American health care system was working well, as contrasted with two thirds of their leaders and one fifth of the public at large. Of the physicians in the study, 59 percent thought that the cost of hospitalization was unreasonably high and attributed this to expensive technology, an aging population, the expense of malpractice insurance, government funded programs, employer-provided health insurance, excessive ordering of lab tests by physicians, and unnecessary hospitalization. A majority also believed that the third-party system was a major contributor to increased health care spending and that there is price competition in the present health care system. (Three fourths of the public believed that there was no competition, and only 16 percent of the public had ever chosen a physician because his fees were lower than those of another doctor.)

Doctors were pragmatic in that they found cost containment policies acceptable when such policies were effective and believed that increased cost sharing by patients would be an effective policy. The majority also endorsed changes that would reduce hospitalization and discourage duplication of expensive technologies and "superspecialists." There was greater skepticism over the value of utilization review and downright disgust with any attempt to fix physician fees, though it was conceded that this may be effective in containing costs. Physicians also intensely disliked the idea of government price controls, while acknowledging that such controls may be effective.

The physicians surveyed found HMOs unacceptable and IPAs more so. They liked the idea of insurance plans providing individual incentives that would promote healthy living or reduce expenditures, and wished for changes in the malpractice laws that pressure doctors to practice defensive medicine. Doc-

---

[10] *The Equitable Health Survey II: Physician Attitudes toward Cost Containment,* March 1984.

tors varied in their acceptance of nurse practitioners, midwives, and physicians' assistances, and were skeptical of using these paraprofessionals as a means of controlling costs. They disapproved of cost-shifting. Younger doctors were less conservative, but the doctors surveyed, in general, were out of step with the nation on many key issues, though more willing than their leaders to accept change. Hospital managements were found to be much more willing to accept alternatives to the traditional fee-for-service doctor/patient relationship than were the doctors surveyed, and this is crucial to anything that management may wish to consider in relation to managing its physicians.

CHANGING PHYSICIAN BEHAVIOR—THE PROBLEM

A review of the studies devoted to identifying cost and quality problems and to attempting change reveals that doctors are responsible for up to 80 percent of the costs of health care.[11] However, most analysis of practice variation is of limited use as far as cost management goes. Nonetheless, the redefinition of practice standards and the introduction of new styles of practice may have far-reaching implications for cost containment. Variations in diagnosis and treatment are large.[12,13] (As an example, 25 percent of women in one town had had a hysterectomy by age 75, as compared with 70 percent in another 30 miles away.) These differences are only explicable on the basis of physician supply, M.D. practice style, and reimbursement incentives.[14,15] It is not

---

[11]E. Tell, "Changing Physician Practices: A Key Piece in the Health Management Puzzle," in *Health Cost Management at the Community Level: Doctors, Hospitals, and Industry,* ed. R. Egdahl and D. Walsh (Cambridge, Mass.: Ballinger, 1983), pp. 1–28.

[12]M. A. Heasman and V. Carstairs, "Inpatient Management: Variations in Some Aspects of Practice in Scotland," *British Medical Journal* 1 (February 27, 1971), pp. 495–98.

[13]J. Wennberg, "Factors Governing Utilization of Hospital Services," *Hospital Practice,* September 1979, pp. 115–27.

[14]S. Schroeder, A. Schliftman, and T. Piemme, "Variation among Physicians in Use of Laboratory Tests: Relation to Quality of Care," *Medical Care* no. 8 (August 1974), pp. 709–13.

[15]N. Roos, L. Roos, and P. Henteleff, "Elective Surgical Rates—Do High Rates Mean Low Standards?" *New England Journal of Medicine* 297, no. 7 (August 18, 1977), pp. 360–64.

just large numbers of doctors (e.g., surgeons) but also the lack of a medical consensus regarding the marginal benefit of many surgical procedures that leads to variations.[16,17] Particularly lacking are criteria for patient selection, indications for post-op care,[18] and assessment of the relative value and risks of procedure. The reimbursement system provides financial incentives to perform surgery and provide services.[19] Thus, more surgery is done and more patients admitted in fee-for-service practice than in prepaid groups.[20] Costs follow accordingly, not only financial costs, but also the cost of risk, including mortality. This occurs because physicians are risk averse, focusing on the risks of disease more than on the risks of treatment.[21] (Besides, the latter are often not reliably known.)

Variations in hospital use, which may be as much as 38 percent below the national average,[22] equal variations in surgery, but there does not seem a relationship between hospitalization and morbidity or disability. Reimbursement favors inpatient use. Variations in length of stay relate to financial incentives, bed supply, and lack of consensus regarding appropriate time of discharge, as well as to hospital efficiency and management and availability of alternative settings. Shorter stays appear to be associated with a hospital management aware of

---

[16] R. Nickerson, T. Colton, O. Peterson, B. Bloom, and W. Hauck, "Doctors Who Perform Operations: A Study on In-Hospital Surgery in Four Diverse Geographic Areas," *New England Journal of Medicine* 295, no. 18 (October 28, 1976), pp. 982–89.

[17] D. Detmer and T. Tyson, "Regional Differences in Surgical Care Based upon Uniform Physician and Hospital Discharge Abstract Data," *Annals of Surgery,* February 1978, pp. 166–69.

[18] O. Echeverri, C. Manzano, A. Gomez, M. Quintero, and A. Cobo, "Postoperative Care: In Hospital or at Home? A Feasibility Study," *International Journal of Health Services* 2, no. 1 (1972), pp. 101–9.

[19] J. Eisenberg and A. Rossoff, "Physician Responsibility for the Cost of Unnecessary Medical Services," *New England Journal of Medicine* 299, no. 2 (July 13, 1978), pp. 76–80.

[20] E. Carels and C. Tabatabai, "Increased Utilization of Laboratory Tests and X-Rays: Effect on Quality and Cost of Health Care," *Quality Review Bulletin,* June 1980, pp. 5–9.

[21] L. Myers and S. Schroeder, "Physician Use of Services for the Hospitalized Patient: A Review with Implications for Cost Containment," *Milbank Memorial Fund Quarterly/ Health and Society* 59, no. 4 (1981), pp. 481–502.

[22] F. Norbrega, I. Krishan, R. Smoldt, C. Davis, J. Abbot, E. Mohler, and W. McClure, "Hospital Use in a Fee-for-Service System," *Journal of the American Medical Association* 247, no. 6 (February 12, 1982), pp. 806–10.

comparisons and greater specificity of medical support departments.[23,24]

There is also gross overuse of diagnostic[25,26] and therapeutic procedures.[27-29] Test results are often useless or ignored.[30-32] And there is no evidence that more testing equals better care.[33-36] The reasons for excess testing include physician training which emphasizes use of technology and reliance on technology in diagnostic decision making. Physicians fail to understand the overall

---

[23]J. E. Simpson, A. G. Cox, T. W. Meade, P. J. Brennan, and J. A. Lee, " 'Right' Stay in Hospital after Surgery: Randomized Controlled Trial," *British Medical Journal*, June 11, 1977, pp. 1514–16.

[24]A. Innes, A. Grant, and M. Beinfield, "Experience with Shortened Hospital Stay for Postsurgical Patients," *Journal of the American Medical Association* 204, no. 8 (May 20, 1968), pp. 647–52.

[25]B. Wolcott and C. Tabatabai, "X-Ray Utilization as a Result of a Patient Care Evaluation Study," *Quality Review Bulletin* 6, no. 7 (July 1980), pp. 3–8.

[26]P. Griner and B. Liptzin, "Use of the Laboratory in a Teaching Hospital: Implications for Patient Care, Education, and Hospital Costs," *Annals of Internal Medicine* 75 (1971), pp. 157–63.

[27]C. Kunin, T. Tupasi, and W. Craig, "Use of Antibiotics: A Brief Exposition of the Problem and Some Tentative Solutions," *Annals of Internal Medicine* 79 (1973), pp. 555–80.

[28]G. Gray and R. Marion, "Utilization of Hematology Laboratory in a Teaching Hospital," *American Journal of Clinical Pathology* 59 (1973), pp. 877–82.

[29]J. Showstack, S. Schroeder, and M. Matsumoto, "Changes in the Use of Medical Technologies, 1972–1977. A Study of 10 Inpatient Diagnoses," *New England Journal of Medicine* 306, no. 12 (March 25, 1982), pp. 706–12.

[30]J. A. Stilwell, D. Young, and A. Cunnington, "Evaluation of Laboratory Tests in Hospitals," *Annals of Clinical Biochemistry* 17 (1979), pp. 281–86.

[31]R. Dixon and J. Laszio, "Utilization of Clinical Chemistry Services by Medical House Staff," *Archives of Internal Medicine* 134 (December 1974), pp. 1064–67.

[32]S. Erickson, J. Bergman, R. Schneeweiss, and D. Cherkin, "The Use of Drugs for Unlabeled Indications," *Journal of the American Medical Association* 243, no. 15 (April 18, 1980), pp. 1543–46.

[33]C. W. Blair, M. Anderson, and M. McNamara, "A Comparison of Diagnostic Costs for Hospitalized and Ambulatory Hypertension Patients."

[34]S. Schroeder, A. Schliftman, and T. Piemme, "Variation among Physicians in Use of Laboratory Tests: Relation to Quality of Care," *Medical Care* 12, no. 8 (August 1974), pp. 360–64.

[35]M. Daniels and S. Schroeder, "Variation among Physicians in Use of Laboratory Tests II. Relation to Clinical Productivity and Outcomes of Care," *Medical Care* 15, no. 6 (June 1977), pp. 482–87.

[36]E. Carels and C. Tabatabai, "Increased Utilization of Laboratory Tests and X-Rays: Effect on Quality and Cost of Health Care," *Quality Review Bulletin*, June 1980, pp. 5–9.

expense of many apparently inexpensive routine diagnostic tools.[37,38] Excesses may also be attributed to a desire for protection against malpractice charges or criticism, to patient expectations, and to environmental incentives such as automated lab technology. A major factor is poorly designed incentives.

Prepaid group practices tend to have lower rates of hospitalization than do fee-for-service practices. Variations in age, sex, mortality, etc., do not account for more than 15 percent of the variation. Perhaps the lower hospitalization rates are due to fewer available hospital beds, but there is little evidence of this, and even mature group practices that have their own hospitals have similarly low use rates. Is the cause of the difference in utilization the organization into group practice, or is it the method of reimbursement? Groups with salaried doctors or with fee-for-service reimbursement do tend to be similar, so if there is a range of acceptable practice, groups tend to perform in the way that they have been structured and doctors rewarded. Physician incentives may not necessarily be conscious, as for example, the value attached by professionals to self-esteem and peer regard. The setting as well as the institution are important in that two physicians, one conservative regarding costs, the other not, would self-select given different settings in which to practice. In a fee-for-service environment, the cost-conservative physician would not make enough money while his nonconservative counterpart would. Each would therefore leave the setting that is wrong for the individual. In an uncrowded, well-insured fee-for-service environment, each might find a niche corresponding to his own style. There are, in current market conditions (except under DRGs), strong incentives not to be conservative and thus the nonconservative practice pattern becomes the norm.

If we follow this line of reasoning, it is the external incentive of competition with other HMOs and conventional physicians, rather than prepayment or the internal organization of the HMO, that supplies an HMO with the incentive for conservative

---

[37]S. Dresnick, W. Roth, B. Linn, T. Pratt, and A. Blum, "The Physician's Role in the Cost-Containment Problem, *Journal of the American Medical Association* 241, no. 15 (April 13, 1979), pp. 1606–9.

[38]H. Fineberg and L. Perlman, "Low-Cost Medical Practices," *Annual Review of Public Health* 48 (1981), pp. 225–44.

practice.[39] But it may be the internal incentive structure that determines how conservative and efficient the HMO becomes. Data are lacking with which to test the theory.

There are important implications here for medical education, because physicians learn a conservative or nonconservative style as they receive their education. Conservative styles are not lesser in quality and should be encouraged.

CHANGING PHYSICIAN BEHAVIOR—APPROACHES

There is room for change in how physicians practice, specifically in the reduction of length of hospitalization and in the use of ancillaries and of diagnostic and surgical procedures. Quality of care may well be improved as a result. This must be the conclusion of the numerous studies cited above. Reviews suggest that there are six basic strategies that have been used to attempt to change physician behavior, including information, education, peer review or audit and feedback, administrative changes, participation, and financial incentives or penalties.[40-43]

It is difficult at times to distinguish between approaches involving information and those involving education. Pure informational approaches provide data, often numerical, to physicians, and assume that simple data feedback will produce results. Educational approaches involve the broader use of data in a designed discussion setting.

Clinical information systems can assist physicians in the prudent use of clinical resources, but in practice, cost savings

---

[39] W. McClure, "Toward Development and Application of a Qualitative Theory of Hospital Utilization," *Inquiry* 19 (Summer 1982), pp. 117–35.

[40] Tell, "Changing Physician Practices."

[41] J. Eisenberg and A. Rosoff, "Physician Responsibility for the Cost of Unnecessary Medical Services," *New England Journal of Medicine* 299, no. 2 (July 13, 1978), pp. 76–80.

[42] S. Kelman, *Improving Doctor Performance: A Study in the Use of Information and Organizational Change* (New York: Human Sciences Press, 1980), pp. 47–61, 93–145, 159–208, 298–309.

[43] E. J. Carels, D. Neuhauser, and W. B. Stason, eds., *The Physician and Cost Control* (Cambridge, Mass.: Oelgeschlager, Gunn & Haig, 1980).

were seldom realized by implementing such systems.[44] In fact, on occasion, the new system cost more per day per bed than the conventional system.

Educational programs assume that the basic problem is an inadequate understanding of the specificity, sensitivity, and costs of procedures. The approaches include discussions, seminars, workshops, case reviews, mortality conferences, cost-containment directives, and newsletters. Most pure educational approaches have temporary effects only, unless there is regular and consistent reinforcement. So it is important to present a variety of educational methods and topics, together with reinforcement. The educational approach should also be tailored to the individual physician; it must be relevant to his or her value system and address his needs.

Education with feedback tends to be somewhat more useful. Methods include sending copies of bills, calculating percentile ranks, and conducting chart audits, as these play on the physician's sense of achievement and desire to excel. Such feedback systems may be expensive and seem to be most effective if they focus on areas of inappropriate utilization, on problems, and on areas where physicians themselves serve as participants in the review process, directing the feedback efforts toward potentially remedial utilization patterns. Such programs assume that there is a deficiency in both knowledge and attitudes and that physicians need to be inspired or motivated.

Didactic programs tend to be unsuccessful. Successful programs are mainly one-on-one and assume the need to *un*learn as well as to learn. Inclusion of a respected senior clinician, i.e., an opinion leader, is helpful. Change must include attitudinal, peer behavior, environmental constraints, and incentive factors. The overall conclusion is that these programs may result in some change but are not self-sustaining unless there are other incentives. Most programs studied to date were carried out with house staff or residents, generally in teaching hospital settings,

---

[44] R. Johns and B. Blum, "The Use of Clinical Information Systems to Control Cost as Well as to Improve Care," Transamerican Clinical and Clinical Association 90 (1978), pp. 140–50.

and therefore their applicability to full-time senior clinicians or fee-for-service attendings is distinctly questionable.[45-55]

Peer review approaches to changing physician behavior rely on the fact that physicians value the support and approval of their peers, and that approval is important in motivating and sustaining any kind of physician behavior. Variance from the peer group is therefore more likely to result in change. Methods used draw on adult education theory.[56] Both altruism and economics are important and may conflict. Most problems are not due to lack of knowledge or skills, but involve attitudes, procedures, policies, or habits. For success, the trainer must be sure of the facts, take the right approach, state the problem specifically, state the desired solution, be prepared to answer the "so

---

[45]A. Martin, M. Wolf, L. Thibodeau, V. Dzau, and E. Braunwald, "A Trial of Two Strategies to Modify the Test-Ordering Behavior of Medical Residents," *New England Journal of Medicine* 303, no. 23 (December 4, 1980), pp. 1330–36.

[46]L. Klein, P. Charache, and R. Johannes, "Effect of Physician Tutorials on Prescribing Patterns of Graduate Physicians," *Journal of Medical Education* 56 (June 1981), pp. 504–10.

[47]S. A. Schroeder and A. R. Martin, "Will Changing How Physicians Order Tests Reduce Medical Costs?" *Annals of Internal Medicine* 94, no. 4 (April 1981), pp. 534–35.

[48]R. Lawrence, "The Role of Physician Education in Cost Containment," *Journal of Medical Education* 54 (November 1979), pp. 841–46.

[49]C. Lyle, R. Bianchi, J. Harris, and Z. Wood, "Teaching Cost Containment to House Officers at Charlotte Memorial Hospital," *Journal of Medical Education* 54 (November 1979), pp. 856–61.

[50]J. Stross and G. Bole, "Continuing Education in Rheumatoid Arthritis for the Primary Care Physician," *Arthritis and Rheumatism* 22, no. 7 (July 1979), pp. 787–91.

[51]P. Greenland, A. Mushlin, and P. Griner, "Discrepancies between Knowledge and Use of Diagnostic Studies in Asymptomatic Patients," *Journal of Medical Education* 54 (November 1979), pp. 863–68.

[52]R. Rhyne and S. Gelbach, "Effects of an Educational Feedback Strategy on Physician Utilization of Thyroid Function Panels," *Journal of Family Practice* 8, no. 5 (1979), pp. 1003–07.

[53]E. Leist, "A Blueprint for Antibiotic Utilization Review," *Hospital Medical Staff,* May 1981, pp. 19–24.

[54]E. Hirsch, "Utilization Review as a Means of Continuing Education," *Medical Care* 12, no. 4 (April 1974), pp. 358–82.

[55]S. Schroeder, K. Kenders, J. Cooper, and T. Piemme, "Use of Laboratory Tests and Pharmaceuticals Variation among Physicians and Effect of Cost Audit on Subsequent Use," *Journal of the American Medical Association* 225, no. 8 (August 20, 1973), pp. 969–73.

[56]W. Jessee, "Improving Patient Care by Changing Physician Behavior," *Hospital Medical Staff,* January 1982, pp. 2–8.

what" question, not force the issue, and use concurrent monitoring.

Economic sanctions may include mandatory preadmission review of elective admissions; mandatory consultation or surgical assistance; reduction, modification or suspension of hospital privileges; sanctions under the Professional Standards Review Organization (PSRO) law; denial of insurance payment; and suspension or revocation of licensure. Persuasion is usually viable because reasonable people dealt with in reasonable ways are professional. Confront but do not attack, consider alternatives, avoid bureaucracy, and reward positive behaviors.[57,58]

Administrative changes include eliminating routine requirements, requiring the writing of orders, requiring physicians to fill in their own request forms, limiting the number of tests, requiring prior approval, and requiring that clinical criteria be met. These changes may be instituted by the hospital or by a third-party payer. Included in this category is the use of protocols. Protocols have been used quite successfully and have produced some reduction in costs.[59-63] Individual protocols may lack comprehensive monitoring and compliance mechanisms.[64]

---

[57]C. Buck and K. White, "Peer Review: Impact of a System Based on Billing Claims," *New England Journal of Medicine* 291, no. 17 (October 24, 1974), pp. 877–83.

[58]R. Brook and K. Williams, "Effect of Medical Care Review on the Use of Injections: A Study of the New Mexico Experimental Medical Care Review Organization," *Annals of Internal Medicine* 85 (October 1976), pp. 509–15.

[59]D. Brand, W. Frazier, F. W. Kohlhepp, K. Shea, A. Hoefer, M. Ecker, P. Kornguth, M. J. Pais, and T. Light, "A Protocol for Selecting Patients with Injured Extremities Who Need X-Rays," *New England Journal of Medicine* 306, no. 6 (February 11, 1982), pp. 333–39.

[60]W. Craig, S. Uman, W. Shaw, V. Ramgopal, L. Egan, and E. T. Leopoid, "Survey at 19 Hospitals and Results of Antimicrobial Control Program," *Annals of Internal Medicine* 89 (November 1978), pp. 793–95.

[61]F. Dyck, et al., "Effect of Surveillance on the Number of Hysterectomies in the Province of Saskatchewan," *New England Journal of Medicine* 296, no. 23 (June 9, 1977), pp. 1326–28.

[62]P. Griner and B. Liptzin, "Use of the Laboratory in a Teaching Hospital Implications for Patient Care, Education, and Hospital Costs," *Annals of Internal Medicine* 75 (1971), pp. 157–63.

[63]J. Eisenberg, "An Educational Program to Modify Laboratory Use by House Staff," *Journal of Medical Education* 52 (July 1977), pp. 578–81.

[64]R. Saltman, *The Prognosis for Protocols: Organizational and Behavioral Issues in the Design of Medical Ordering Standards* (Boston, 1974), pp. 1–17.

Because physician incentives are professional, financial, and personal, reinforcement tied to prestige rather than to finances may be more successful. A properly designed system must be based on an average treatment pattern and must be culturally targeted to behavioral incentives affecting physicians' clinical decision making. It must include positive incentives for compliance and be implemented by physicians who themselves will be held accountable but will be adequately supported by management.

Financial rewards and penalties have included denying billing claims, claims review, offering financial rewards, and DRG-type systems. The most convincing evidence of the effectiveness of financial incentives in altering physician risk behavior comes from the success of HMOs and IPAs[65-68] in reducing hospital and ancillary use.

The evidence seems fairly strong that where there is risk sharing, savings can be considerable.[69] It also appears that where there is decision sharing with physicians there may also be some degree of improvement of cost behavior. In general, the participation of physicians in identifying savings and the changing their own patterns of practice does seem to result in successful programs.[70,71]

It has been proposed that if peer review finds a hospital stay is unnecessary, the assumed cost should be split among the patient, the physician, the hospital, and the insurance company.[72]

---

[65]J. Eisenberg and S. Williams, "Cost Containment and Changing Physicians' Practice Behavior. Can the Fox Learn to Guard the Chicken Coop?" *Journal of the American Medical Association* 246, no. 19 (November 13, 1981), pp. 2195–2201.

[66]H. S. Luft, "Economic Incentives and Clinical Decisions," in *The New Health Care for Profit,* ed. B. H. Gray (Washington, D.C.: National Academy Press, 1983).

[67]S. Schroeder and J. Showstack, "Financial Incentives to Perform Medical Procedures and Laboratory Tests: Illustrative Models of Office Practice," *Medical Care* 16, no. 4 (April 1978), pp. 289–96.

[68]C. Buck and K. White, "Peer Review: Impact of a System Based on Billing Claims," *New England Journal of Medicine* 291, no. 17 (October 24, 1974), pp. 877–83.

[69]S. Moore, "Cost Containment through Risk-Sharing by Primary-Care Physicians," *New England Journal of Medicine* 300, no. 24 (June 14, 1979), pp. 1359–62.

[70]J. A. Rice and R. K. Keck, "Motivating and Sustaining Involvement," in *Persuading Physicians: A Guide for Hospital Executives.*

[71]J. U. Stoelwinder and P. S. Clayton, "Hospital Organization Development: Changing the Focus from 'Better Management' to 'Better Patient Care,' " *JABS* 14, no. 3 (November 3, 1978), pp. 400–414.

[72]J. M. Eisenberg and A. J. Rosoff, "Physician Responsibility for the Cost of Unnecessary Medical Services," *New England Journal of Medicine* 299, no. 2 (July 13, 1978), pp. 76–79.

Due process should certainly be available to the physician, as well as to the hospital and patient, and there must be mechanisms for resolution of disputes. Any control system must give adequate recognition to the doctor's professional status and allow the physician latitude to exercise judgment. While it is difficult to estimate whether the administrative costs of the peer review/cost sharing system described would offset the potential savings, the advantage of this proposal is that it leaves responsibility for determining the level of medical care in the hands of the physician and his peers.

Those studies dealing with HMOs and IPAs do not isolate financial incentives from the other forces that may be improving cost behavior. The more conservative use of resources in HMOs and IPAs may be a function of peer pressure and utilization of information, e.g., collegial rather than financial. A major problem in the effective use of financial rewards is that, except under DRGs,[73,74] hospitals do not necessarily realize the savings gained from efficiencies.

In summary, for a successful cost-reduction program, the involvement of physicians, the definition of the problem, and the design of the solution are critical, the involvement of physician opinion leaders is important, and the fostering of attitude change, in addition to the transmission of new knowledge, are key. A supportive and reinforcing financial and administrative environment is also important.

Few studies give actual estimates of financial savings.[75-80] In some instances, savings involve items such as shortened length

---

[73]M. Lawrence, "The Impact of Physician Compensation Arrangements on Hospital Financial Management," in *Topics in Health Care Financing* (Rockville, Md.: Aspen Systems, 1978), pp. 27–34.

[74]L. Myers and S. Schroeder, "Physician Use of Services for the Hospitalized Patient: A Review, with Implications for Cost Containment," *Milbank Memorial Fund Quarterly/ Health and Society* 59, no. 4 (1981), pp. 481–502.

[75]A. Martin, M. Wolf, L. Thibodeau, V. Dzau, and E. Brunwald, "A Trial of Two Strategies to Modify the Test-Ordering Behavior of Medical Residents," *New England Journal of Medicine* 303, no. 23 (December 4, 1980), pp. 1330–36.

[76]L. Klein, P. Charache, and R. Johannes, "Effect of Physicians Tutorials on Prescribing Patterns of Graduate Physicians," *Journal of Medical Education* 56 (June 1981), pp. 504–10.

[77]F. Nobrega, I. Krishanf, R. Smoldt, C. Davis, J. Abbott, E. Mohler, and W. McClure, "Hospital Use in a Fee-for-Service System," *Journal of the American Medical Association* 257, no. 6 (February 12, 1982), pp. 806–10k.

of stay, which may produce an increased cost per diem or a reduction of occupancy rate! Moreover, it is usually the less expensive part of the stay that is abbreviated. Cuts in the use of diagnostic facilities may not produce savings for there are fixed costs associated with these. The exception is significant cuts that allow the hospital to dispense with people and machines. Similarly, a shift to ambulatory surgery will only result in cost savings when inpatient facilities can be closed.

In conclusion, it is salutory to recall that the practicing physician feels that differences in physician practice style are legitimate and part and parcel of a professional's autonomy.[81] Normative error is the stylistic idiosyncracy of a particular attending. This helps explain why it is so difficult to change physician behavior and why so many of the approaches described above have been ephemeral with sketchy results unless physicians are heavily involved. Physicians deal with deviation by remaining silent but not referring patients to the questionable practitioner.

COMPENSATION AND FINANCIAL INCENTIVES AS A TOOL FOR CHANGE

Compensation approaches are many and varied.[82,83] Only selected comments on their managerial implications will be made here. A favored model is a fixed salary with variable incentives that reward designated performance. Performance can include "devotional" activities, such as participation in staff functions and on

---

[78] J. Wennberg, L. Blowers, R. Parker, and A. Gittlesohn, "Changes in Tonsillectomy Rates Associated with Feedback and Review," *Pediatrics* 59, no. 6 (June 6, 1977), pp. 821–26.

[79] O. Echeverri, C. Manzano, A. Gomez, M. Quintero, and A. Cobo, "Postoperative Care: In Hospital or at Home? A Feasibility Study," *International Journal of Health Services* 2, no. 1 (1972), pp. 101–9.

[80] D. Detmer and T. Tyson, "Regional Differences in Surgical Care Based upon Uniform Physician and Hospital Discharge Abstract Data," *Annals of Surgery,* February 1978, pp. 166–89.

[81] C. L. Bosk, *Forgive and Remember: Managing Medical Failure* (Chicago: University of Chicago Press, 1979).

[82] H. Adolfi, "Compensation for HMO Physicians: Pay Policies for Staff Retention and Motivation," *Health Services Manager,* March 1980, pp. 8–9.

[83] H. Adolfi, "Compensation for HMO Physicians: What Program Is Best for Them and Their Patients," *Health Services Manager,* February 1980, pp. 5–8.

committees, or increased productivity. A performance-based plan should include incentive bonuses oriented to departments and to individuals.[84] Most incentive schemes fail because the amount of the bonus is too small a proportion of pay as a whole or because it is not tied to specified performance under the control of the physician or physician group concerned. There is nothing wrong with most performance-based incentive schemes; any fault lies less in their design than in their implementation. It is extraordinarily difficult to ensure consistent and thorough performance evaluation. In all honesty, evaluation can be a tedious, though worthwhile pursuit. As physicians increasingly contract with hospitals, whether as full-time employees or as members of physician groups, good design in compensation plans becomes more salient. The well-designed plan takes into account the various factors contributing to productivity and under control of the physician or the department, and provides incentives to enhance productivity.[85,86]

In arriving at a proper compensation level for full-time physicians, three major factors must be taken into account: prevailing practices in similar institutions, compensation requirements of the physician, and attitudes of the private practitioner.

Compensation may be fixed, variable, or a combination of the two. These possibilities are applicable whether the physician is an employee or an independent contractor. Different models have different effects on the information and data-management system of the institution, on the physician and on hospital utilization level, on tax-exempt status, on the physician's authority, on the involvement of the physician, on participation in medical staff activities, on legislation, on retention of physicians, on the capacity to renegotiate, and on developing good working relationships.

Each model has its pluses and minuses. The independent contract limits the physician's authority in the hospital and his or her responsibility and accountability. Offering a percentage of

---

[84]R. Cooper, "A Performance-Based Physician Compensation Plan," *Journal of Ambulatory Care Management*, May 1980, pp. 19–33.

[85]P. Trenz, "Compensation—Part II. How Important Is Your Happiness?" *Group Practice Journal*, May–June 1982, pp. 32–49.

[86]K. Johnson, "Fair Share Formula: A Direct Expense Profit Center-Based Plan," *Group Practice Journal*, September-October 1982, pp. 6–7.

net provides the physician with greater incentives to be cost effective than does percentage of gross. Under a leasing arrangement, the physician has an independent operation within the hospital and has total authority, responsibility, and accountability for all departmental activities.

Generally, the employer-employee relationship increases physician-hospital involvement, while the independent contractor relationship tends to place physician goals in conflict with hospital goals. Other models have predictable effects on reducing costs or increasing volume, on enhancing or diminishing involvement. Additional benefits can include life insurance plus pensions and tax-deferred annuities, and paid time off for professional development or for short-term disability.[87]

Physicians with the greatest earning power do not like income distribution systems that reduce their income below what they might obtain competitively. One solution is the direct expense profit center plan which attributes productivity for services to the individual doctor, attributes cost within the doctor's control to the physicians, shares cost for items not under physician control, attributes profits from ancillary services according to utilization, and allows physicians' incomes within the group to approximate what their incomes would be outside the group. To the total annual revenue for a physician, a collection adjustment is made, and then personnel costs, drugs and supplies, equipment, liability insurance, and fringe benefits are deducted, resulting in the adjusted revenue. This is multiplied by, say, 60 percent to obtain the clinic income. (The percentage is the clinic's profitability.) Further income is derived from laboratory, radiology, and cardiopulmonary ancillaries which augment income. This, plus fringe benefits, is the practice-related profit.

Many contract hospital-based physicians are compensated on a percentage of gross or percentage of net. If the hospital increases prices, reimbursement to the hospital-based physician is automatically increased.[88] The physician's responsibilities may be assigned to specific categories that require payment, includ-

---

[87]J. D. Browdy, *Health Care Executive Compensation: Principles and Strategies* (Rockville, Md.: Aspen Systems, 1983).

[88]R. Cotner, "The Contractual Flexibility between Physicians and Hospitals," *Hospital Financial Management*, August 1980, pp. 37–38.

ing administrative management, personnel staffing and selection, scheduling, ordering and supplies inventory, etc. Also, professional supervision, evaluation of technical and other workers, and supervision of education may be included. Dollar values can be assigned to each responsibility. Reimbursement may be a flat dollar amount, or a dollar value per relative value unit or procedural count. Deductibles can include billing costs, uncollectables, etc.

One problem with all these alternative compensation plans and financial incentive designs is that they rely on the historical status quo. And historically certain specialties, based on the demands of the marketplace, have been able to command higher prices for their services than others. The most highly skilled internist cannot command the same amount of money for an hour's work that a less skilled surgeon receives. These differences, which some might term inequities, are perpetuated in most incentive schemes. Existing systems favor technology-intensive procedures and place lower value on cognitively intensive procedures.

Some attempt has recently been made to use the relative value scale.[89] It was developed in 1956 in California and was based on the existing median charges of physicians statewide. The scale takes into account resource costs, time taken to perform service, complexity, cost and duration of physician's training, overhead expense, and malpractice insurance. In one recent study, office visits were found to be undervalued by four- or fivefold, and surgical procedures were overvalued. While implementation of any plan based on the relative value scale must await general acceptance, this is an interesting approach.

The issue of paying for productivity has not yet been widely discussed in health care literature. Yet the efficient use of scarce resources, whether technology or physician time, is becoming a major competitive issue. Some HMOs are attempting to limit the duration of patient-physician encounters as a way of increasing productivity and reducing costs. When productivity is concerned, apart from the specter of lay intrusion into clinical practice, physicians are concerned about the development of

[89] W. C. Hsiao and W. B. Stason, "Toward Developing a Relative Value Scale for Medical and Surgical Services," *Health Care Financing Review*, Fall 1979.

standards; they feel only physicians can judge what constitutes the appropriate length of an encounter with a patient. Yet it is also clear that some physicians are inefficient or lazy. This is less a problem in a fee-for-service office where there are natural pressures to keep productivity high.

The Ochsner Clinic in New Orleans represents an interesting example of the effects of financial incentives on physician control of costs. In this large group practice, physicians are paid a salary as well as a large bonus to which they become entitled once they have generated sufficient resources to cover their individually negotiated salary. The bonus pool is generated by the excess of profits over costs within the clinic. Physicians are therefore at risk for costs, and the clinic is an extremely efficient, low-cost operation. The same physicians practice in the Ochsner hospital, where they receive fee-for-service payment for the time they put in and the procedures that they do with the same patients they treat in the clinic. The hospital's costs are similar to those of any other hospital of its size!

The problem with most incentive schemes is that they are cost rather than productivity oriented. The incentive is based on reimbursing reduction of costs rather than on generating profits. The bonus pool is therefore self-liquidating, for costs are progressively reduced to a level where they can be reduced no further, and ultimately the bonus pool disappears. One way around the problem of tying financial incentives to individual productivity is to give a bonus based on the performance of the organization as a whole, as is done in Group Health Association, a large HMO in Washington, D.C. This does not raise some of the more ticklish moral and design problems, and certainly provides physicians with an incentive to see that the organization performs well in general. The difficulty with this type of incentive is that there are numerous factors other than the physician's own behavior that contribute to profitability. Therefore, there is no direct relationship of the physician's behavior to the rewards he receives. This goes against the basic tenets of incentive design: rewards should be large, should be direct and immediate, and should be under the control of the physician, to be successful.

Group practices generally value higher-producing physicians, and productivity incentives do tend to improve efficiency. But specialties bring in different amounts of money. Moreover, doctors vary in their use of testing, etc. In group practices, to avoid creating separate profit centers, some percentage of profits should be shared equally, but if less than 50 percent of the group income is based on productivity, the arrangement does not offer great enough incentives. Multispecialty groups may have particular problems, because equipment purchases tend to be very different, as is the use of labs, etc.

Productivity is usually measured by gross billings, bookings, or services minus write-offs of uncollectables. Productivity measures should be based on figures for an entire year, and changes in compensation should be gradual. For cost centers, a two-tier system is utilized—one based on the profit generated from gross services, the other on profit-center expenses—to arrive at the profitability total. The same productivity percentages are used to allocate income and to allocate expense. For senior group members whose practice activity is on the decline, minimum compensation can be guaranteed, a set amount can be put aside for the physician's remaining active life, or extra time off can be given, but it is important to define "senior doctor" and what the compensation will be. Moreover, outside activities that benefit the group should be taken into consideration and recognized in dollars to compensate for productivity losses.

The divisional or departmental concept is more complex. It helps to have physicians in the same specialty sharing space. Divisional organization can be a way to deal with some types of group problems.

Teaching hospitals are experimenting with attracting and retaining highly qualified teaching physicians by offering various incentive plans that provide supplemental compensation. These arrangements pool revenues received, or use budgetary allocation or hospital general funds, and distribute revenues or funds according to the plan. Crucial to such arrangements is the development of the right balance of physician efforts between patient care, teaching, research, and administration. Achieving this balance requires that careful attention be paid to the specific performance measures that will be rewarded.[90] Different plans will have different consequences for aspects of hospital function, in-

---

[90] G. Eiland, "Putting Incentive in Physicians' Pay," *Health Services Manager*, February 1981, pp. 13–14.

cluding the hospital information system,[91] as well as for financial management of the hospital.[92-94]

An important question facing managers concerned with influencing physician behavior is the extent to which it is not just effective but legitimate to influence behavior through the use of financial mechanisms. This is both a practical and a moral matter. As one CEO put it,

> A doctor ought not to admit a patient to a hospital because he will get X dollars back from having admitted that patient there. If we help a doctor locate his office close to the hospital and he admits his patients to my place, it is because it's convenient to him and he's satisfied with the quality. But there is no direct financial incentive, and I am afraid that putting in a financial incentive would raise more questions than it would answer.

However, at least one physician has begun to change his mind on this issue:

> I owned a lab for many years. If you had asked me that question five years ago, I might have said that there would have been a conflict. But now with the limited resources available, with just so many dollars to be paid out, physicians know that you cannot milk the system. Many of us know that. Therefore, if there is a limited amount of revenue, whatever you get you have to protect. Having a financial interest only enhances the system in terms of efficiency.

The crucial issue in financial incentives is the link between physician as agent and physician as provider.[95] The physician as agent ideally would have no personal economic incentives to encourage or discourage additional tests or procedures or to prefer one treatment over another on the basis of cost. Acting for the patient, the physician as agent should be disinterested. In practice, fee-for-time arrangements are uncommon, and even the de-

---

[91]J. Morell and P. Rogan, "Hospital-Based Physician Compensation Concepts," in *Topics in Health Care Financing* (Rockville, Md.: Aspen Systems, 1978), pp. 11–25.

[92]M. Lawrence, "The Impact of Physician Compensation Arrangements on Hospital Financial Management," in *Topics in Health Care Financing* (Rockville, Md.: Aspen Systems, 1978), pp. 27–34.

[93]J. Head, "Regulatory Environment for Physician Compensation," in *Topics in Health Care Financing* (Rockville, Md.: Aspen Systems, 1978), pp. 75–88.

[94]E. A. Kaskiw, "Overview of Physician Compensation," in *Topics in Health Care Financing* (Rockville, Md.: Aspen Systems, 1978), pp. 1–9.

[95]H. S. Luft, "Economic Incentives and Clinical Decisions," in *The New Health Care for Profit*, ed. B. H. Gray (Washington, D.C.: National Academy Press, 1983).

partmental revenues of salaried medical school faculty are dependent on fee-for-service billings. Economic factors are present even in an HMO where the capitation payment will cover a certain amount of care and no more, and net income will be smaller if there is an excess of treatment.

Most physicians claim that financial incentives do not influence their patient-care decisions, although physicians in prepaid plans like the fact that their patients have comprehensive coverage so economic issues are not in the forefront in these situations. (This is less true now. With competitive pressures on premiums and therefore costs, there are significant economic pressures on HMO physicians, for example, to improve productivity and shorten the patient encounter.) The physician as provider obviously has considerable interest in what he or she provides, and economic incentives do have an impact here. As an example, clinical decision-making patterns in prepaid groups do seem to be different from the patterns in other types of practice.

There may be a difference among physicians in the use of technologies that have clear-cut and specific benefit and those with obscure or marginal benefits. The latter technologies tend to be used for reasons other than efficacy, such as fashion or social control.[96] Variations in practice patterns may be explained by clinical choices made in these gray areas—preferences that have no scientific basis, yet are self-reinforcing.

The law requires people such as physicians who are in positions of trust, to subordinate their self-interest to the well-being of their charges, for physicians have a fiduciary relationship to patients.[97] Because physicians receive secondary income from treatment they advise, there is a possibility of wrongful manipulation of trust. The physician should exercise judgment in deciding what will benefit the patient.[98] In this context, labeling certain business practices unethical, but not others, may involve

---

[96] A. Sheldon and D. Hooper, "Psychiatric Care in Cross-Cultural Perspective," *Human Organization* 25, no. 1, pp. 3–9.

[97] F. H. Miller, "Secondary Income from Recommended Treatment: Should Fiduciary Principles Constrain Physician Behavior?" in *The New Health Care for Profit*, ed. B. H. Gray (Washington, D.C.: National Academy Press, 1983).

[98] R. M. Veatch, "Ethical Dilemmas for For-Profit Enterprises in Health Care," in *The New Health Care for Profit*, ed. B. Gray (Washington, D.C.: National Academy Press, 1983).

self-interest. In addition, professionals must not lose control of their sphere of responsibility; physicians may be made uncomfortable by the actions of lay management in for-profit corporations. Perhaps doctors feel relatively comfortable with the Health Corporation of America because it is owned by a physician.

To some degree, whether health care is a right is at issue. If it is, then the profit motive is inappropriate. However, the employed professional must not only serve the interests of the client, but also those of the employing organization. Generally speaking, physicians in the 10-hospital study discussed earlier seemed to feel that no incentives should exist to attract volume to a hospital. They feel that hospitals can provide subsidized offices or make the institutions attractive, but physicians should not receive direct payment to bring in their patients. On the other hand, physicians are beginning to support joint ventures in the provision of services; the physicians have a financial interest but do not themselves provide the service.

GOALS AND PROCESSES FOR PHYSICIAN BEHAVIOR-CHANGE PROGRAMS

In selecting goals for a physician behavior-change program, management must choose those of significance to the institution and of importance to the physician. Quality programs, for example, should be aimed at behavior having a significant effect on the welfare of patients, staff, or visitors; that reflect behavior which has been recorded or on which it is possible to collect data; where continued deviation from hospital policy or criteria involves suboptimal care, financial loss, accreditation, or legal risk; or where it is necessary to document causal relationships to facilitate decision making.[99]

What are you trying to achieve? What are the incentives at your disposal? How are you going to design the program? What is the setting and what peculiarities do your physicians have? What motivates or induces doctors to behave in particular fash-

---

[99]T. G. Carroll, *Restructuring Hospital Quality Assurance* (Homewood, Ill.: Dow Jones-Irwin, 1984), chapter 8.

ion? What are the basic assumptions behind the existence of problems? What is keeping things the way they are? Without the answers to these questions, it will not be possible to find some way to alter undesirable behavior.

Is the goal to shift a standard, to reduce minor deviance, or to eradicate a gross deviance? Some programs are intended to shift the normal bell-shaped curve, i.e., to alter the basic standard or pattern of practice. Others attempt to eradicate significant deviance at one extreme of the curve. While the extremes of the poor-quality or the high-cost doctor have been emphasized, there are other extremes of equal importance. In any program intended to enhance quality, it is important to determine and then improve basic standards. Yet, in any attempted improvement, it is the extremes that are all important. If patients have to wait too long to see a physician, and average waiting time is improved by 10 minutes, this is relatively trivial. It is the four-hour wait that creates the story that reaches everyone, including the board. Programs intended to upgrade quality must aim at cutting off that devastating extreme, must, in other words, improve consistency.

The opposite may be true for costs, where it is the sum of small deviances that may be telling. For example, at one hospital, DRG data on 15 physicians in one department who together admitted 85 percent of the total cases, showed that patients of the four highest admitters all had lengths of stay only about one day above the state mean, although these doctors admitted one half of all the cases. A few other doctors had patient lengths of stay grossly above the mean. What should management do about these data? Should attention be paid to the gross deviance? Or to the small departures, which added up to major costs? This is obviously not simply an economic problem, but also a political one, because it is not easy for management to put pressure on high admitters.

Cost programs of interest to a hospital, rather than a regulator, may have as much to do with increasing productivity as with reducing cost abuses. If capital-intensive resources can be used more efficiently, if FTEs (Full Time Equivalents) can produce more, then a hospital will perform better under DRGs, and more competitively in its efforts to become a low-cost provider. Therefore, cost per unit of resource, rather than absolute costs, becomes the important goal. Relatively few studies seem to have been done on this issue. Financial incentives may be important here, for excesses or abuses are not as salient as efficiencies. Can one instill in physicians that kind of pride that managers call "running lean"?

Once a goal is determined, appropriate measures for achieving that goal must be identified. Of importance is whether these measures are part of routine operations or will have to be specially introduced. To the extent that programs intended to improve performance can be institutionalized and routinized, they will be that much more effective.

The next step is to determine what behaviors appear to relate to the target goals, and what causes unwanted behavior. Is the unwanted behavior caused by ignorance, expectations, or standards? Is the behavior occurring because doctors do not believe, do not know, or do not care? Is there fear of litigation? Do doctors justify their actions or simply act out of habit? What influences on this behavior come from fellow physicians, from the organization itself, or from external factors such as the nature of the reimbursement system, which may support undesirable behavior? What kind of relationship does the physician have to the organization that might be amenable to change? It is crucial to explore these basic factors, for it is on a profound understanding of why doctors are doing what they are doing (and not what the organization wants), and what motivates them, that any successful program will depend. This is shown schematically in Figure 6–1.

Managers may be tempted (and often are) to adopt, for simplicity or cost reasons, standardized programs packaged attractively, to solve their problems. These may, on occasion, be both appropriate and efficacious. It certainly can be a major undertaking to design and implement a program (though this is by no means always true). But there is no real replacement for a dedicated program designed to suit the particular setting, situation, and target.

Programs may be episodic or ongoing, systematic or special, personal or institutional, sequential or one-shot. Many programs are one-time affairs aimed at remedying a particular problem, as opposed to an ongoing institutionalized attempt to keep a particular behavior within specified limits. Are programs aimed at specified individuals, at a group, at a division or department, or

FIGURE 6-1 Factors Involved in Physician Behavior-Change Programs

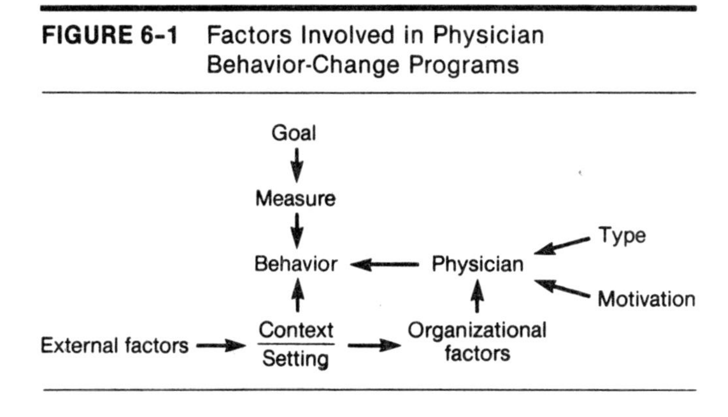

at the organization as a whole? What is the role of management versus that of other staff and in terms of systematic procedures? Do the planned incentives have value for the target group? Is that value higher than the value of factors that may be keeping behavior at an undesirable level? Incentives must be designed carefully and targeted to the goal. If incentives are financial, they must be large in comparison with other forms of compensation, equitable, and without adverse consequences, such as stimulation of competition resulting in an unforeseen reduction of crossreferrals.

An example of the kind of analysis recommended in a behavior-change program is use of information feedback. Any information the physician is to receive has to compete for physician time, and physicians have little discretionary time. Therefore, any successful information feedback must be pointed, unavoidable, and repetitive. To get the physician's attention, the context must be relevant, salient, palatable, and probably personal. When thinking about how to reach the doctor through alternative formats, such as a house organ, a newsletter, a personal letter, the use of audio or video presentations, or a computer, it is important to consider the different kinds of physicians targeted and their most likely use of media. (How many own/use computers? Might it be worth supplying doctors with terminals?) One alternative obviously is face-to-face communication, but this is expensive and time-consuming, and doctors have as little time for this as anything else. A useful format for getting the attention of doctors is the medical chart on which the physician must record certain kinds of information. It is indeed unavoidable. However, because physicians are notoriously bad at completing charts, even this is by no means foolproof. It is the consideration of such detailed items as this that yields a successful program.

Summary of M.D. Behavior-Change Programs

To sum up, a program for physician management needs to deal with the following issues.

The first task is to determine the basic goal of the organization with regard to the relationship between physicians and the organization. Everything follows from this. Does the organization see the doctor as a competitor, a contractor, a consultant, an employee, or a partner?

Depending on the nature of the relationship, what structural relationships are desired? These have to do with control and power. What is the relationship between management (the operation of the organization), the physicians, and care (control over the work of the organization)? What kinds of new roles are envisioned to facilitate the articulation of physicians and management? Does this include a vice president who is a doctor, and/or an ombudsman?

How are physician values and needs articulated with institutional values and needs? Do the physician and the institution have similar views about physician performance? How are differences dealt with? Are these methods of dealing with differences acceptable to both parties?

Measures. What measures are used to determine the goals of a program directed toward influencing physician relationships?

How do you measure loyalty? By percentage share of physician's practice? Volume of admissions? Crossreferral within the system? Does the hospital have a strategy for a targeted share of physician practice? That is, does it want a lot of a few physicians' patients or a few patients from many physicians? Higher commitment by physicians involves more hospital vulnerability. Lower commitment involves less influence over them.

How do you measure physicians' devotion, i.e., amount of time given to institution? How do you measure competition for physician time taking into account that the physician gives time to several hospitals, to his or her office, to other businesses, and to nonbusiness activities? How do physicians spend time in the organization, i.e., on patient care, on administrative matters, or on professional matters?

How do you measure physician performance, i.e., cost, case mix, productivity, dollar volume of admission from ancillaries? Are goals set?

Assumptions. What are the assumptions about physician behavior on which a program is based? What is the role of ignorance and knowledge, of money, of professional pride, in the design of a program? For example, is the volume of admissions believed to be a function of the convenience of the hospital to the doctor and patient; of the degree of access to or control over facilities by the doctor; of the state of the relationship of the doctor to key people in the institution, such as the department chief; or of the additional income to be derived from ancillaries such as EKGs or echo sound? The beliefs about what doctors get out of a particular behavior or their basic motivation will determine the nature of a program. Do physicians have to be bullied, bought, bedeviled, believed, etc.? Do they want power or control or just a fair share? Incentives will not work if based on incorrect assumptions: productivity incentives may fail with lifestyle oriented M.D.s, e.g., effectiveness in a group practice differs from that in an HMO.

Incentives. Are incentives clearly related to specific goals or of a general nature? Are the goals known and the incentives familiar? Are the incentives addressed to the basic assumptions about physician motivation, and are these assumptions correct? Incentives may include tax write-offs, sharing in nonpatient-care revenues, or income protection. Does the hospital feel it has to be the dominant partner, or can it allow physicians autonomy to develop activities in which the hospital may take a share?

Policies for Deviance. Are physicians aware of hospital-defined undesirable behavior and hospital goals to eradicate this? Are there clear-cut policies for deviance? Is there a culture in which deviance can be discussed and dealt with? What kinds of deviance are regarded as matters for concern by the hospital and by the doctors? Are there different policies for different types of deviance such as outliers, high-volume small deviance, changes in normal patterns?

RECRUITMENT

Physicians welcome the involvement of management in identifying gaps in the range of specialties involved in their health organization and in helping them recruit for these specialties, but expect to retain control of recruitment. This is true whether the physicians are in an HMO, a fee-for-service group, or a department of a teaching hospital. Recruitment still tends to be restricted to the identification of the need for a particular specialty and selection on the basis of clinical credentials. Neither physicians nor management have yet given much attention to the practice style of recruited physicians, with its dramatic impact on the health organization's performance, though HMOs have begun to attend to this.

Health organizations are changing from being like mom and pop stores with idiosyncratic variability and charm, to more highly specialized institutions akin to supermarkets or gourmet boutiques. As specialized, designed institutions, health organizations must offer products that are much more highly tuned, and their staffs must fit the product and the organization more closely. If you are going to practice efficient, cheap medicine, then you have to have doctors who will do that. If you are going to go for quality, then your doctors must exemplify it. Selective recruiting is an important way to influence costs, quality, and case mix. As one physician put it, "I think there will be finer tuning of the physicians in terms of who gets on staff and who doesn't get on staff. Who will play the game with certain numbers in terms of dollars, and who will not play the game in dollars."

This issue is of particular gravity to HMOs. The HMO product is quality, comprehensive health care services provided in a cost-efficient manner. The HMO's ability to alter the traditional practice patterns of the primary care physician to more cost-conscious alternatives is key. Regardless of the operating model, the primary care physician is the central player in providing quality services and in cost performance.

Quality services are ensured first by selecting the right physicians. In staff model HMOs, the outlook for attracting quality physicians is improving as the number of physicians increases. Only a few years ago, HMOs had difficulty attracting quality providers, and in some instances, settled for foreign-trained physicians who often created an image problem. Today, staff model HMOs are able to recruit well-trained, board-certified physicians in most primary and specialty care areas. Typically, new staff physicians are recent graduates of residency programs.

In open-panel HMOs, physician selection is extremely important because the organization's reputation is derived from the reputation of the physicians chosen to participate in the HMO.[100] Key physician selection criteria include:

Board certification/eligibility in their selected specialty.

Affiliation with quality hospitals.

Sophisticated technology in the office to limit referrals to diagnostic tests.

Available capacity in practice to ensure accessibility for the new HMO patient.

Strong interest in participation in an alternative health care system.

To be successful, the HMO core product—medical care—must be high quality. Historically, consumers' perceptions have lagged behind reality. The Harris poll found a smaller percentage of HMO members than nonmembers saying they were very satisfied with the quality of their doctors. Yet, empirical research findings suggest HMOs are quality providers. Numerous studies have indicated that the quality of services at an HMO is, at the very least, equal to that of the fee-for-service system. Even the American Medical Association, in a 1980 report on HMOs, found the medical care delivered by HMOs, "appears to be of a generally high quality."[101]

---

[100]*The Health Maintenance Organization Industry,* Basic Report 84-67A (W. Blair and Company, 1984).

[101]L. Harris, *Medical Practice in the 1980s: Physicians Look at Their Changing Profession* (Menlo Park, Calif.: Henry J. Kaiser Family Foundation, 1981).

Much of the mixed perception of quality results from the difficulty closed-panel HMOs have had in recruiting the highest-quality physicians. In its early years, the HMO industry had difficulty recruiting physicians to meet membership growth. However, the growing supply of physicians and the propensity of young physicians to select group practice settings should improve recruitment in closed-panel HMOs. Open-panel models, with strict selection criteria, should be immune to mixed perceptions of quality because members can choose or remain with physicians in whom they have confidence.

Another significant recruitment issue is the extent to which medical staffs are open or closed. Medical staffs must control accreditation of and granting hospital privileges to potential new members. This is done through hospital bylaws[102] to ensure effective peer review and quality assurance. Medical staffs may close because there is a limit to the number of physicians that can service a given number of beds, or because of competition. Accreditation does ensure that only those with appropriate academic qualifications are granted privileges to practice or teach. Sometimes closure of a staff may, as in the case of one small community hospital on the East Coast, reflect the desire to restrict competition but will eventually hurt the hospital, for new blood is kept out while the existing staff ages. Where reasons for closure are ethically questionable, such as in instances of racial or religious exclusion, management has a major responsibility to pressure the medical staff to open up, and to override the staff if they resist. Resistance may take subtle forms. Applications may be considered, but reluctantly, so that processing is delayed while physicians grow impatient and seek privileges elsewhere.

---

[102]J. C. Goldsmith, *Can Hospitals Survive? The New Competitive Health Environment* (Homewood, Ill.: Dow Jones-Irwin, 1981).

CHAPTER SEVEN

Managing Change and Conflict: Monitoring Physician Response

Who shall decide, when doctors disagree, and soundest casuists doubt, like you and me?

Alexander Pope

MANAGING CHANGE AND CONFLICT

The problems involved in managing both conflict and change are discussed together because in everyday practice, they are much intertwined. Indeed, one cause of many conflicts is an attempt to bring about change. The ensuing shift in the stabilizing but debilitating forces is what precipitates the conflict. One principle of managing change should be that if the dynamics of maintaining the status quo are not understood, do not attempt change. In managing physicians, the conflicts faced may be of several types, as listed in Table 7-1.

The situation at "Pym Medical Center" reflects the complexity and touches on most varieties of physician conflict. In the summer of 1985, a group of cardiologists called a meeting to set down their grievances regarding Dr. Charles Hassall, the department chairman, and to ask the chief executive officer of Pym to remove Hassall. The CEO knew that Hassall was an excellent researcher and respected clinician, but also that he could be arbitrary and autocratic. While the petitioners constituted a minority of the cardiology group (14 of 33), their grievances clearly could not be ignored. As with so many crises, there was a long history to this situation.

The dissidents were all fee-for-service attendings. Those not involved were either disinterested or allies of Hassall. The dissidents listed numerous complaints in writing, although the request for resignation was made verbally. The complaints were various: there had been three serious incidents involving differ-

TABLE 7-1 Types of Physician Conflict
Interpersonal
Interdepartmental
Generational
Strategic
Growth
Evolutionary

ent physicians; a staff person's firing was questioned; and there were some supposed threats against physicians. Some complaints were over access to remunerative technologies such as arteriography and echo reading. The dissidents also felt that they had not fully participated in key department decisions. They concluded their written statement: "These incidents have created an overall atmosphere of rudeness, anger, distrust, loss of confidence, and low morale within the department which has permeated beyond it."

Dr. Hassall had been hired 10 years previously, following the retirement due to illness of the previous incumbent, a powerful man who had not only been chief of cardiology but also medical director and chief of medicine, and somewhat autocratic himself. Dr. Hassall had been brought in by management, as a well-trained and qualified academic, because the hospital wished to upgrade the quality of care in the department and its teaching-hospital status. Management wished to develop the teaching program and especially fellowships in cardiology. Hassall's job was to rebuild the cardiology department, and this he did well, making many contacts outside the hospital and increasing referrals significantly, especially catheterization referrals. But as a consequence of his success, he recruited to run the catheter lab, a second full-time cardiologist, also a well-trained academic skilled in angioplasty. The two attending cardiologists who had previously monopolized cardiac catheterization resisted the new arrival because they feared a loss of income. Hassall largely referred to the new man, while most department referrals went to the old-timers. The more energetic of the two attendings was able to maintain his referral flow, but the other suffered a distinct drop in referrals and income; the two were key dissidents.

There had also been a shift in the ethnicity of the department. Originally dominated by Irish physicians, the department had become dominated by Italian Catholics, many of whom were generalists "grandfathered" into the department, and not highly trained cardiologists. The new chief and his assistant were both Jewish academics.

At the time of the crisis, the new assistant chief performed 300 procedures a year, while the more active of the two old-timers also performed 300 (a drop from 400) and the other 200 (down from about 350). Hassall himself did very few, but was responsible for referring more than 200 procedures to his assistant and fewer than 20 to the two old-timers.

When the CEO looked into the allegations, it turned out that the staff person who had been dismissed had worked closely with the two old-timers and was unable to adjust when Hassall arrived and made somewhat different demands. The three cases involving physicians included an anesthesiologist who had fallen sick and for whom Hassall provided a backup, but Hassall's action had been misconstrued. A second, an Italian doctor, had been invited to join the hospital and was offered EKG readings as a financial inducement, but was not competent to read them. Nevertheless, he was supported by his Italian colleagues and put on the EKG rotation, although he later had to be removed. A third was a cardiac surgeon whom Hassall had openly criticized at a mortality conference, and who had threatened suit. The surgeon was later found to lack malpractice insurance and subsequently had his privileges removed.

Physicians denied the EKG rotation were not trained cardiologists. This was part of Hassall's attempt to improve the quality of care in the department, as was Hassall's decision to read echograms himself, for none of the existing cardiologists were trained in the technique. Hassall had had no salary increase for a number of years because it was not included in the hospital's budget. He had threatened to increase his private practice and, therefore, cut his teaching. As a result, the hospital gave Hassall a percentage of the echogram revenues for reading them. This was meant as a temporary measure until they could put a salary increase into the budget. (Management wanted Hassall to continue teaching fellows and residents, because teaching was not being adequately done by the other cardiologists.) Finally, Has-

TABLE 7–2 Underlying Issues in Physician Conflict

Underlying Issues
Economics/income
Power/control
Recognition/status
Competence/respect
Style
Race/religion
Constituencies

sall had got out of practice in doing arteriograms and decided to refurbish his skills by doing a few. He tactlessly and thoughtlessly bumped one of the old-timers from the schedule on one occasion.

The situation at Pym reveals a number of underlying issues and dynamics which it is clearly crucial to comprehend for any solution of physician conflict to be possible. They are also listed in Table 7–2.

It turned out that the members of the dissident group were reacting to a series of personal concerns, each somewhat different, with but one focus in common: they blamed Dr. Hassall for their problems. For some, the issue was economic in that a change in hospital strategy diminished their income. For others, the issue was power and control. The attendings had had considerable power, as is often the case in mixed teaching/community hospitals. With a shift to more full-timers, they were experiencing a loss in control. For yet others, it was a matter of status and recognition. As one cardiologist put it, he had been there many years and had worked hard for the department but had no title that recognized his efforts.

Dr. Hassall, coming as he did from an academic background where discussions of quality were abstracted from the personal, failed to recognize that attendings were sensitive about the quality of medicine they practiced and resented his critical comments, at the same time that they needed his advice about their patients. They wanted their competence, perhaps not up to that of full-time academics, to be respected for what it was. The racial and religious undertones were perhaps less a function of outright prejudice than of constituencies or networks that had grown up over the years, of people with similar backgrounds referring to one another. It was in their interest, therefore, to support each other and those they knew intimately. Finally, Dr. Hassall's style was, by his own admission, sometimes abrasive and less than tactful.

The CEO realized that great delicacy was required, and moved cautiously to work through the medical system. An ad hoc committee of department physicians, joined by the hospital CEO and two other senior managers, was appointed to look into the matter. This committee recommended formation of an annually elected advisory committee of three members of the department that would meet monthly with Dr. Hassall and discuss ongoing problems. Dr. Hassall was reappointed for five years, with a six-month cancellation clause, and a director of noninvasive services was recruited, although Hassall was authorized to continue billing for reading echos and phonos until the person was appointed. Hassall also met with an organizational consultant and agreed to tone down his management style.

One year later, the problems, while less critical, still lay smoldering beneath the surface, and it seemed that the steps taken had merely removed their sting rather than resolved them. A comprehensive assessment done at this time indicated that three approaches were possible, each with different consequences. Nothing further might be done, on the basis that the problems had diminished in intensity and might ultimately burn themselves out. Second, Dr. Hassall could be encouraged to leave; the dissidents would have won, and the hospital would have to give up its strategy of improving its teaching status. Third, the key dissidents might be fired or persuaded to depart.

The dilemma facing the hospital was that it was in essence on a cusp. On the one hand, in an era of competition, it needed the high-quality image associated with Dr. Hassall to compete successfully as a teaching hospital. But it also needed the considerable volume of procedures and admissions brought in by the attendings. The attendings saw themselves competing with full-timers for a diminishing private-patient market, with their power and control in the institution also diminishing. From Dr. Hassall's point of view, any significant relaxation of standards would jeopardize his goals.

The greater involvement of the attendings in the department's processes, and sharing more of the economic benefits of new technologies with them seemed like a reasonable step. But the long and rancorous past history colored these actions for the attendings, who saw them as a sop rather than a solution. While management had bent over backwards to work through the medical system and to work slowly and tactfully toward resolution, management was correctly perceived to be fundamentally backing Dr. Hassall. In situations like this, which are not uncommon, there is no solution that will or indeed can, please everyone. When health organizations make strategic shifts, they are taking action that will hurt some and help others. There are, as stated elsewhere in this book, winners and losers in a competitive situation—not everybody can win.

A not dissimilar situation was faced by Dr. Jack Dempsey at "Eastern Neurologic Center (ENC)," but here the problem was hospitalwide. Dempsey, an aggressive surgeon-researcher, had been recruited one year previously to head ENC, which consisted of two separate institutions, a research institute and a neurologic hospital. The two institutions shared a physical site with nearby Eastern Community Hospital with which they also shared a number of ancillary services, such as radiology, laboratories, etc., as the hospitals were too small to comfortably afford separate services. Because Eastern Neurologic Hospital served a specialty market, while Eastern Community served a community market, the ancillary services that had evolved were of higher quality than those usually found in a community hospital, but uneasily straddled the two hospitals' somewhat different needs.

With the advent of enhanced competition, Eastern Community had strategically restructured and implemented a broad range of ambulatory services and diversified businesses, strengthening its link with physicians in their community-based private practices. Eastern Neurologic had recruited Dempsey to upgrade its specialty status, and he had ambitions for it to become a major national and international referral center. Dr. Dempsey's plans included recruiting high-quality academics and weeding out the community physicians, a number of whom had joint appointments at ENC. He planned to replace the lost patient revenues in the short run by seeking research grant money and ultimately by developing high-technology applications. The older general physicians and surgeons who used Eastern Neurologic were much threatened by his intentions, though the younger ones were generally supportive. The older doctors hoped that Dempsey would make sufficient mistakes that they could exploit their long-standing contacts with the board to secure his removal. He, in turn, hoped and expected that the board, which had specifically recruited him for the strategic purposes he had in mind, would support him in any showdown.

Once again, the underlying issue here is one of a strategic shift that threatens the livelihood and power of established doctors. No real compromise is possible for the new strategy to succeed. But in the meantime, it is the management of the turbulent transition period that should preoccupy Dempsey and the board so that they can secure their long-run objectives. These long-run objectives are, to some degree, only to be attained by sifting out doctors through a recruitment of physicians who endorse the new goals and have practice styles compatible with them.

These kinds of dilemmas are not restricted to teaching hospitals, but are commonly found in health organizations across the board. HMOs are facing uncomfortable transitions as they find that they have to grow aggressively if they are to survive. Midwest, for example, is a flourishing and successful staff-model HMO serving some 50,000 members in four centers. It plans to add five more centers and develop IPAs in low-density areas. But while management is happy with Midwest's progress and is considering for-profit status, the physicians, many of whom joined the HMO for the undemanding security that it gave them and its support for their comfortable lifestyle, are finding that growth and competition have placed an unwelcome burden on the productivity of their clinical practices. With growth and the aggressive recruitment of new physicians who are dispersed geographically, collegiality has become all but impossible. With competition, extended hours are now necessary, and this means more demands on physicians' time or convenience. Financial incentives cannot make up for this alteration in physician work- and life-style. Moreover, the nature of rapid growth in an HMO, with periodic understaffing, meant excessive workloads for considerable periods of time. What the physicians face, therefore, is an alteration in their work setting from the one they expected when they joined to something unpalatable and unwanted. Yet they have little or no control over the strategies that have led to this state of affairs, and moreover, as is not true in hospitals, physicians are rarely on the board in HMOs. The issue for management is how to handle the transitional process. If management fails to do this, they will lose physicians at a critical point in their growth curve or find themselves unionized.

Interpersonal conflicts generally involve style, whether managerial or verbal. Physicians are sensitive about their prerogatives and about the care they give. They are concerned that their competence is respected and their prerogatives preserved. In a prolonged transition period, with the role of physicians changing, such sensitivities are enhanced to the point that physicians are far more likely than hitherto to regard criticism as grounds for a lawsuit, even if this criticism takes place within the setting of peer review.

Interdepartmental issues are generally around turf and technology.

> I've had some insoluble problems, a philosophical and patient-care controversy with the anesthesia department. I had a patient with whom I had discussed a general anesthesia. You go to the room and the anesthetist is preparing a block. The patient had said he wanted to go to sleep and did not want a block, so you tell the anesthesiologist, and he says it is his decision and bug off until I get through. I will not work under those circumstances. There is no need for me to start a case with an adversary relationship with anybody in the room, because the only one who is going to lose under those circumstances is the patient, and I have had that happen before.

Here, a difference of opinion or misunderstanding escalated to an issue of control, by anesthesia or by surgery, with the anesthesiologist acting as though the surgeon is attempting to give him orders. This is a situation in which the problem must be referred to the department chairmen concerned or to the chief of staff, with management involved if the issue cannot be resolved. The patient's well-being is at stake.

Another version of a similar conflict, this time handled successfully:

> We recently had one over who was going to use a microscope, of which we have only one, and the opthalmologists and the ENT people were scheduled on the same day. That was dealt with very straightforwardly. The two parties involved sat down with the head of the operating room, the chief of the surgical service, and myself and hashed it out and came to an understanding, in about an hour, which was fairly reasonable and satisfactory.

Generational problems are more subtle and obviously extensive. As one doctor commented:

> I had just come out of training and we were doing things differently. The older doctors are good, solid, and well trained, but they were not updating and starting to change what they were providing patients and what the patients now wanted. They had a good thing and they wanted to keep things exactly the way they were instead of making progressive changes that were needed.

These sorts of generational problems—a group of physicians that has practiced in a certain way and had certain powers finds themselves slowly displaced by a younger generation, or the younger generation is frustrated by the fact that older doctors will not give way—are not uncommon but are compounded by the evolutionary changes taking place in many general hospitals. With prospective payment systems, DRGs, and competition, general hospitals are tending to "upgrade" and shift delicate balances. Whether this is the balance of general/specialized care, or public/private care, any shift means a change in the power of certain physicians over others. Generally, the shift is one from indigent to private-pay patients, from lower- to higher-quality care, and from less highly specialized to more highly specialized cases. Subspecialties thus gain power and access to the resources of the institution at the expense of the general attendings, who then feel that they supply the bread and butter for the hospital but get less than their share of resources. Income-producing technologies that were the preserve of the private physician are used to provide revenues to pay full-time subspecialists (as was the case with Pym described above). These are real changes and cannot be mitigated to any significant degree.

But, as one CEO points out, some apparently major conflicts are

> trite as it is, because of a lack of adequate communication. Doctors wonder about numerous issues, and because they are busy people, they do not have the time to do the personal reading that is required to understand the many facets of an issue. They really do not have the time to [satisfy] their curiosity by stopping by the administrator's office and checking [whether] something is fact or fiction. This type of communication requires a certain amount of energy on their part, as well as a willingness on the part of administration to say come on in and let's talk about it. It is this lack of infor-

mation about numerous issues that contributes to the paranoia of physicians.

The final word on this might be drawn from a vivid description of yet another pressure on the private physician, coming this time from a house staff member.

> Their interests are different. The attending wants to keep sick patients in and administer a complete battery of tests, the residents want only the most interesting patients in and getting them out as soon as diagnosis is made. The full-time salaried are in between. In the old days, private physicians enjoyed "unmitigated control over their cases and their practices." They could do whatever they pleased with their patients without having to rely on the cooperation and participation of other physicians or the hospital. In recent times, however, medical practice, technology, and organization have changed in such ways that other parties increasingly intrude on the formerly private relationship between the physician and the patient, and the doctor in private practice has increasingly become alarmed about a loss of control, autonomy, and money.[1]

In the resolution of conflict, communication is important for the creation of trust and must involve the solicitation of advice.[2] Communication, however, is not as simple as it sometimes sounds. It is not just telling more, for as stated earlier, this may simply result in information overload. Instead, communication involves a broad understanding of the nature of the physician and of the physician's changing world. Some managers seem to imagine that communication is a tranquilizing drug, and that if physicians can only be encouraged to talk more and listen more, their sensibilities will be lulled and problems will go away. While talking is an important prerequisite, it is not a solution. Conflicts involve real differences of interest that must be managed effectively and not simply placated.

Important facets of this process include preventive planning and staging through early discussion of controversial issues. A structure should also be provided for making decisions. Many HMOs could manage their planning processes more effectively than they have. As young organizations, they have relied on the enthusiasm of their equally young staffs to create a new organization. Professionals and lay managers have joined together and

---

[1]M. Millman, *The Unkindest Cut* (New York: Morrow, 1977).

[2]D. H. Hitt, "Grounding the High Intensity in Physician-Hospital Relationships," *Hospitals*, April 1984, pp. 91–95.

worked extraordinarily long hours with few resources to make HMOs succeed. But now most HMOs are maturing and what once was tolerable is no longer acceptable. Slippage in planning is no longer excusable once an organization is mature. What many HMOs are finding is that what once was forgiven is now criticized.

Deliberations must be scheduled and participative. Consultants may usefully be involved to reduce organizational strains, and can be effective in diverting tensions away from management on controversial issues. Key subordinates can also be asked to perform unpopular tasks to deflect criticism from senior management![3] Formal mechanisms must be in place for soliciting requests and complaints, and standing committees should exist to address major concerns such as patient care, professional standards, and education. Such committees might take the form suggested in Shortell's parallel organization.[4] Hospital executives should also routinely participate in medical staff organization as discussed in Chapter 4. Medical staff officers should be selected for managerial and leadership ability.

In essence, what management, whether lay or physician, must do is not only talk but also ensure that due process is carried out. What physicians want is equity and fairness. Moreover, it is critical to distinguish perception from reality. In the Pym case discussed earlier in the chapter, there were some real problems but also many perceptions that had developed among the protagonists that bore little or no relation to reality. Realities are amenable to rational discourse, but perceptions are based on beliefs and cannot be dealt with rationally. Often managers will find themselves dealing more with perceptions than with realities. Perceptions are rooted in feelings that lie deep, feelings about the changing world of the doctor that may provoke silent questions about a whole career and its meaning. Perceptions have their own stubborn life, and must be acknowledged and dealt with on their own terms, with sensitive understanding.

Given that behind some of the more intractable conflicts lie differences of interest and deep feelings, it is important for man-

---

[3]Hitt, "Grounding the High Intensity."

[4]S. Shortell, "The Medical Staff of the Future: Replanting the Garden," *Frontiers of Health Service Management* 1, no. 3 (1985), pp. 3–48.

agement to understand the dynamics that have given rise to these feelings. They must assess with a cool eye the damage that may arise from alternative solutions, the damage that will take place in morale or climate, and the damage to the institution. They must keep an eye on the future and on what they want to have happen. In this respect, they must be tough minded, for the desired outcome may involve not only discomfort, but also a battle in which some have to go. Sometimes it is important to move in early to nip possible problems in the bud, as suggested by Dr. R., a canny physician manager whose style is discussed at length in Chapter 9. Sometimes problems need to be allowed to fester, for until a problem is of sufficient intensity and extent to attract the energy and concern of many, an attempt at solution will be suboptimal.

There are no easy answers to conflict resolution in any organization, let alone when dealing with such complex people as physicians. Justice, fairness, patience, a sympathetic ear, and a firm hand are beginnings.

PRACTICE PATTERN IMPACT ASSESSMENT

When the health environment was slowly changing, health delivery organizations themselves changed little from one year to another and had few, if any, momentous decisions to make. Today, in a fast-moving and rapidly changing, highly competitive environment, more decisions have to be made rapidly, with relatively little information, with potentially great consequences, and therefore with heightened risk. Anything that can be done to reduce risk in managerial decision making therefore reduces the cost (actual or potential) of any particular decision.

Many of the decisions facing the board and management of health delivery organizations have profound consequences for physicians, whether these physicians are employees of the organization or in private practice. Decisions may not only help or hurt the physician within the institution, but may also affect the physician's private practice or his practice at other institutions. Where the physician is not involved in decision making, or finds it inimical to self-interest, he or she can still vote with his feet.

Even though fee for service may be on its way out,[5] in most areas of the United States it is very much alive, and the physician is a major influence in the patient's choice of where to seek health care outside the doctor's office. In the study described below, for example, 76 percent of patients questioned placed their loyalty to their doctor above that to their hospital. (Only 12 percent placed their loyalty to the hospital first.) Physicians confirmed their patients' estimates. Therefore, before a health delivery organization engages in actions that might have adverse consequences on physicians' use of the institution, it might be well for them to consider attempting to determine the potential risks of such decisions.

While the study cited below is specific to a particular situation in which a teaching hospital was considering alternative relocation options, this kind of *practice pattern impact assessment* can be useful in all types of health delivery organizations, and can be valuable for reviewing the potential impact of alternative courses of action and in assessing and mitigating risk. It would seem not only prudent but responsible for boards or managements to engage in such studies, even though the studies are not inexpensive. The particular study discussed involved extensive interviewing of numerous physicians, patients, and community leaders, and cost some $150,000. This figure is only .25 percent of the total cost of a potential building project estimated at $60 million. (When architectural costs or the cost of insurance may be as high as 1 percent of the total, it would seem a small price to pay for risk reduction.)

A Case Study

An urban teaching hospital was considering a number of alternative rebuilding options, including a move to a neighboring medical school. The physicians favored rebuilding on the present site and were concerned about a move. Therefore, it was decided to assess their views both qualitatively and quantitatively and to

---

[5]K. Hunt, "Do They Really Have the Guns to Kill Fee for Service?" *Medical Economics*, April 2, 1984, pp. 145–60.

attempt to determine the likely impact of the alternative rebuild options.

Future possible behavior, which can never be assessed with certainty, is the focus of studies such as this. There is always the question: will doctors say certain things because they believe they can have an impact on the decision but not mean what they say when it comes to reality? The only way that this can be dealt with, as in any kind of market research, is to approach what doctors say about what they will do from a number of different points of view, as well as to attempt to determine whether what the physicians say they will do is feasible and likely. Market research, for all its occasional widely publicized flaws (the Edsel, "new" Coca-Cola), has been successful far more often than the opposite in indicating the likely success or failure of some future enterprise. If the critical question being asked can be framed correctly, market research, or impact assessment studies, can be fairly accurate.

An important first step, therefore, in the study described was the use of selected focus groups to refine the basic questions. Initially it was felt that there were four possible alternatives: rebuild on the present site, rebuild on the medical school campus as an independent entity, rebuild with administrative integration with the medical school, and rebuild with full integration (including clinical services) with the medical school. The value of using a focus group of selected physicians, representing a cross-section of full-timers and attendings and of different specialties, was that it allowed reduction of the four alternatives to three, for the latter two were felt to be essentially identical. The focus group is a speedy and relatively inexpensive way to refine the questions used as well as to get an early idea of answers, so it is important to carefully select members. Such focus groups can be quite small, in this instance, half a dozen physicians.

Sampling design is also important in proceeding beyond this exploratory phase. Because the major concern was what patients would do as a result of what their doctors tell them, this study solicited a broad range of physician opinions as well as the opinions of patients of the physicians interviewed, to see whether patients and physicians agreed.

The extent and nature of the interview process is a function of cost, available resources, and credibility. The utility of increas-

FIGURE 7-1 Rating Scale for Hospital Location Alternatives

0	1	2	3	4	5	6	7	8	9	10
Very undesirable					Neutral					Highly desirable

ing information may diminish. That is, one can learn a great deal from the first set of interviews with little added in subsequent ones. However, larger numbers of interviews may be needed than might be used in a smaller sample study to support quantitative conclusions and enhance credibility. Thus, 63 physicians were interviewed in person by a trained interviewer and the remainder of physicians on the staff of the teaching hospital were sent a self-administered questionnaire covering much the same ground. The basic questions are listed below.

Impact assessment instrument. The physicians were asked to supply the following information:

Name, specialty, position in hospital, multiple affiliations.

Admissions, procedures, consults and office consults—number per month and percentage of each.

Income distribution across salary, admissions, consults, office, and procedures.

Desired practice pattern—same/different, reasons and changes desired.

Referral patterns: percentage from doctors and others, percentage from primary affiliation and other affiliations, percentage to primary affiliation and other affiliations.

Reasons for use of primary and other affiliations.

Estimated patient loyalty to primary affiliations, to other affiliations, and to physician.

Patients adverse to primary affiliation, lost to M.D. or lost to primary affiliation.

Patient characteristics, i.e., payer source, location.

Physician choice of hospital action under consideration rated on a scale of 0 to 10 with reasons. (Figure 7-1)

Estimated impact of hospital action on services, teaching program, patients, and admissions.

FIGURE 7-2 Change in Share of Practice under Different Location Alternatives

Alternative						*Change in Share (percent)*					
A	0	10	20	30	40	50	60	70	80	90	100
B	0	10	20	30	40	50	60	70	80	90	100
C	0	10	20	30	40	50	60	70	80	90	100
Now	0	10	20	30	40	50	60	70	80	90	100

Physician action given each alternative hospital action: would physicians stay/leave, be happy/unhappy, shift hospital affiliation, shift admissions?

Estimate of share of practice given to primary hospital and changes in it due to alternative hospital actions. (Figure 7-2)

Physician estimate of change in referral pattern.

Detailed estimate by physician of whether the following items would remain stable, go up, or go down given alternative hospital actions: (Figure 7-3)

Total practice.

Total referral pattern.

Total admissions.

Share to primary affiliation.

Total number and percent to primary affiliation.

Consults to primary and other affiliations, percentage and number.

Procedures to primary and other affiliations, percentage and number.

Office consults, percentage and number.

Conditions and circumstances under which physician would consider alternative hospital actions.

A simpler version of these questions was used in the self-administered questionnaire, which was coded for easy tabulation. The questionnaire was sent out with a covering letter from senior hospital management and the hospital's chief of staff. In-

FIGURE 7-3 Physician Estimate of Impact of Location Alternatives

		Alternative		
Factor	*Change*	*A*	*B*	*C*
Total practice	+ 0 −			
Total referral pattern	+ 0 −			
Total admissions (percent)	+ 0 −			
Share of admissions (percent)	+ 0 −			
Total impact on admissions (percent)	+ 0 −			
Total impact on admissions (number)	+ 0 −			
Consults at this hospital/others (percent)	+ 0 −			
Consults (this hospital) total impact (number)	+ 0 −			
Procedures at this hospital/other (percent)	+ 0 −			
Total impact on procedures (number)	+ 0 −			
Office consults (percent)	+ 0 −			

terviews were scheduled in the teaching hospital. Physicians were given advance notice, appointments were made, and reminder telephone calls made the day before the scheduled interviews. A letter describing the intent and goals of the study was sent out to all physicians. It was signed by senior management and the chief of staff and indicated the importance of the study and the attention management would pay to the study in making their final decisions and recommendations to the hospital's board. Few physicians failed to come to their interviews, although returns on the self-administered questionnaire were predictably much lower, with only about one third of physicians surveyed responding. However, the interviewees were selected to represent the majority of the full-time physicians, heavily weighted to represent high-volume admitters, and stratified to include all specialties; there was also some representation of medium and low admitters. The 63 doctors interviewed together with the 96 who returned questionnaires represented 72.8 percent of the total admissions to the hospital and therefore a reasonable universe. (Physicians overestimated their own admission rates by just under 20 percent, so this was taken into account in correcting subsequent estimates.)

The rationale for interviewing was that, while it is more expensive and time-consuming, interviews made it possible to get a better quality of answer and greater detail concerning complex issues than was possible using the self-administered questionnaire. With experience it became possible to reduce the length of the interview from one hour to 30 minutes.

A large sample of patients was also interviewed over the telephone following, once again, the use of focus groups to refine the questions that would be used and to sharpen the issues. These focus groups confirmed that there were three (not four) options, and that there were three distinct groups of patients with quite different opinions about the options represented to them: private patients from the city in which the teaching hospital was located, private patients who lived outside the city but came to the teaching hospital for their health care, and clinic patients. Therefore in the larger study, three samples were drawn, each representing one of these groups and consisting of 250 patients.

Key findings that indicate the nature of impact studies include the following: of the patients surveyed, 85 percent ranked their doctor's recommendation as very important; additional important factors included good care, location, and the recommendation of someone they trusted. (The relative importance of these factors differed among the groups.) As shown in Table 7–3, 76 percent of patients indicated that they chose a doctor first, 12 percent chose a hospital first, and 12 percent said the choice depended on their needs. Again, patients differed, with more pri-

TABLE 7-3 Patient/Physician Loyalty: Initial Choice—Hospital or Doctor?

	Patient Group			
	Private City	*Private Suburban*	*Clinic*	*All Patients*
Hospital first	11.3%	1.8%	23.2%	11.8%
Doctor first	80.0	85.4	61.6	75.9
It depends	8.3	11.7	14.8	11.7
No answer	0.4	1.1	0.4	0.7

vate patients than clinic patients choosing a doctor first. Fewer clinic patients than private patients ranked their doctor's recommendation as very important in choosing a hospital.

The key question was whether patients would return to the hospital in the survey if their doctor no longer used it. Of private city patients, 47.4 percent said they would return without the doctor recommending it; similar responses were obtained from 41.4 percent of clinic patients, but from only 9.9 percent of private suburban patients, as Table 7-4 shows. So, while there would probably be a very significant drop in the use of the hospital by any patients if their doctor was no longer there, this trend was much more marked for suburban than for city patients. Patients were also asked whether they would use other hospitals in the area if their doctors suggested it. Responses are given in Table 7-5. Even with favorable doctor recommendation, far fewer patients were willing to use other hospitals than were willing to use the hospital in the survey. While upward of 90 percent of each of the three groups were willing to use this hospital if their doctor suggested it, roughly half of the private patients and less than 40 percent of clinic patients would go to another teaching hospital in the area if their doctor proposed it.

There were some interesting by-products of the physician study. Physicians gave as their primary reasons for using the hospital studied, rather than other alternatives, the availability of technical and subspecialty resources and geographic convenience, and this suggests significant implications for health organizations concerned about attracting and retaining physicians. Moreover, while patients commonly choose internists and

TABLE 7-4 Continued Patient Use of This Hospital without Physician Support, Given Three Location Options

Patient Group	Option		
	Current Site	*Relocate*	*Integrate with Medical School*
Private city	47.4%	43.5%	41.7%
Private suburban	9.9	9.1	10.6
Clinic	42.4	41.2	36.0

TABLE 7-5 Estimated Percent of Patient Use of Area Hospitals with Favorable Doctor Recommendation

	Patient Group		
	Private City	*Private Suburban*	*Clinic*
This hospital	94.8%	96.4%	91.8%
Other teaching hospital	54.3	55.7	36.8
Medical school hospital	47.0	46.4	35.6

family practitioners, specialists rely on the physician referral network to give and to receive patients, and this network is given as a not unimportant reason for choice of hospital. One of the reasons physicians fear relocation is that members of their referral network will leave. Thus, with a move, there is a distinct domino effect, which suggests the need to identify key practitioners and make particular efforts to retain them. Finally, physicians gain approximately one third of their income from admissions and almost equal proportions from their office practice and the performance of procedures. While consults account for only 10 percent of physician income, these are important because they lead to lucrative procedures. Thus, in evaluating organizational alternatives, it is important to estimate their impact not only on admissions, but also on consults, procedures, and office practice. Such an evaluation in terms of the study hospital's relocation options is shown in Table 7-6.

TABLE 7-6 Estimate of Impact of Location Options

Option	*Change in*			*Change in Physicians' Office Practice*
	Admissions	*Consults*	*Procedures*	
Rebuild on site	15.1%	14.0%	7.3%	5.0%
Relocate to medical school campus as independent hospital	(40.7)	(28.0)	(3.2)	(3.7)
Integrate with medical school	(51.1)	(40.0)	(22.9)	(8.7)
Relocate medical school campus integrated with medical school				

TABLE 7-7 Physician Feelings about Relocation*

Option	*Very Positive*	*Positive*	*Negative*	*Very Negative*	*No Response*
Relocation as independent hospital to medical school campus	0	12	20	16	15
Integrate with medical school	0	3	16	29	15

*Figures are number of physicians interviewed holding that opinion.

Physicians overwhelmingly chose the rebuild-on-site option and expressed intense negative feelings about locating on the medical school campus as Table 7-7 shows. Many said that they would either seek additional affiliations or increase the proportion of patients they admitted elsewhere, should their disliked alternative be chosen. Given that many of them already had multiple affiliations and were admitting elsewhere, or had been approached to do so, for the most part the doctors felt it would be easy to make such a shift. Only a small number of subspecialists requiring highly specialized resources that are not easily obtainable stated that it would be difficult to move.

TABLE 7-8 Estimated Overall Impact of Location Options on Hospital Admissions

Option	*Estimated Change in Admissions (percent)*
Rebuild on site	5%
Relocate as independent hospital to medical school campus	(24)-(28)
Integrate with medical school	(37)-(43)

The overall impact on admissions was that the most favored option, rebuild on site, would result in an increase of 5 percent, independent relocation would reduce admissions by some 26 percent, and integration with the medical school would drop admissions by some 40 percent (see Table 7-8). These are fairly dramatic findings. They obviously have considerable implications for the decisions made by top management and the board. Physicians also estimate that their consults, procedures, and office practice would be hurt by the less-favored options, though these would not be harmed as much as admissions. The fact that physicians do make a distinction between the impact of the alternatives on these different modalities of practice gives some additional credibility to the figures.

This study provided valuable data to the planning committee, enabling it with some confidence to recommend to the full board the steps that should be taken regarding rebuilding. In view of the fact that there had been political pressures favoring certain options, the thoroughness of the study provided not only data but also convincing support for a course of action that had to be defended in a wider area.

The study described was particularly extensive in view of the importance of the set of decisions involved, and somewhat expensive. However, impact studies, if carefully designed, can be done by the smallest organization for relatively modest amounts of money. This is particularly true if the concern is with actual impact rather than with defending a position or establishing credibility. In the example given, a much smaller sample of physicians could have been interviewed or sent the questionnaire, with much the same results and at much lower cost. But then the results of the study might have been questioned and, given the political nature of the ramifications, it was felt that a more extensive approach was desirable. As a general rule of thumb, an adequate impact study can be done for somewhere between 0.5 and 1 percent of the cost of a particular action such as building a surgicenter or funding a new service.

Regardless of extent, there are three elements that should be included in any impact study: use of focus groups to refine the questions and issues; direct interviews to provide depth; and self-administered questionnaires for breadth. Impact studies are potentially extremely valuable market research tools that, used judiciously, might well help health delivery organizations avoid making embarrassing and expensive mistakes.

PHYSICIAN-MANAGEMENT RELATIONS MONITORING (PMRM)

Another important area in managing change and conflict is the relations between management and physicians. In view of this, it may be worth considering periodic systematic assessments of the relationship. A quite small sample of physicians is adequate, as long as they are drawn from the variety of constituencies, namely from among those holding elected/appointed positions, from full-timers and physicians at large, and from different specialties and subspecialties. A sample of 10 physicians will give an indicative reading. Each of the items dealt with in the assessment can be ranked on a scale so that a simple quantitative tabulation is possible.

This assessment can be done internally, jointly with a consultant, or by a consulting company. In the pages that follow, two forms are provided: the first is a simple questionnaire that can be used internally without consultants and can be administered quite inexpensively. The second is a more comprehensive assessment that probably requires additional resources to use.

It is helpful to remember that a certain level of "noise" is always appropriate to any healthy organization. "Noise" comes from the natural and inevitable conflicts that arise when groups with different interests express these interests openly and work together to resolve them. What is critical for a health organiza-

Physician-Management Relations—Short Form

Loyalty and Devotion

How loyal do you feel?
How devoted do you feel?
How would you assess what the organization has done to win your loyalty and devotion?
What should the organization do with regard to winning loyalty?

Physician Voice

How would you assess existing mechanisms for informing physicians?
Are physicians educated and informed appropriately?
Is the influence or voice of physicians over the following adequate and appropriate:
- organizational goals and directions?
- major capital projects?
- clinically related activities?
- acquiring physical equipment and staff resources?
- problems in the work setting?

In general, is the influence or voice of the physician over the direction of the organization and over management affairs adequate?
Do the mechanisms work well or not?
What changes would you recommend?
To what extent do formally appointed physicians act effectively in the physicians' interest?
Are there any notable conflicts between physicians and management?
Do existing conflict resolution mechanisms work effectively or not?
To what extent does management encourage effective confrontation and conflict resolution?

Management and Medical Affairs

Do adequate quality mechanisms exist?
- Do such mechanisms work effectively?

Do adequate cost-control systems exist?
- Do they work effectively?

Are adequate recruiting mechanisms in place?
- Do they work effectively?

Is management's role in these processes appropriate?
Are there any significant physician-physician conflicts?
- Are conflicts resolution mechanisms adequate to handle these?

tion is to assess whether noise is within reasonable limits or is excessive. If the latter is the case, the causes of unusual conflict must be identified. The goal should not be to eradicate noise altogether, for that will force natural and healthy conflict under the table. Physicians in today's health environment will experience some degree of dissatisfaction both in their private practices and in their association with a health organization.

Sometimes it may be useful to consider dong a more substantial and broader assessment of physician-management relationships. This will probably entail using some form of consulting help.

Comprehensive Assessment of Physician-Management Relationships

---

Basic facts and structures

How big is the organization?
What services are offered?
What are the proportions of medicare, medicaid, and indigent to private pay patients?
What is the total number of physicians on staff and age? How many are active (10+ admissions)?
  How many are high admitters (50+ admissions)?
Are physicians largely (50 percent) fee-for-service, single specialty groups, or multispecialty groups?
  If groups, of what size?
What is the main competition for the organization, i.e., other hospitals, other types of health organizations?
What is the size and structure of the board, especially are there physicians on it and do they represent the organization? How are they elected?
What is the balance of the organization's mission toward academic/city-indigent/community-private pay?
What is the basic medical structure, i.e., the format and election process for officers, the size and electoral representation of the medical executive, subcommittees of the medical executive, do management reps sit on medical executive and other medical department or other committees?
What key management committees are there, i.e., capital, long-range planning, etc., and do physicians sit on these?
What is the market area, primary and secondary, for the health organization?

Details about doctors

Years in the practice of medicine.
Formal appointments and positions held, past and present, in organization.
Other organizational affiliations.
What is the share of the practice given to each health organization, and rationale for this breakdown.
Other health care delivery financial interests.

Loyalty and devotion

How is loyalty measured? How loyal do you feel?
How is devotion measured? How devoted do you feel?
What characteristics constitute extraordinary loyalty and devotion?
What has the organization done, and what might it yet do to maintain and enhance the loyalty and devotion of its physicians, i.e., marketing,

additional staff, additional physical facilities, additional conveniences?
What might department heads do to support loyalty and devotion of clinical faculty?
How should the organization reward those who are particularly loyal?
Where is the attachment of loyalty in the physician?
What is the feeling of the physician about joint financial ventures between the organization and the physician?
How should such ventures be offered and to which physicians?
How can an organization attract and keep new physicians?
How can an organization increase its share of practice of existing physicians?

Voice or influence of physician

Given the existing mechanisms for physician management interaction (medical structures, board representation, physicians and managers sitting on each other's or joint committees, informal), are these mechanisms adequate for ensuring that the doctor's voice is appropriately heard?
  Describe the formal and informal process.
  Are the structures adequate or do they need changing?
  Do they work well or do they need changing?
  Are changes needed in those who administer the structures?
Are physicians educated and informed appropriately?
  What formal mechanisms exist, and how well to they work?
  Do they need changes?
  What informal mechanisms exist and are they adequate?
  Do they need changes?
What characteristics constitute an influential or politically successful physician?
Is the influence or voice of the physician over the following decisions adequate and appropriate:
  organizational goals and direction.
  major organizational capital projects.
  new clinically related activities.
  closing services.
  acquiring physical equipment and staff resources.
  problems in the work setting.
In general, is the influence or voice of the physician over the organization adequate and appropriate?
Does the physician feel there is any value to having a paid physician manager in the institution?
Are there any particular conflicts between managers and physicians?
  How frequent and/or severe are they?
If there are conflicts, how, generally, are these conflicts resolved?
  Do they tend to be resolved rationally or politically? Confronting management, at one extreme, or at the other, by sitting, bitching, end running, or somewhere in between?
To what extent does management encourage direct confrontation or indirect power plays?
To what extent does management encourage participation on the part of physicians?

How extensive is this participation and what kinds of physicians tend to be most involved?

Clinical affairs

How are physicians recruited?
What is management's appropriate role in physician recruitment, if any?
What are the quality control mechanisms for managing variations in physician quality?
Are there graded responses possible to physician failure to cooperate?
If such mechanisms do exist, how well do they function in practice?
What remains to be improved, and how?
What is management's appropriate role?
With regard to the cost of care, do mechanisms exist for admissions and ancillary use?
If the mechanisms exist, but do not function adequately, why not, and how should this be remedied?
What is the role of management in intervention here?
Is there any attempt to influence physician case mix by management?
If so, how, and is this legitimate?
Has research on the patterns of practice been brought to bear on altering patterns of practice here?
What, if anything, is being done about potential conflict of interest regarding diminishing patient costs with possible consequent poor care?
Regardless of DRGs, is the organization attempting to influence patient costs, and if so, how?
Does the physician know true costs and prices?
Is information easily available?
Are there productivity incentives of any kind, financial or otherwise, and what is the physician's view about these?

Physician-physician conflicts

Have there been conflicts in the following categories?
Conflicts of loyalty such as not admitting fair share.
Are there minimum requirements, and what are penalties for admissions?
Physicians who fail to attend committee meetings regularly. (Are there penalties for such failure?)
Conflicts over turf, jurisdiction over technology, access to resources such as the operating room, between chiefs and Indians?
How are such conflicts characteristically resolved?
What is management's role, if any, in intervention?
Do such conflicts tend to get resolved through a consideration of fact and patient or organization interest, or through the exercise of power?
Have generational conflicts surfaced between different generations of physicians with different views of quality of care or direction of institution?
Is the organization evolving from a general to a more subspecialty institution?
If so, is this producing conflicts between physicians?
Do physicians vary in their perceptions of the existence of problems or the adequacy of mechanisms?
If so, on what basis is there this variation?

CHAPTER EIGHT

Sorts and Settings

Every physician almost has his favorite disease.

Henry Fielding

DOCTORS ARE NOT ALIKE

Just as physicians are different in what they want, how they like to work, and what is important to them, so too do organizations differ in their characteristics and culture. They also differ in the key tasks they must manage to be successful. Both physicians and health organizations are changing. Physicians, like anyone else, self-select for the setting in which they feel they will be happy and productive. The ones who are successful find a fit between their values and those of their chosen organization. But, as organizations change, that fit may be strained. And as physician values change over time, organizations may find themselves dealing with a different kind of doctor.

Traditional physicians, found most commonly in fee-for-service solo practice, value autonomy and independence, the right to control their clinical practice and to preserve what they cherish about the physician/patient relationship. As health organizations become more demanding and more intrusive, conflicts develop. Physicians attempt to influence health organizations to preserve their cherished values, as organizations seek to alter physician behavior.

Managers must have an understanding not simply of physicians in general, although doctors worldwide do share some common characteristics arising from similarities in training and in basic motivation, they must also recognize the diversity among physicians, for different kinds of doctors are found in different settings. Managers must also comprehend the characteristics of different settings, each with its unique problems of physician management.

The most identifiable characteristic of doctors is the specialty they choose. There have been a number of studies of differences between specialists. As an example, one suggests that surgeons tend to be males, come from large families, tend not to be academically outstanding, are low on neuroticism, and are thick-skinned and self-confident. More extroverted than those in other specialties, surgeons are emotionally expressive and not very reflective. Among practitioners, they are the least interested in the interpersonal aspects of patient care. They are aggressive and tend to trust logical thinking rather than feeling. Psychiatrists tend to be only children with less-educated parents, have the highest grades in college, are very nervous, and place a high value on interpersonal relationships, i.e., are pretty much the opposite of surgeons. Internists tend to have higher grades than surgeons and have strong intellectual interests, but are otherwise average. Obstetricians tend to be more religious, more conventional, and more deferring. Pediatricians are the most humanitarian.[1]

Surgeons, when asked about their choice of specialty, talk about technology and its appeal. (One was influenced when he read about the Hufnagel heart valve.)[2] Some talk about their capacity to produce immediate results. "You can take a patient who is very sick, do your thing, and a week later that patient says thank you and goes home." They like speed. "I'm impatient. I like to do things and get results fast." One has always used his hands, "I've always been a carpenter, an electrician, a plumber's assistant" because of the instant gratification, and that brought him to orthopedics. He then moved on to plastic surgery, limb salvage, and reconstruction. He liked manipulating materials. Another started as an X-ray technician and through that got into orthopedics.

Physicians emphasize quite different things: "I like people to get real sick and then well. I love dealing with children and I like to be rewarded. I do not like diseases that are life-style and peoples' fault." Doctors like variety, the puzzle of diagnostics, and unraveling a problem—especially a complex problem. Internal

---

[1]H. Wechsler, *Handbook of Medical Specialties* (New York: Human Sciences Press, 1976), pp. 108–19.

[2]10-Hospital Study.

medicine offers a mixture of intellectual challenge and altruism, but basically it is the problem solving that practitioners enjoy. Family practitioners unsurprisingly "like dealing with people in the broad range." They like the fact that they see the young and the old, and that their broad-ranging practices do not fall into any particular patterns. They like the balance of healthy and sick, and seeing patients through the phases of life.

To some degree, doctors choose specialties from a negative point of view, that is, on the basis of what they do not like about other specialties. One family practitioner avoided becoming an internist because he felt that all his patients would be dead or dying 10 years into his practice. All an internist sees "is cancer, end-stage coronary disease, severe emphysema—and no one ever gets well."

Obstetricians like dealing with basically healthy people and enjoy doing preventive medicine. They like the long-term nature of their specialty for "If you screw something up today, it lives for 35 or 40 years. If you do something right, it's very lasting." The doctor quoted was scathing also about internists, "People who do critical care think they are on the cutting edge of big-time medicine. So they added another 30 days to somebody's life—big deal!" Obstetricians enjoy the combination of medicine and surgery and the wide scope.

Pediatricians obviously enjoy kids, as well as the admixture of science and population studies. Those who elect to become hospital specialists—radiologists, pathologists—are avoiding surgery or internal medicine, and enjoy problems that do not require involvement. According to one hospital specialist: "It is the variety and the ability to deal with multiple specialties in all parts of the body. The ability to see a lot of different things but not to be involved with them all the way. I find it stimulating to see hundreds of different things a day with a hundred different people." These specialists prefer dealing with things rather than people.

Based on the above, it seems that there are doctors who enjoy dealing with people (obstetricians, pediatricians, family practitioners), who like dealing with things (pathologists, radiologists), who like dealing with practical problems (surgeons and internists), and who like dealing with knowledge (academicians).

Doctors themselves have a number of different ways of categorizing their fellows. At one extreme, "There is the physician who is in pure fee for service and is reimbursed on a procedural basis, the general practitioner in the community to whom Blue Cross will give $10 for every suture put in."

For the private practitioner time is money, whether this physician is in an office or the hospital, and that is something the manager needs to remember. Private practitioners contrast themselves with the full-timers, whether hospital based or HMO based, and ask of their full-time colleagues

> Is there something the matter with them? Is there some reason they are not out with the rest of the world practicing on a fee-for-service basis? Could they not make it in the real world? Had they some problem, maybe not good technique? Maybe they do not want to go through the business aspect of it or the pain of bill collecting.

The full-timers see the other side of the picture:

> The attendings who make the most trouble may be the poorest ones who need us most, but we need them to send us patients. The full-timers set the role model and the tone for the fee-for-service doctors and determine what new drugs will be adopted or what doses are appropriate. The attendings know that the full-timers know more and do follow them, even if they may resent them at times. The attendings will always be angry at the full-timers because they are secure especially if they are threatened by [the full-timers], such as when their cases are questioned. But they know also that it cannot be a doctors' hospital without surveillance, because they all admit to those second-rate hospitals and know that they get better care in a teaching hospital. [The full-timer] therefore tolerates the fact that most of his doctors are fee for service and what this means and tries to influence them rather than push them around.

Surgeons are more stubborn than internists, and internists feel as though they know about everything and do not ask for help as often as a surgeon, who may be aware of his or her limitations quicker. "Surgeons are often wrong but never in doubt," contrasts with internists who "are always in doubt and seldom wrong."

At the other end of the spectrum is the HMO doctor who is attracted by freedom from administration and the opportunity to live a chosen lifestyle without excessively demanding hours. While fee-for-service doctors may respond to financial incentives, HMO physicians will not. This is indeed a problem for HMOs, for with competitive pressures, cost reduction and productivity must be stressed, and yet doctors that self-select to work in HMOs do so for lifestyle reasons and not financial ones. How does the manager get them to be efficient?

> You have to create incentives that relate to quality. You can say we are going to institute a method of monitoring quality that says if you exceed 90 percent on the process of audit of screening for colorectal cancer, and control your hypertensive patients, and make appropriate use of drugs, you'll be given an extra week of vacation.

Then there are the young doctors and the older doctors. "The group of physicians coming out of medical school now are not as conservative as they were 15 or 20 years ago. They're not less aggressive, but they are more prone to discipline. They are more interested in lifestyle."

Older doctors, as they near retirement, may be less open to change and more threatened by what is happening. (Surgeons may feel that they are losing their dexterity.) Older physicians can easily feel trapped, though more now are becoming interested in new opportunities such as HMOs, but the ones who do feel economically trapped are difficult to work with.

Of increasing importance to organizations are "those who are motivated by power and involvement in the decision-making process. They will do very well for organizations because they will join in and be part of the problem when regulatory or fiscal problems come along."

Some join organizations "to be protected from financial issues in terms of security or wish protection because they acknowledge the reality that people have to be paid but find that that intrudes."

This suggests that there are doctors who are truly interested in administration, those who are research oriented, the academics, and those firmly committed to the clinical setting. Doctors who are strictly technical are often seen by their fellows as having "a terrible bedside manner" when compared with doctors more concerned with primary care, such as family practitioners.

Hospital-based doctors are less concerned generally with personal economics, although some do combine intellectual concerns with private practice objectives. A new group emerging encompasses entrepreneurial physicians who "view that anything that happens in the future should happen between the doctor and the hospital as a partnership and are interested in joint ventures. This is a new group of doctors that sees itself economically leading the hospital." This group often is very energetic in working with management to start new ventures that will benefit both.

Physicians contrast their own approach with the one they attribute to managers:

> A physician is more people oriented, the manager system oriented. Sometimes the manager is more interested in the institution than in the patient. That is dumb because 80 percent of the institution's budget is people, so you need to be interested in developing and working with people. We are all taking managerial courses. One of the frustrations is that if you want to be honest, for things to work you should send managers to take physician courses. There's a lot of quackery and eggheadedness in management, as there is in medicine.

Emerging trends seem to indicate a shift from the traditional physician—stereotypically an independent fee-for-service solo practitioner who worked excessively long hours, cared deeply for his patients and was well paid for doing so—toward somewhat different kinds of doctors choosing to work in different kinds of settings. Physicians are beginning to be lifestyle oriented, entrepreneurs, or bureaucrats. More work in groups, even if for administrative convenience only, and many more are full-time employees of health organizations. The greatest strains and conflicts will be experienced by those physicians brought up with traditional values who find themselves working in settings for which they were not trained and which constrain their opportunities to live their values. As new physicians, trained more appropriately and more fitted to the new settings, emerge, such strains and conflicts may well diminish.

SETTINGS AND THEIR MANAGERIAL CHARACTERISTICS

As with specialties, doctors choose their work settings for both positive and negative reasons. Many choose community hospitals for both practice and personal reasons. For example, they like the rural setting and the range of work:

> I had a residency in a highly academic center. I hated writing and felt strongly about some of the kinds of inhumanity I saw going on in that academic center, which I did not feel could be eradicated by me. I spent six months of my residency in a community hospital and decided that that was the way to practice medicine.
>
> In a community hospital as an anesthesiologist, you can have fingers in the intensive care area, pain therapy, obstetrics, whereas in a university hospital people tend to subspecialize. I could practice in more than one dimension.
>
> I like knowing my neighbors.

Often the geographic area appeals to the family. Sometimes the decision is based on economic considerations:

> I was in academics, I liked them, but I got a little tired of doing a very narrow thing. I was only doing breast cancer, and there are lots of other things I was interested in, and the political climate was heavy, and the driving force was ego. So I went into private practice with people whom I'd trained with, people I got along with well, where the politics is just as bad but the driving force is economics, not ego.

Some found they could make no money in an academic setting, others felt that there was less patient contact there and more time "spent on one person to the detriment possibly of other patients." In a community hospital, "there's a more friendly collaborative atmosphere" and it is more possible to treat people rather than diseases. Those with a particular interest in private practice find it attractive, and they can indulge their lifestyles more easily. "I wanted a place that was small enough so I could live in the country but big enough for me to practice my subspecialty with some academics available and good quail hunting." Yet others went back to where they were born or where they felt there was a need for doctors.

Those who choose the academic life do it for the teaching and the resources. "I'd walk out tomorrow if there weren't any students. There's nothing else that keeps me here." "I'm a nephrologist. In 1965, the artificial kidney machine was the most exciting thing that an internist could be involved with." "There's a challenge, some ego and power. This is the best hospital with the sickest patients."

Today there is a broader range of alternative settings in which physicians can practice than ever before in the history of health care. Academic medical centers, teaching hospitals, community hospitals, HMOs, IPAs, group practices, convenience centers—each in this bewildering array offers different opportunities to the physician. In this section, some of the managerial characteristics of each setting will be discussed, characteristics that raise issues for the management of doctors within them.

Teaching hospitals obviously tend to be much larger than their nonteaching counterparts. Medical staff size is also larger, although as hospitals get bigger, sheer size tends to be more important than whether or not they are teaching.[3] There is more management structure in teaching hospitals than in community hospitals of similar size, and more service chiefs, i.e., more paid than voluntary physicians in teaching than in nonteaching hospitals. There are more physicians on boards of community than of teaching hospitals. Those hospitals with greater medical-staff resources, such as teaching hospitals, have more formal committee activity, more generalist physicians under contract, more physician participation in decision making, more physicians who are involved in more than one hospital, and a smaller percentage of hospital-based radiologists and pathologists.[4] For-profits tend to be high on physician participation and low on communication control. Control in for-profits is achieved less through the committee structure than through greater medical staff participation. Smaller hospitals tend to have a local orientation with less committee activity and physician involvement.

Academic medical centers often are located in deteriorating inner cities, are large, and need a lot of research money.[5] As salaries have increased, teaching costs have risen and must be paid for at the same time that new reimbursement systems disallow teaching costs. As a result, teaching hospitals have had to be-

---

[3]M. Kessler, "Survey Compares Medical Staff Organization in Teaching and Non-Teaching Hospital," *Hospital Medical Staff*, August 1976, pp. 19–24.

[4]S. Shortell and C. Evashwick, "The Structural Configuration of U.S. Hospital Medical Staffs," *Medical Care*, April 19, 1981, pp. 419–30.

[5]D. E. Rogers, *American Medicine: Challenges for the 1980s* (Cambridge Mass.: Ballinger, 1978).

come increasingly competitive with community hospitals for local private-pay patients because traditional sources of funding have dried up; these institutions have also become innovative in attracting tertiary care patients from afar.

Academic medical centers differ from teaching hospitals in one major regard; they tend to have more full-time faculty and require all physicians to have medical school appointments (which teaching hospitals do not). Because both academic medical centers and teaching hospitals teach and do research, they have similar problems in funding and are taking similar measures to seek additional revenues: namely, encouraging faculty to engage more in the private practice of medicine through, for example, faculty group practices. Academic medical centers usually place some limit on the income to be derived, the excess going to the department. Teaching hospitals are tending to emphasize, as do other hospitals, the development of ambulatory systems. For academic medical centers with a high complement of teaching and research faculty, this emphasis may present recruitment and organizational problems because the kinds of physicians needed to practice in ambulatory systems are similar to those in HMOs or private practice who have different motivations and different styles from those of academic doctors. They therefore need different incentives, and it is possible that academic requirements may need to be relaxed to recruit them, because most teaching hospitals do not have sufficient medical staff to start up such systems.

Community hospitals face much the same reimbursement problems as their academic and teaching counterparts, but their strategic moves to deal with a stringent competitive environment tend to involve enriching their mix and joining multihospital systems. This places an emphasis on the development of subspecialists at the expense of generalists, and creates the problem of working within a larger system that may create identity problems. The advent of more full-timers, and especially of paid physician managers, whether chairmen or medical directors, places a medical management layer between the physicians and administration that troubles fee-for-service attendings. Hospitals, as they move toward direct marketing to potential patients and innovative services, often find that they have to seek full-time physicians to staff the services, even though opportunities may be offered to fee-for-service attendings. This creates the specter of internal competition.

The growth of for-profit or proprietary health systems has been a startling phenomenon on the U.S. health scene. These systems have grown not only by acquisition of community hospitals, but also through management contracting, which often subsequently leads to acquisition. How doctors feel about working in these systems was investigated in the 10-hospital study which involved five Health Corporation of America (HCA) hospitals and five similarly sized not-for-profit hospitals situated in the same competitive markets. The hospitals concerned ranged from around 100 beds to around 500 beds, and included both community and teaching hospitals. Some of the hospitals were owned by HCA, some were under management contract.

In the contract situations (three hospitals), arrangements were too recent for physicians to have clear ideas about any specific effects HCA might have had on the practice of medicine. General impressions were of firmer, tougher management, which physicians welcomed. If anything, they could detect some increased responsiveness to their concerns as private practitioners, particularly in obtaining equipment and in upgrading facilities and nursing staff. In one instance, a cut in the number of nurses, attributable to concerns with cost and efficiency, was resented by doctors. In general, physicians said they were unaware of prices and costs, although HCA was willing, if pressed, to give cost and price data. Doctors' impressions were that HCA prices were somewhat above community levels, but justified by the higher quality of care physicians perceived HCA to be giving. This was more marked in the two HCA-owned hospitals.

While, with rare exceptions, physicians could not identify specific actions of HCA that made them uneasy, there was a generally prevalent disquiet about what HCA might do at some time in the future if the corporation felt it was in their interests. As one physician put it, "We're looking after our interests, and they theirs, and at the moment, they happen to be congruent." However, when pressed, physicians admitted that HCA managers were unlikely to behave very differently from managers in any other toughly managed institution concerned with survival. Major concerns in this respect were the possibility of the hospital or corporation starting new health care ventures and bringing in physicians to compete with existing doctors. A couple of misunderstood instances, described below, had fed these myths.

The major differences between HCA and non-HCA hospitals which doctors experienced might to some degree have been a function of the size of the institutions involved. The two hospitals owned by HCA were small, and physicians there felt that they had direct access not only to all levels of management, but also to the CEOs. They also felt that the HCA philosophy was to allow such opportunity for physician influence, as reflected in the fact that both these hospitals had heavily physician-dominated boards. The doctors recognized, however, that the hospitals were small in comparison to competing institutions, and that while the HCA philosophy of management was different, larger hospitals had more bureaucracy and more committees, which resulted in slower decisions and less responsiveness to physicians.

HCA managers stress making their hospitals extremely attractive to their doctors and patients and responsive to their needs. Physicians can get patients in and out easily. Patients liked the food, the physical plant, and the nursing attention. Physicians were spoiled, often getting meals late at night when cafeterias were closed and such amenities were not available at competing hospitals. HCA hospitals were especially responsive in obtaining equipment for physicians.

Where physicians' requests were denied, the doctors felt that the consideration process was prompt, clear, and direct. They understood why, on rare occasions, "no" was the answer, and they were told promptly. In competing hospitals, the approval process was often lengthy and ambiguous, and requests disappeared into limbo.

In general, physicians felt that HCA hospitals were more open to physician influence, more responsive, and clearer in their responses. Physicians saw no difference in quality between HCA and non-HCA hospitals, and no intrusion into what they regarded as proper medical matters in HCA hospitals.

The comparison and contrast between competitive hospitals can be made quite sharply using the example of South Town because physicians in this area had privileges at both Community (HCA affiliated) and City hospitals. One doctor was particularly articulate about the comparison. Community had a lot more foresight as to what was happening in the town, where the growth was going to be, and in meeting the need before it became manifest (even when not obvious). City, its competitive neighbor, allowed things to happen and then had to respond to them. Community was more nurse oriented, part of being better at creating a favorable patient climate, better at responding to and anticipating physicians' needs, and better at consulting physicians. Management was also more aggressive, especially in obtaining equipment that physicians cherished. A gastroenterologist wanted an endoscope and went to City, which denied him. Community got him the equipment, and City ended up having to play catch up.

> While a hospital being nonprofit appeals to the senses, and if somebody is turning a profit you would expect to pay more, in fact, while Community is a little more expensive, it provides more for that little. Its physical plant is better, and when a family member needed hospitalization, we chose Community.

The practice of medicine was not, however, significantly different, as must be intuitively obvious given that the physicians are the same.

Doctors are unanimous that HCA has been particularly effective in its community relations. The corporation made an effort to become participating members of the community, supporting the United Way and many other activities, and of course, contributed, as City could not and did not, to the tax base.

The CEO at Community was quite successful at dissipating the ever-present paranoia concerning the corporate structure. Doctors knew there was a national corporation and that some decisions were made there, but saw their own CEO as very independent and, indeed, as making improvements for which he had not sought corporate clearance. The CEO was also praised for his accessibility and responsiveness. However, whether this accessibility and responsiveness were a function of personal style, of HCA corporate management style and philosophy, or of hospital size, was not immediately clear. Certainly HCA hospitals tend to be smaller, and City is significantly larger than Community. But the CEO at Community believed that it was philosophy rather than number of beds that made the difference. "If you think that the doctor is important and you can do your paperwork or pay attention to the doctors, you make your choice. And if you care about your relationship with doctors, you get someone else to do the paperwork."

Indeed, the CEO emphasized to his subordinates the need to avoid the *rigor mortis* that tends to set in as the organization grows and management becomes layered. The CEO ate lunch in the cafeteria because doctors got free lunches and so many ate there also; eating there was a good way to keep in touch and give physicians opportunity to take their shots at him.

However, this CEO also gave his version of one of the situations in which HCA seemed to compete with its own physicians. He became aware of a surgicenter being built in their market and was very threatened. He went to the owner of the building and asked whether the owner had signed a lease with the competing physicians who had planned to take it on. He was able to get the owner to sign with him and then turned to Community physicians to try to get them to run the surgicenter. He was even willing to help them financially, but they turned the proposal down and left him holding the bag with a lease he still has. Now he plans to sublease to another group that is going to put in an urgent care center. Even though this group runs the Community ER, the group will still be seen by the attendings as competition because of the potential for taking away some of the attendings' patients.

The CEO was, in fact, thinking of additional aggressive moves, because the corporation plans to start a physician referral service and market services directly to potential patients, especially in obstetrics. Because most local obstetricians work at City, they will not be competing with Community doctors. The CEO prefers, of course, to support his own doctors. When one group of Community doctors bought some land for development as medical office space and needed money, HCA's real estate people cosigned the note and guaranteed 50 percent of the space, even though the physicians did not need the space. This is perhaps a measure of the lengths to which HCA is willing to go to support its physicians in a competitive environment.

This CEO was particularly articulate about the ways in which he implemented HCA's mandate. He agreed with the doctors that HCA was indeed more aggressive about attending to doctors and their needs. Five physicians serving four-year rotating terms are on the board. City has had the same single doctor on its board for 20 years.

While City was the leading hospital—it is larger and older—they did no more than was required to stay competitive.

> They follow from the front, i.e., they drive along looking in their rearview mirror and when they see us putting on our turn signal, they turn. We jack up the standard of care in this town, we set the pace, and they follow, in fact. But is this because we are HCA? Maybe if we were the only hospital in town, we would behave just like City.

Doctors at all the HCA hospitals commented favorably on its responsiveness to their need for new equipment. How does this work?

> At Community, the capital budget period begins in July, and as early as the following fall, as the year goes on, the director of surgery will talk, for example, with the surgeons, and they catalog requests. Management puts a notice in the physicians' newsletter about any requests for equipment just before the capital budget period, but the process has led to the departments themselves deciding on what they need, so that there are few surprises. Priorities are set, for resources are not unlimited, but, in fact, they are able to fund 90 percent of what is requested.

About recruitment of physicians and their quality, Community's CEO acknowledged forthrightly that being the newer, younger hospital, they did not have as much choice as the older, more established institution. In his view, HCA did influence the practice of medicine, not directly by telling the physicians what to do, but indirectly by creating a climate conducive to good care by providing excellent support staff and excellent equipment. HCA is also aggressive in trying to stay current. It could afford numerous experts and staff specialists to discover what was new, or invent it, and was therefore able to move quickly to implementation in the hospitals. This national expertise is always available at the end of a telephone line. Somebody in an HCA hospital has usually implemented similar procedures elsewhere, and that knowledge and experience is available, so that the wheel does not have to be reinvented.

The differences in hospitals remarked on by the physicians extended beyond ease of access to managers or obtaining equipment. Accreditation for particular technologies was also different at the two hospitals. City tended to be more rigid and more political, restricting the use of certain technologies to particular people (probably for economic reasons). Community had fewer constraints, and their physicians found that if they were interested in practicing a particular technology, they were encouraged to do so. This may be due to the fact that City is bigger and has more subspecialists and therefore more turf over which to be jealous. With more generalists at Community, there were fewer specialists to seek jurisdictional control over specialized technologies that enhance income.

With physicians admitting to both hospitals, how did they decide which one to use? Doctors said that first they asked the patient. Those who did not express a preference tended to be admitted to Community because the physicians found they could work them up quicker and get things done faster. A cardiologist doing a stress test could save one or two days of hospital stay at Community.

What seemed to determine patient choice? Geography and physical plant for those familiar with the hospitals. Community had a more attentive nursing staff and a nicer, cleaner plant, and patients preferred being there. If patients had not been to either hospital and family or friends had no experience with either, then when the differences were explained, patients still tended to chose Community.

When then did physicians admit to City? The answer, for some at least, was that they preferred to admit all their patients to Community, but that City offered some specialized services unavailable at Community.

While physicians, in general, agreed about the differences between the hospitals, there was some difference of opinion in the touchy area of the indigent. One doctor saw no difference between the two, both being rigorous about nonpaying patients. Another saw Community as more rigid and stricter in its indigent policy than City, and felt that indigent patients were turned away quicker at Community. This, he felt, resulted in doctors with patients lacking funds directing those patients toward City rather than Community.

Physician comments at other HCA hospitals range from their delight at HCA's responsiveness to their apprehensions about what HCA, or any management, might do at some time in the future. Several doctors from different HCA hospitals give their views:

There's a totally different personality in the two hospitals in this town, and having never worked in another town, I can't really relate to another city. In Community, it's very easy to talk to administration, it's very easy to talk to people in [corporate headquarters], if you've got equipment that's needed to upgrade the care of medicine, if you've got equipment that needs to be updated, new equipment, it's easy to go to them and explain to them, and if you explain reasons for that, it's easy to get that equipment and have it fixed to where it's very usable. The allowances [are] there of allowing one to do what; they're fairly strict on your qualifications, but if you're qualified, it's OK.

There's a dichotomy here. The institution (HCA) would like to have all of us seeing patients eight hours a day, all from the suburbs, all with numbers, being able to generate income. It's perfectly reasonable for them to expect that. The medical school, on the other hand, wants us to be eight hours a day teaching, and the promotional boards want us to be eight hours a day doing research. That mix has been difficult for a lot of us. I am not a researcher. I am a physician and a practicer and a teacher, so when I tell you I want to see HCA talk to me, to develop technical equipment, and I want to see lower costs, those are the kinds of things I'm looking for.

I don't think they would hesitate to do whatever's in their best interest. You want it to be friendly, but they've got to show a profit. Everybody's equal, but some people are more equal than others. I have the power of admitting to their hospital, and it's all friendly, but both sides need to understand who's coming from where. I was on the faculty of the University of California, and when I came here I was supposed to have space. The other hospital took me in. I came over here and still got all the business, so some of their administrative decisions as they relate to me were incorrect and were done because they thought it was in their best interests. It was in my best interest to forget about it. Them, too. There's a lot of stuff that goes on between [corporate headquarters] and here which affects physicians that we have no input into, like they were building an office building here. I know there are secretive things that need to go on because of certificates of need, etc. I asked the architect what they were going to do with this building, and he showed me the plans and talked about dedicated dollars. That night we had a meeting with the board and the executive committee to discuss what we should do. It was an orchestrated meeting for the doctors to have input into what I already knew had been a fait áccompli.

I'm sure that in 20 years from now what a physician will be is dramatically different. I think there's going to be a total change in structures, and I could elaborate on that, but I'm sure you know them better than I do. I'm often reticent to recommend that my sons go into medicine. But I think I'm trying to analyze for you what I think the difference would be if I was sitting in Lowell General, Choate Simms, Waltham, South Shore Hospital, Carney Hospital, what would be the difference from an HCA hospital. The difference, I think, is the interface between the supposed three or tripartite elements of governance of the hospital—TAP, the trustee, administration,

> physician nexus. If you were sitting with the administration in any of the other hospitals, you are probably sitting with a very bright group, many probably well trained in hospital management. When you are sitting with the manager of the HCA hospital, you are sitting with probably $3.5 billion of revenue behind him. You know there are structures and purposes being served that may not be totally obvious from the local view. You have to assume there are interests being served.
>
> They've made the hospital a better hospital to be in. They've also made it more appealing, both for the people in here and also the PR is much better. They've accomplished this several ways. People were leaving me because this was the principal hospital I was using. I was lucky in that the hospital needed me. Now you don't get that as much. Straight PR and being able to handle the media has helped.
>
> It's well managed and efficient, which impressed me. There is a distinct orientation toward pleasing professionally and nonprofessionally the medical staff component of the hospital function. There appears to be a trend to strongly consider physician satisfaction. That stands out here. The employees here seem to be contented, most of them, more so than at most places I've worked. Also, this hospital maintains more of a general hospital in its function and seems to be less specialized, which I view as a negative thing, but that may be viewed administratively as a positive thing. The wards are all general, the specialty care orientation is not strong.

Interestingly, some have experience with or know doctors at other for-profit health corporations and they do make distinctions between their styles. "We have friends who are employed by Charter Medical. I sense that the crispness of management here at HCA is reflected from top to bottom. In Charter I sense a much higher level of disorganization and probably a less active interest in physician satisfaction."

In fact, Charter Medical has specialized in the psychiatric and substance abuse areas and is now the second largest such company, just behind HCA.

For-profits obviously differ in their strategies, and some of these differences may have considerable implications for their physicians. While HCA makes an explicit effort to support the private practice of its physicians, the corporation is also expanding into full-service health systems in some regions, and this may result in competition with doctors in the ambulatory area. Humana, on the other hand, has already made a major commitment to enter the primary care market through the establishment of its health services division. It now operates 140 ambulatory centers, each supporting four to five physicians. This has resulted in much animosity, especially because the physicians who have become involved may eventually find themselves under critical utilization review scrutiny. Most for-profits are getting into the insurance end of the market, are acquiring HMOs and PPOs, and are marketing "hard" to physicians.

There are many different kinds of group practice, including multiple specialty groups, general practice groups, mixed groups, single specialty groups, as well as diagnostic clinics and medical school or hospital groups. Single specialty groups have increased faster than the other types. Regardless of the kind of group, there are four basic kinds of organization: partnerships, corporations, associations, and sole ownerships.

Groups differ from fee-for-service solo practices in providing a broader range of service and higher standards; they counter fragmentation of care with continuity and tend to be more efficient than solo practices.[6] Groups have significant management problems in that they tend toward democratic anarchy. Physicians who join them like the idea of practicing with other doctors but retain many of the values and attitudes of the solo practitioner with regard to independence and autonomy. So physicians in groups tend to have veto power over executive decision making and resist the formation of an executive committee, preferring decision making of the whole. For this reason, it is often difficult for groups to agree on compensation schemes and incentive systems. What is valued is the opportunity to work with respected colleagues while enjoying managerial support that is removed in some degree from clinical practice, freeing physicians from administrative headaches. There are in essence two major types of groups—those that physicians form purely for administrative convenience, while retaining their essential freedoms, and those that are formed because physicians truly wish to collaborate clinically.

In one study of group practice, physicians interviewed felt that patients in group practices were less considerate, grateful, satisfied, and willing than were their fee-for-service counterparts.[7] Patients saw doctors as cold and unsympathetic, accord-

---

[6]F. E. Graham, "Group versus Solo Practice: Arguments and Evidence," *Inquiry* 9 (1972), pp. 49–60.

[7]E. Freidson, *Doctoring Together: A Study of Professional Social Control* (New York: Elsevier, 1975).

ing to administrators. Physician overload was a chronic problem in group practices; when the number of patients increased, there was always a delay in increasing the number of physicians.[8] Doctors therefore tended to desire more freedom to come and go as a way of making up for this. Doctors felt they accepted their responsibility to see patients and were conscientious. Administrators, however, felt that doctors could not always be trusted; for example, there were times when physicians should make house calls and did not. Physicians were adamantly against rules, and so there were few rules.

In a group practice there are no economic barriers stopping the patient from visiting the doctor, so the doctor becomes more of a servant rather than a consultant. Physicians in a group practice may feel trapped, in part because of the nature of the contractual relationship, in part because the patient cannot see their doctor of choice. Because of this contractual relationship, adept and aggressive patients know their rights, but it is difficult for physicians to accept the fact that patients have a right to demand things. The nature of practice is therefore quite different from that found in solo fee-for-service practice, but is very similar to that found in most HMOs. In group practice, doctors dislike overloads, not only because of the pressure, but also because this reduces their time to be personal with patients. They therefore feel that quality suffers. In addition, patients may demand tests and X rays that physicians feel have no direct relationship to diagnosis but which patients feel they are entitled to under the contract.

HMOs are group practices with prepayment added. In staff model HMOs, physicians are employed directly and usually receive a salary plus a bonus based on the HMO's cost performance and/or profitability. In the group model, the HMO contracts with a multispecialty medical group to provide facilities and administrative support; physicians receive a fixed capitation fee for each member on a monthly basis. In the group network model, the HMO contracts with several medical groups, which are paid a capitation fee for each HMO member, but the physicians also maintain fee-for-service practices.

---

[8] E. Freidson, "Prepaid Group Practice and the New 'Demanding Patient'," *Milbank Memorial Fund Quarterly,* Fall 1973, pp. 473—88.

With an independent practice association (IPA), the organization contracts with numerous independent physicians who are paid either a fee for service, a capitation fee, or some combination. As with group practices, IPAs relieve the physician of the management burden, but present them with a different kind of relationship to the patient. The problem for IPAs is that strategically they face the same management issues as HMOs, because IPAs must provide cost-effective quality care, but they have to cope with numerous independently practicing physicians over whom they have relatively little control. Many physicians join IPAs for purely defensive reasons and really wish to continue to practice as they had previously. They may be reluctant to acquiesce to cost- and quality-control measures. Unlike the case with an HMO, in an IPA there is little to bind the physician to corporate management unless the association retains a high share of the physician's practice.

HMOs face a number of management challenges, as rapid growth overloads professional staff and geographic decentralization reduces colleagueship. The rapid growth of HMOs has also resulted in their recruiting relatively inexperienced mangers who often lack basic management skills and an understanding of the HMO environment.[9] However, the increase in size of HMOs and the formation of HMO chains have enabled them now to offer competitive salaries and thus to recruit management that was hitherto inaccessible.

Neighborhood health centers have to deal with a number of somewhat different management issues. As have other kinds of health delivery organizations, they have found their traditional funding running out and can no longer expect subsidies for their care for the indigent. They have therefore had to turn to the private pay market, as have teaching hospitals, but with fewer physical and professional resources to do so. Neighborhood centers also have one unique problem. Historically they have attracted ideologically committed young physicians who join because of the center's social mission. While neighborhood centers have been able to keep their costs low because these committed physicians were willing to work for little, the shift toward com-

[9]D. H. Harrison and J. R. Kimberly, "HMOs Don't Have to Fail," *Harvard Business Review*, July–August 1982, pp. 115–24.

peting in the traditional health market for private pay patients has been ideologically difficult for such young physicians.

Initially freestanding ambulatory centers, "doc in the boxes," fast medicine centers, etc., relied on moonlighting residents and doctors between jobs for staff. As they have grown and had to produce a reliable quality of medicine as well as control costs, these centers have begun to rely on a more stable cadre of doctors. Young doctors burdened by the cost of malpractice insurance or of setting up their own practices and older physicians not wishing to continue in private practice have been attracted to these centers as well as to HMOs. The public has found these centers, which serve the "convenience market," attractive. Current licensing pressures on these centers may reduce their rate of growth or increase their costs, for licensing usually means regulating equipment, space, and staffing. From a medical point of view, continuity and quality are certainly in question. Such centers also attract entrepreneurial physicians who see in them an opportunity to combine clinical practice and capitalism.

ORGANIZATIONAL PREPARATION

Medical schools are responsible for training doctors, but emphasize the basic sciences and clinical medicine. Only recently has there been attention to the behavioral and social sciences, and there is still little attention paid to giving young physicians any understanding at all of management or of health organizations. Yet today even the fee-for-service private practitioner finds himself running a small business, and most young physicians will spend much of their professional lives working in organizations. All physicians find that they must deal with regulators and with management matters, and indeed, that they have to devote significant time to such issues, but there is little teaching of these subjects during their training, for the medical school curriculum is full, and internships and residencies are as overburdened. Yet the evidence is that all of the settings in which the future physician will practice will place management demands on them. These management demands are not extrinsic to clinical practice, for they have already become part of it. Judgments about health and illness, diagnosis, and treatment involve complex decisions that must take into account societal, patient, and organizational interests.

While mature doctors are satisfied with their clinical preparation, they agree that their training lacked essentials that would have better prepared them for the world in which they now find themselves.

> I see it as a given that medical school curricula will include much more material than they do now about management and cost-effective decision making.
>
> We need to know how money is generated and spent, trends of the future. You come out of school and you do not know what is going on.
>
> We're going to have to teach doctors more about the political process and the choices that have to be made.
>
> We need more training in managing our practices, in marketing, in patient relations, in finance, in medical economics.
>
> There should have been some training in managing a practice, what to use in terms of equipment, dealing with patients' emotions.
>
> Medically it was fine but it was poor from an economic standpoint and philosophically in terms of dealing with patients and death and dying.
>
> We lacked training in the business aspect and the personal patient aspect.
>
> I had absolutely no preparation except for acute hospital care. I trained at a 3,000-bed New York City hospital, and I had never stepped into a doctor's office until I stepped into my own.
>
> It seems to me that we are still training doctors to be private practitioners whereas most of them are going to work in organizations. Are we training them to function in that setting? No. Somebody said we are going to have to learn organizations like our grandparents did farming. That's a fact.

This is indeed a major challenge for the training institutions and teachers of tomorrow.

CHAPTER NINE

Management Style and Management Skills: Lay and Physician Managers

Honor a physician with honor due unto him
for the uses which you may have of him:
for the Lord hath created him.

Apocrypha xxxviii.1.

MANAGEMENT STYLE AND SKILLS FOR THE LAY MANAGER

The central argument of this book is that in a health environment which is competitive and/or requires the prudent disposition of scarce resources to deliver equitable care to all sectors of the population, physician behavior must be modulated to reflect not only physician concerns but also community needs and the concerns of the health care delivery organization. Physicians must therefore be managed, but managing takes on a special meaning where professionals are concerned. Even though the role of physicians is changing, even though more are becoming organizational employees, there are still areas where their expertise must be respected. Managing therefore does not mean ordering but influencing, and that is a two-way street, for managers will achieve more if they are open to influence. As one physician put it,

> I take offense at the idea of managing physicians. It is like we are subservient, but there should be an open line of communication. Both sides should be aware. Physicians should be involved in decision making. What is important is that management should be available to staff. Their offices should not be set apart. Let us tear down the ivory tower. Walk the corridor and say "hello" to people.

The manager must be tactful, and the successful manager will use a variety of forms of influence. Some types of manage-

FIGURE 9-1 Influences on Physician Behavior

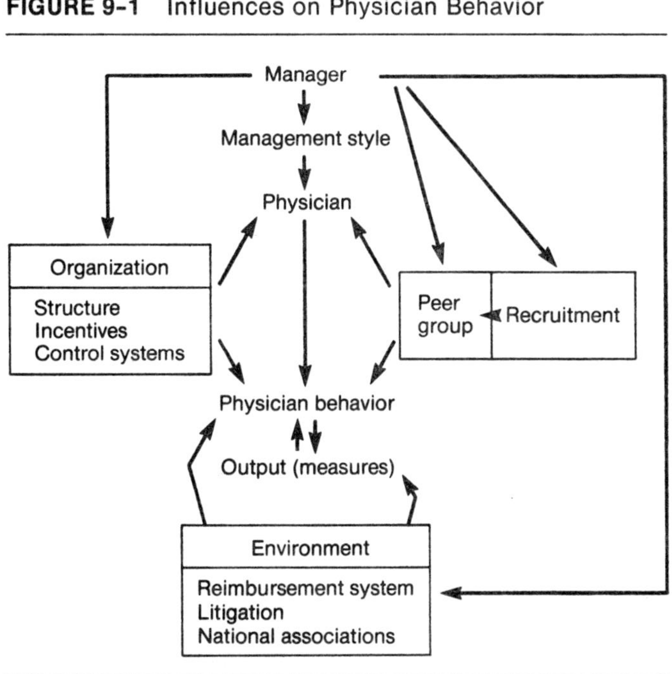

ment influence, as well as other influences on physician behavior, are shown in Figure 9-1. There are many ways in which influence can be brought to bear on physician behavior and on physicians. The most direct is the impact of personal style in face-to-face situations. Management style then becomes critical and physicians have much to say about the styles that they find effective or frustrating. Management style must depend on an understanding of physicians in general and of different physicians in particular. (See also Chapters 3 and 8.)

Physician behavior is also influenced by environmental factors such as the nature of the reimbursement system, fear of litigation, or pressure from national associations (Figure 9-1). To some degree, managers may be able to affect some of these factors and thus to influence physicians. Managers can also bring influence to bear on the peer group of physicians within the organization, through the example of respected opinion leaders or through selective recruitment. Organizational structure, incentives, and control systems can be altered to modify physician behavior. In some instances, simple feedback on the relationship between physician behavior and output measures will be sufficient to alter physician behavior. For example, in Ireland, general practitioners were given information about the costs of their prescriptions, resulting in a significant reduction of these costs.

One clear message from the 10-hospital study of CEOs and doctors is the importance of understanding where doctors are "coming from"—for example, that they like to use data and that they are concerned about patient care. While doctors expect respect, they themselves respect firmness, openness, and honesty. They want to be worked with, not told what to do. Here is what some of the CEOs in the study said in their own words:

> If there's another hospital within 20 miles, don't act arbitrarily, capriciously, or unreasonably just because you have the power. Second, you must be strong people and be comfortable enough with yourselves.
>
> First, you have to understand physicians and their makeup. You have to have a feel for their education in terms of the specifics, the orientation, what they're taught, what they're not taught. Medical schools have an approach and a style—physicians get presented with facts and make decisions quickly. They're still taught they're the captain of the ship and responsible for patient-care decisions. That orientation gets translated into nonclinical activities. Medical schools have not started to teach things like teamwork, the importance of communication skills, getting a good feel for what a hospital is. Administrators have to understand that.
>
> One of my saving graces has been to put myself in the place of a physician in terms of the behaviors he has been through in his formal academic environment. Dealing with data helps me deal with physicians. We can get bogged down with emotions, but physicians can handle data concretely.
>
> To any problem, there is a defined methodology to come up with a solution. Get data so when physicians make statements you don't understand, you don't need to ask for further information. From there, you need to help them flesh out the criteria they're using to make their value judgments. Then you need to gather data to make your assessment. Once you've made an assessment, go back to the source and present it to them to get them to buy into it. If you can't, you have to kick it up to the higher powers that be in the structure so they have to do the negotiations to get the solution implemented. So it's education, data gathering, and implementing.
>
> The thing I'm learning is don't promise anything you can't deliver. Be there if they want to talk and then listen. Work out problems together. Use the system and keep them informed.
>
> Speak softly and carry a big stick. It would be to your benefit to firmly and without question about your intent tell a particular person what you

think ought to be and leave it up to him to correct or better the situation on his own or with his colleagues. Actually being there and directing or trying to influence the process would not be well taken.

You have to have a low ego, be able to communicate very well, and be able to work at establishing personality identification patterns as to what they like to hear and they don't like to hear. Some physicians have abrasive personalities, and you can't be offended by them. Don't take things personally. You have to provide them with the knowledge that lets them make decisions. At the same time, maintain charge, and I wouldn't recommend anybody get in this business.

Develop a spirit of team with them. Always try to see their side of it. As I said earlier, you know, most of the time if they come in here with a gripe, it is a legitimate gripe—probably a little bit overblown in their own minds. I treat them as something special for one thing and then appeal to their sense of fairness, like if they're going to be a dictator, they need to be a benevolent dictator.

Primarily listen before you start to communicate. Each physician is an individual; it is by nature that he went into medicine [because] he is a highly aggressive individual and has very definite ideas about any subject matter that you breach, and I think you have to get to know the people before you can effectively communicate with them.

Like the one guy that's a high admitter. When I ask him to do something that may not be exactly in his best interest, but it is in the best interest of the staff, I always preface it by saying, "You know that as powerful as you are in this hospital, that if you say that I've got to do it this way, I'll be doing it that way." However . . . and maybe it's a little trap, maybe it's a semantic thing that gets to where he can't answer it any other way, but it works.

The most important is to be upfront, honest, and communicate with the staff. Management and the staff have a good working relationship. That's not by accident. The fact that we include physicians in the major things that go on, i.e., I put together an operating plan every year which is shared with the medical staff, they're asked for input through the medical executive committee and departments, so if people have a thought about it, we can know about it. At the same time, any time we go out and come up with something new during the year, we involve the staff. Any memos which affect physicians that either of us is going to send out are reviewed before they go out so we aren't shooting bullets at one another. There's a medical needs assessment committee which is a physician-run committee. That's the group which looks to bring in other physicians. In most hospitals, that's done by the board of trustees and the staff only has input.

Loyalty is basic to any hospital operation. Our physicians are loyal. We have to continue by increasing our communication. The federal government is trying to get hospitals and physicians to compete. As soon as that starts, we'll start cutting one another's throats. When we come up with new projects, i.e., PPOs, IPAs, HMOs, we talk about them with the medical staff.

Always tell the truth, regardless of how it sounds, because you will destroy your integrity, especially a new manager or a new doctor or a new administrator that goes into any area. When you're young and aggressive, you tend to want to be hell fire and show everyone what you really know and it's really to your advantage to sit back and show them what you don't know at least until you get on solid ground.

Some comments of physicians on what they look for in a manager:

Get into a relationship with your medical staff where you're extremely well informed. Efficiency of management breeds efficiency among physicians. Bring facts and figures and have a continuous method of communication.

The essence of that is how to be a diplomat and yet not give the impression of being too suave and slick. It comes down to a certain sense of earnestness. It is important for an administrator to interact with at least certain key physicians, to maintain a liaison with leading physicians. Then things run more smoothly. One must be cordial and responsive to needs.

Make sure doctors feel they've been listened to and be available for discussions as necessary. Most problems come from isolation.

Communication—always be willing to listen to their side and be willing to see their point of view and be willing to compromise if necessary, but keep the basic principles intact. Physicians have tremendous egos, and sometimes it's hard to work around that, so you have to change your personality depending on the physician you're with. Some you can be aggressive with, but with others you have to be very passive.

Most physicians feel they know more about patients and what patients need by virtue of training and experience than most managers. When we ask for something—diagnostic equipment, laboratory procedures, whatever—we feel we're asking for that because it benefits the patients and we should be listened to, and administration should not say "no, it's too expensive." We think they ought to give, and in the long run the return will be there financially because it will be used. To me what is important is for the administration to handle the administrative part and let the physician have a lot of input.

Be personable, available, and good at what you do.

It depends on the hospital and its tradition. Physicians have been in control and need to be shown what their responsibilities are. If they're willing to do the necessary things, management has to show them what they have to do.

The most important thing is to keep an open door, listen to physicians. Many problems are temporary, and they have to vent their wrath, sometimes not more than that. The other thing is management has to be available to all departments and, if possible, to all personnel. You can do it in a small hospital, but it's harder in a big one.

The biggest thing, as with patient contact, is to give the physician the feeling that he has been heard, that his opinion has been solicited, that his advice is valued. He needs to think that the person who is making the decision understands your position.

Need to communicate with physicians. Lack of communication is very common. If you knew about something and you knew the reasons and you knew it was coming, you'd be much more [amenable] to it.

Physicians stress that what is most important to understand about them is their preoccupation with clinical care. This is stressed over and over.

The primary purpose of a hospital is to deliver health care, and the physicians are the ones who have the license to do that. Then managers can delineate their own role in this area. They can demand that physicians be accountable for what they do.

In general, doctors are concerned with the care of their patients. There are exceptions, but if you provide them with the base of delivery of care, there won't be problems.

I don't think managers understand the physician's exposure every day with every patient interaction to both legal liability and the psychological aspects of being a physician. I don't know what it's like to manage an institution where you have the economic well-being of hundreds of people as your responsibility. Some people care more about their economic well-being than their health, obviously. Physicians and managers come at things from very different directions.

You ought to tell them, for the next 10 years, I still really believe that our interests in taking care of patients is highly overdetermined and we are as much committed to set things right for people, the healing tradition, so they should address doctors not only in terms of what's good for the bottom line, because doctors find that offensive. I wouldn't be surprised if there was some backlash against the health care industry. It started with mixing cost-benefit analysis—that kind of terminology. They ought to remember that doctors will still respond best when you put it in terms of what's good for patient care. If it's not, and you have to address bottom-line issues, it will be more meaningful to doctors when you can put it in terms of what's good and best for our patients.

If you go in a courtroom, remember you're as smart as anyone in there. If someone can't explain something to you, it's their fault, not yours. I won't accept from a manager anything if they don't understand the medical implications. When you're talking the same language, you can then more effectively communicate.

A good manager has to be very aware of and comfortable with the reality that physicians are motivated by power and autonomy and tend not to relate well to hierarchical situations. Unless that's firmly meshed, that physicians like to help make big decisions but don't like to be stuck with the responsibility of implementing them, that if they perceive a manager as committed to making the practice environment function efficiently and smoothly, that can go a long way to physicians' willingness to give up some autonomy. The whole tension between licence and liberty, between freedom and discipline, ends up having to be further on the freedom side than managers might understand. The worst mistake a manager can make is to overstep the line between decisions which are managerial and those that begin to be professional.

Physicians would like managers to understand the way they think and work, and ideally to have had some actual experience that would support this understanding.

For a manager to be really effective with physicians, he should have experienced some of the things which physicians experienced in their training that bring them to think in a certain way and set their priorities in a certain way. I don't know if you can do that without having served in the trenches.

It would depend on the setting and the doctor, but the most important thing is not to infringe on the doctors' medical turf unless he had problems. Physicians get upset when nonphysicians mention medical topics. They also like to consider themselves administrators, so even though they don't want you on their turf, they don't mind infringing on yours. Tell them what you want to do. Be honest and strong.

Physicians are trained and function with a sense of immediacy. Problems can't be put on the back shelf. Management and trustees have to respond in that way. If they say they want an NMR [Nuclear Magnetic Resonance] machine tomorrow, the board has to say we will make a decision on that issue after we study it and we will have the decision for you in March. They then have to produce that decision in March. Medical staff unrest is strictly on the basis of unfulfilled promises. It's OK for the answer to be no, although the administration and the board are reluctant to say no. So they say maybe, and that's worse than no.

He doesn't have to be medically trained, but he has to understand how doctors work. He has to keep an open mind as to what doctors' needs are. If he loses sight of that and looks only at economics, the physical building, he will lose his doctors. Listen and understand, and if you have a better way, you have better rapport.

One thing is it's almost essential to be a doctor. Hospital administrators have become managers and doctors are leaving issues of support personnel, etc. to administrators. They do want to be involved in major decisions, but not be the guy who has to go to all the committee meetings. To be successful . . . I believe in medical management, especially in a compartmentalized complicated hospital. The administrator can manage a lot of these things. It helps to understand where the doctors are coming from, and a lot of administrators are good at that. It helps to be recognized as one of them who has a slightly different point of view. Maybe a person with a macro view can help a person with a micro view. From my point of view, the physician has to meet the qualifications of being one of the boys; someone who has had some successes, some knowledge and expertise, is appreciated.

The first thing they should do is try to learn as much medicine as they can so when discussions turn to substance, they will have a working knowledge of what's being discussed. They won't be able to be buffaloed. The second thing is to be aware of the money, to consider physicians' incomes, but not only that. The third thing is that physicians are very proud. Even though the profession is tattered and torn, physicians expect to be treated with deference. A good manager should have good manners.

What doctors want most in managers is openness, sincerity, credibility, integrity. They expect managers to be straightforward with them.

You have to err on the candid, open side, and hope you're making such a good decision, that the power which rises against you will be small, and that most people will see the wisdom and honesty of your decisions. As soon as you become secretive, you start losing your ability to convince anyone else.

Sincerity is one, but the thing is how do you provide sincerity? That's a very tough thing. Honesty and reliability and going in one direction and sticking to it is another, but you're always going to ruffle feathers. It's very hard to get around doctor apathy, insecurity.

Avoid as much bullshit as possible. No self-serving soliloquies. Don't jump the gun. Listen to see where the flow is going before making statements. Be candid as to goals and objectives so people understand what you have to do. Work at establishing joint partnerships.

Number one is integrity. You can't do one thing and say another. [Second,] don't adopt the attitude that physicians are in adversarial positions. Deal aboveboard, treat them as though they're not adversaries, make them feel like kingpins. Third, you need the ability to listen and hear what is being said. Fourth, you need to have the kind of makeup to say that it's okay to agree to disagree. You don't have to win them all because you're really after a result, so it's important that you develop that sense. It's probably a negotiating talent.

Two things. Credibility and stability. If they are consistent, even if it's not what you want and it's not what you are thinking about, if you're consistent, it can be dealt with. If an administrator does what he says he's going to do, you have confidence and trust in him. Both of our administrators are like that.

Sometimes there is nothing that is effective. To be honest and straightforward, to be well organized in discussion and show physicians the advantages and disadvantages of what they do.

I like people who are honest about what's going on and where they are and what they're trying to accomplish. If somebody can't do something, just say you can't do it. Don't tell me that you're going to and then not be able to do it, and if you do tell me you're going to do something, then you better be sure you can do it. I think that and a sense that, if somebody talks behind backs, that makes everybody nervous. The honest, upfront, this is what's going on, I can or cannot do this.

The major thing [doctors] respect is being straight, upfront, and honest. The major problems I've seen with anything is when the doctors feel they're in competition with the administrators.

Be open. Recognize that you're wrong when you are. Be honest when you don't know what to do. Leo's been good at this. Beyond that, it's a daily kind of communication.

The thing that doctors respect most of all is being honest with what you say, that is, even in this town in the past, there have been some administrators who moved too fast, who said one thing and did another, and that's bad. You don't know where you stand. You've got to be honest and straight. Be aboveboard.

Physicians do not like to be bullied and expect managers to be reasonable and rational as they feel they themselves are.

Don't tell a physician it's going to be this way whether you like it or not.

An absolute don't is a way of dealing with people that tells them, "Do it." There's no way to bristle a doctor quicker.

I prefer to be led rather than driven, to have at least the illusion that decisions are mine.

Doctors don't like having something pushed down their throats. When asked for an opinion, you must assimilate that opinion.

Dictatorial attitude turns doctors off. Be available and listen and mediate. Get other physicians' ideas, work with them, don't dictate.

The best thing is don't come in like a wind out of the west and try to change everything over night. Evolve into the position, establish credibility.

With a reasonable request or solution, and the reasonableness can be demonstrated.

Know what you're talking about and be fair.

I think the key thing I would tell any administrator is tell people where you are coming from.

Assuming they're dealing with rational physicians (and there are some irrational ones), if you're professional about your job and demonstrate respect for physicians' knowledge, you'll get along pretty well. When you begin to get into each other's business, you're in trouble.

When a physician comes to you with a problem, you have to note that problem. Then you have to investigate it, because a lot of times a problem is nothing. There are some physicians who create problems to make themselves feel better. But valid problems need recognition and follow-up. If nothing is done, then you get the feeling that if you have another problem, nothing will be done.

And finally, physicians want managers to be available, to communicate well, to mix, and to take the time and have the patience to educate doctors when needed.

> Not being able to get in touch with them. At the medical center, it's hard to get in touch with [the administrator], and he doesn't listen to what you say, he doesn't care. Here it's different. They're responsible to higher-up people and they've got to make sure the hospital makes money and physicians use it. Try to accommodate us without being servile.
>
> Be available and visible. Backslapping turns doctors off. Working with them in committees and being open helps.
>
> Try to get very close to the doctors, attend meetings, keep the office near the mainstream, be available, and don't try to avoid issues.
>
> They have to work on communication, take time to explain how you see it and what it means. Bend over backwards to let everyone know what you're doing. The worst thing you can do is present a conclusion before its time. Be very open. We got into some problems with secretive meetings.
>
> Physicians don't want to feel they've been given lip service. They realize they have to become involved. Back in the early 1900s, they were very involved, then they lost it, and now it's happening again.
>
> Educate [physicians]. That won't make them agree with you, but they'll understand the issue.
>
> Don't forget to talk to doctors in terms of what's good for patient care, and also to tell them to create an atmosphere where you bring doctors in and say we have this problem and how can you help us with it. Even if you have your predetermined management ideas how to solve them, at least include the doctors and dignify their presence with the assumption that they might come up with some imaginative ways to deal with those problems.

THE PHYSICIAN MANAGER

While physicians expect managers in a health delivery organization to be knowledgeable about medicine, they do not necessarily prefer a physician manager over a lay manager where there is a choice. The role of the physician manager is difficult because the position, paid for as it is by management, is naturally suspect. As with other authority positions, myths grow up about the incumbents that have less to do with the reality of who they are or what they do than with what physicians choose to believe about them. Such myths, where negative, are not easily dissipated by facts, for the basis of myth lies in emotions and beliefs. Because the role of the physician manager may be to exert influence over the practice of physicians, the manager's effectiveness lies in an understanding of what physicians will and will not accept in the way of supervision.

Doctors value supervisors whom they judge to have professional competence, diagnostic skill, knowledge of therapy, ability to establish rapport with patients, skill in dealing with the social problems of patients, extensive knowledge of medical facts, the ability to work with nurses, the ability to get along with colleagues, and knowledge of community agencies. Specialties differ in what they value and appreciate: surgeons value therapy above knowledge of medical facts, while diagnostic skills are valued more by physicians than by surgeons. Psychiatrists value rapport and knowledge of therapy.[1]

Physicians feel that their actions cannot be supervised unless the supervisor has seen the patient. Authority relationships are therefore restricted to administrative rather than professional areas, while professional work requires an advisory relationship. Regardless of the qualifications that supervisors possess, unsolicited advice from a supervisory physician will be received as an adverse reflection on the physician's professional competence. However, if the supervisor is a professional peer or superior, physicians are more likely to regard comment as helpful and review it carefully, so professional competence is more important than rank. But it is not so much professional competence that secures compliance with decisions as it is the physician manager's intimate and firsthand knowledge of the medical subculture that enables these managers to know in advance which decisions they may make with assurance and that will be accepted.

Therefore, in attempting to make a difference in the lives of the doctors reporting to them, physician managers must exert influence rather than power, and so use persuasion, reward and punishment, participation, and trust. The power of the position is insufficient influence. It is also important that supervising physicians continue to practice as a way of achieving credibility.

---

[1]M. Goss, *Physicians and Bureaucracy: A Case Study of Professional Pressures on Organizational Roles* (New York: Arnow Press, 1980).

Credibility will also be established by the quality of the decisions physician managers make and the way that they successfully manage conflicts.[2,3]

There are eight basic tasks that physician managers generally have to deal with: determining/improving medical practice; dealing with problems or conflicts; evaluating physician care; advising, counseling, and motivating doctors; recruiting; improving quality; dealing with outside organizations; and improving their own professional knowledge and skills.[4] These tasks may vary with different definitions of the physician-manager's role and in different settings. The HMO physician manager, for example, may be significantly involved in physician productivity and compensation and in quality-of-care assurance and recruitment. Dr. Barrett, Medical Director of Dynamic Health, commented on his key tasks as follows:

> The way I see it, the long-term success of Dynamic Health will depend on our ability to attract and retain quality physicians. . . . Salaries are my biggest problem at this point in time. The physicians have submitted a formal request for a 20 percent salary hike next year. . . . One problem that I am working on now will have implications for the long-term future of Dynamic Health. The board and executive director need to be aware of the role of physicians in this organization. I do not believe they entirely understand the sensitive position I hold with the responsibility to motivate the medical staff while keeping one eye on the budget. . . . The experience of increasing referrals and hospitalization, which caused the plan to fall short of the budget last year, has focused attention on physicians although the philosophical issues have been entirely translated into dollars and cents. The increased patient-care expenses apparently represent to the board a potentially serious problem, and they would like to resolve the ambiguous role of the medical staff, particularly with respect to financial accountability. . . . Patients' best interests do not in all cases coincide with those of a prepaid plan, particularly when you realize that providing patient services costs the plan money and does not necessarily produce money in return. I feel this conflict has been very evident in my role, in that I must value the corporate and financial interests on the one hand while on the other I represent the doctors and the quality of the clinical care they deliver on behalf of the plan.[5]

---

[2]I. Rubin, "The Managerial Role," in *The Physician in Management,* ed. R. Schenke (Washington, D.C.: American Academy of Medical Directors, 1980).

[3]J. Royer, "The Dual Role Dilemma: A Perspective from Medicine," in Schenke, op. cit.

[4]C. Slater, "The Physician Manager's Role: Result of a Survey," in Schenke, op. cit.

[5]*Dynamic Health: A Case Study,* Proceedings of the Medical Directors Conference 5, no. 1 (Medical Directors Division, GHAA, 1980).

This cogently expresses the dilemma that any physician manager faces, and particularly the dilemma facing medical directors in prepaid plans.

In addition to the eight basic tasks there are additional tasks peculiar to particular physician-manager roles. These include training and orienting, placing and promoting, disciplining, determining remuneration, improving productivity, and development of medical education programs. Physician managers in prepaid plans will be more concerned with personnel administration, while those in teaching hospitals are more concerned with clinical care, recruitment, problem solving, and conflict resolution.

To be effective, the physician manager must speak many languages, be an integrator, and work on the interface of management and medicine.[6] There are many problems involved in these tasks, including the time and effort to get information, the fact that you are in the middle and viewed as neither clinician nor manager, the ill-defined nature of the role, the reduced personal satisfaction of working through others rather than doing clinical work, the need to think like a manager without training, the excessive load, the constant pressures for solutions, the inroads of regulation, the lack of professional peers, and the difficulty of working with doctors who prize their individuality. Indeed, an agonizing dilemma faced by many physicians who drift into or select the managerial role is finding that the direct satisfactions they gained from clinical practice are not so easily gained in working through others. It is not, therefore, surprising that many physician managers continue some clinical practice, not only for reasons of credibility, but also to be able to continue to feel competent and rewarded by their activities.

One problem common to many physician managers is that they were brought up as physicians! Physicians are trained to act autonomously, to be individualistic, and to make solo decisions based on information collected from many sources and analyzed internally. Managers work with others and must make public decisions based on shared information. So the natural

---

[6] L. Kaiser, "The Physician Manager as an Interface Professional," in *The Physician in Management*, ed. R. Schenke (Washington, D.C.: American Academy of Medical Directors, 1980).

skills and abilities that lend themselves to being a good physician may be liabilities in a physician manager. One study of physicians in management, for example, showed that physician managers tend to be very selective in the groups they join, do not need group involvement, do not care about conclusions, and have little concern about prestige or what others think; they are detached, independent, and self-sufficient.[7] Physician managers prefer to remain distant. When things go smoothly, they tend to be supportive, but when confronted with opposition, stress, or conflict, they share a tendency to withdraw and become more authoritarian, using position and professional status to overcome opposition. They are uncomfortable with conflict and prefer to avoid and withdraw and become stubborn.

Doctor R. is chief of medicine at a 925-bed teaching hospital and professor of medicine. He has a number of full-time physicians and many residents and interns reporting directly to him, and he also has to work with a large independent attending staff. He is also a particularly effective physician manager. How does he go about completing the difficult tasks facing him?

> There is [an] interesting little aspect right here, and that is that if you run an organization with all volunteers and they are incompetent or they fail at the jobs they are given, they don't go away. They remain here for another 40 years because this is their practice base, so that as one begins to cull out people who perhaps in an industrial situation might be fired, you still have them on board. They are still able to influence the policy decisions of the hospital through various selections of staff committees and so on. They still admit patients so that one has to live with whatever one inherits and accumulates over time, over long time spans. So this, too, may play a part.
>
> They must feel that I'm their man. That I represent their interests and that I understand what their problems are. And I think that this is the essential feature, in the fact that we've had a common development. It's easy for me to deal with doctors, since I can use shorthand—I can take short cuts. I know how they think. I know what their problems are, and I have to totally change my style when I have to deal with administrators and people who have a totally different background, and I find that I can't deal in the easy, quick way that I do with physicians.
>
> My view of a chief of medicine is that he must be a peer of his staff and he must be regarded as a first-class clinician by members of the staff in order to accomplish some of the derivative functions such as discipline, demand for standards or for quality control. So I see my first major task is to

[7]M. Kurtz, "A Behavioral Profile of Physicians in Managerial Roles," in Schenke, op. cit.

maintain my clinical skills and expertise and still be regarded by members of my staff in that fashion, rather than [as] the manager of some enterprise who really doesn't understand what the problems are. I think that's the key to the entire operation of a volunteer staff that must do all the things that have to be done in order for a chief to accomplish his goals.

How does Dr. R. find out about what is going on so that he can deal with problems? Because this is a teaching hospital,

the chief medium through which we monitor is our house staff, and one of the difficulties that we've had, as the hospital has grown so large, is that we cannot have house staff involved in the admission of every single patient. In those instances where the house staff is involved in patient care, if strange things are happening, we learn about it very promptly. In the areas of the hospital where there are no house staff involved, we usually hear about strange things either through the medium of the nurses or after the fact.

The house staff is being monitored by attending staff and the full-time staff and so on. So a major task is to have an information system that alerts us so that poor patient care, whether medication errors on the part of nurses, poor practice of one sort or another, or abandonment of patients by physicians, comes to our attention. Then we can do something to try to solve those problems.

Generally the information system is extremely effective. The jungle telegraph in any hospital is incredible. Something happens in the emergency room and I know about it within three or four minutes, and I'm not sure how that telegraph works.

Why are people willing to tell Dr. R. what is going on? After all, the quality of his information system must depend on the climate that he is able to create.

I think it's maybe because we don't make a big deal out of it. In the example I was mentioning, we would see the patient, I would call the doctor and say, "Hey, this really is quite fascinating. We would very much, for educational purposes, like to get some lab work. We'd like you to consider the possibility of diagnosis X, Y, or Z, and we'd like you to sit in as we present this case." He now becomes a part of the team that is taking care of his patient. He's learning something and we are bailing him out. He tacitly knows that. I know that. But we don't say anything about it. He's gone through a learning experience. The patient benefits, and [the physician] feels that he can trust us in that we did not make him look a fool. We didn't say, "Hey, you dummy, you're killing this patient!" We simply provide a climate in which he can do a little better than he was doing before.

But Dr. R. is not averse to judicious confrontation when it seems to be required.

This we usually handle right in this office, nose to nose. I have been known to lose my temper and I have been known to say, "Hey, you dummy, I don't like what you did. If you do it again, you're going to get in a lot of trouble from me," in situations where we're in an intractable flap between two physicians or house staff and doctors. I have often to deal with conflicts between physicians and nurses, physicians and respiratory therapists, and so on. We try to lay those on the table. We do take advantage of the divisional organization. In other words, for example, if one of our pulmonary physicians is doing too many lung biopsies and getting bad results, we put this in the hands of the chief of the pulmonary section and say, "Hey, we're a little concerned about this. Will you please reassure us that this is consistent with good practice throughout the country." And then we allow his peers and himself to debate this issue. We have had situations where we have stopped doing certain procedures because the results have been poor, but we've done it through the medium of peer pressure and laying it out on the table in the interest of good patient care. Those are the easiest problems. Any problem that we can reduce to a problem of "is it good or bad for patient care" is easily resolvable by discussion. Other problems of status and this sort of thing are insoluble and I don't even try.

To some extent it's a confrontation that's uncomfortable, but again, we always try to provide an out. We know that patients will continue to go see a physician who perhaps is not performing as well as he might. We know that some of them will be sick and will be admitted to the hospital and, therefore, the simple confrontation is not quite enough. What we then suggest very strongly is that each time that particular physician admits a patient, he must name a consultant that we approve who is a member of our staff. We've only had to do this in one or two instances, but it works very well. It doesn't go on for very long then. The physician then gets used to admitting the patient to the consultant's service. He continues to see the patient, but we feel better about the fact that one of our recognized consultants is in actual fact running the case. In a way, once again, we don't throw him off the staff.

We try to keep it out of the usual mill of committees and so on as long as possible. However we are not all averse to taking certain instances to our own departmental executive committee. We have an executive committee in the department with whom I share most of these policy decisions, responsibilities and so on, and when we have a real problem we will bring this before the executive committee and we will give the man an opportunity of explaining his actions and so on. We find that this is a very effective. . . . I always try to use the single mechanism of peer pressure. That's the one that works the best for me at this place.

But Dr. R., recognizing that conflicts are inevitable, feels that patience and proaction are important elements in successfully handling situations.

One of the things that has come up a number of times that I think may be a sort of generic problem for chiefs is the tendency to collect a dossier on somebody before you look him in the eye and say, "I don't like what you're doing." I think repeatedly we allow a man to progressively cut his throat. He's not quite aware of it, and we're carefully documenting this case that eventually we're going to use for disciplinary purposes, rather than early on stopping him and saying, "I don't like what you're doing. I wish you'd stop doing it," and most often he's not even aware that he's getting into trouble. I think that the organization tendency is to allow people to go too far before someone has the courage to say, "Hey, we're all very angry at you. We don't like what you're doing, and you know we're going to have a lot of trouble." They tend to say, "Well, get me the documentation of how many times he did this, that, and the other thing," thereby escalating the whole thing and painting the man in a corner that perhaps he can't get out of.

Just to pick up on one little thing in terms of flap, management, and discipline. It seems to me that we get into more trouble by reacting too quickly to people who are unhappy or what appear to be big problems. One of the things that we try to do is allow something to incubate a little longer before we have our confrontations and so on. Every time we acted very promptly to let's say a catastrophe in an emergency room or something, we end up with more trouble than if we had allowed things to kind of jell and situations to present themselves, and then have the formalized confrontations, discussions, and so forth.

I think the basic thing of any organization is conflict resolution. One way or another there are always conflicts because we're so highly specialized and there are always going to be difficulties. The general idea is let's try and keep oiling the machine and let it run as smoothly as it's capable of running and try to solve the problems as they arise and hopefully, try to identify some of them before they occur.

Dr. R. is not at all sanguine about the value of continuing medical education as a way of remedying problems.

I really am not at all convinced that this whole continuing medical education business and going to courses and brownie points and relicensure does anything. I think most physicians learn when they have a need to know, and, therefore, we try to wander through the corridors. We try to be walking consultants. We try to help the physician when he has a problem with whatever knowledge we can pull together at that time, and we think that's the way our physicians get the bulk of their continuing medical education. I suppose that is part of my rationalization to myself for not feeling guilty at all about nosing around, and if I see an interesting case, I'll call the doctor and ask him about it. And the mere fact that we're showing interest in the teaching service improves the care of that patient, I believe.

As a result, he tries to create systems that make it difficult for doctors to engage in the behavior that he wants them to avoid.

I believe in the concept of downtown parking: you put a nickel in and if you want to park longer, you've got to put a dime in, and if you want to park all night, you have to take your lumps when they haul your car away. So that we have tried to set up a series of greater difficulties to make it more difficult to do the wrong thing. At the same time, I think it's our job to make it easier to do the right thing. A couple of simple examples. I'm totally bored with bylaws, rules, regulations, and reports. Occasionally there will be a situation where a physician will not fill in his records for days and days and won't do his chart work and so forth, and it now becomes necessary to jazz him a little. The worst offender, long known to me and to himself, responds in the following fashion. I don't do anything directly. I simply call the record room and say, "Please pull all of Dr. X's records for the last two months." Within one hour, Dr. X knows about that because the girl in the record room, who likes him very much, let's him know that someone has asked for his records. He then promptly brings them all up to date. The records are never moved. I never look at one. I know that he's going to be OK for about three or four months and then the cycle will begin again. So that over the years, I think we've been able to identify certain cyclic things that occur. One of our senior staff physicians is on a five-month cycle. Every five months he comes down and complains about everything. He wants the house staff disciplined and this and that, and the other thing. I agree entirely with him. I know that he would be entirely horrified if I did anything about his complaints, and he'll be good for another five months after the ventilation and drainage session. So that sort of thing goes on. We play little games by indirection very often.

Another and frequent example. In many instances a private physician is doing his very best with a patient, but he knows he's got a little bit of difficulty. He's having trouble with the patient, but he's not quite at the point where he is calling for consultation himself. When I learn about this, I call him and say, "I understand you have a very interesting patient and our house staff would like to see that patient with you. Would you mind?" He almost never minds, and this is a courtesy consultation.

I make it progressively more difficult to gain exceptions to a generally accepted, worked out, sensible, and hopefully less expensive way. I think we've saved a great deal of money on antibiotic ordering. Another example is our pacemaker clinic. By standardizing the pacemakers and really analyzing which ones are the best, I think we've again accomplished some efficiencies.

I'd like to comment on one last thing in terms of management style. There's an old story about this southern governor. When asked why he had all those prison riots he said, "We wouldn't have all those riots if we had a better class of prisoner." In medicine we always say, "If we only had smarter doctors we could solve all our problems." Our answer to everything is: How about more education? Educate the public, educate the doctors, etc., and then our problems will go away. This just doesn't work. So I think we have to accept people for what they are and what their limitations are. Yes, we'll try to educate them. But I think we've attempted to get at a series of constraints where it becomes increasingly difficult to do the wrong thing, and so we do spend a fair amount of time trying to design these mazes where it's easier to run the right maze than the wrong one.

A very simple example. In a period of 10 years or so we went from 2 respiratory therapists to over 100 with demands for more and more. The curve of some treatments was going out of sight. We simply put a stop order on them because it was very clear that many physicians would write an order and then simply allow it to go on and on. So simply saying, "After 48 hours you will stop all of these unless you do something; you have to write another order; you have to fill something out, or it has got to be a little inconvenient for you to allow this to run" began to control it.

Dr. R. has one final comment on his own style.

I have a horror of being a do-gooder. I'm not a do-gooder. I'm a do-badder. I think the world is in a terrible state, namely because of do-gooders. I think that I would much rather have some old crab who knows what he's doing than somebody who wants to save me by taking care of me. I don't think we have to love everybody to do a good job, because that's what you do. There's no point in doing anything else. I think with my boys, with the residents and so on, I want to make pros out of them. I keep telling them, "just because you get paid for something doesn't make you a pro. A pro has good moves. He has economy of effort. He does things with a little style, a little class, and he keeps looking at himself as the chief instrument of what he's doing. So that you must be self-conscious about what you're doing. Recognize the stupidities yourself, and recognize that you're going to want things to happen so that you're not going to observe carefully." I want them to be as tough mentally as they possibly can get as a better protection for their patients than saying, "I'm going to save humanity." I want tough-minded guys. In the long run, that's what I think a doctor is all about.

CHAPTER TEN

The Future of Health Care: The End of Doctoring?

Better to hunt in fields, for health unbought
Than fee the doctor for a nauseous draught.
The wise, for cure, on exercise depend;
God never made his work, for man to mend.

John Dryden

The assumptions under which most doctors entered the field of medicine have changed. Medicine may be alive and well, but doctoring is a dying profession. This is not only because of the industrialization of health care, but also because of a redefinition of medicine's purpose.

The Alma Ata Convention, sponsored by the World Health Organization (WHO), proposed a goal of "health for all by the year 2000" through primary health care. Health is defined by WHO not merely as the absence of disease, but as total physical, social, and mental well-being. However, the doctor's only and proper role is with illness, not with health, and even there the physician is being displaced by technology and events, many of which are beyond the physician's control—escalating costs, competition, litigation, and altered consumer expectations—but some of which are directly due to physician arrogance, abuses, and defensiveness.

The emerging critical health and disease problems both in industrialized countries and in the Third World are no longer amenable to solution by the actions of individual practitioners, even if physicians attempt to respond to demands for plupractice and become "super doc." For the major health problems facing the industrialized nations are those of an aging population, of chronic disease and of poverty. And those facing the Third World largely involve public health and nutrition, requiring economic development more than high-technology health systems. In either instance, remedy lies in the creation of systems of skills utilizing resources economically directed at complex problems. The role of the physician, therefore, is unalterably and inevitably changed.

Attacks on medicine and on physicians are not new, nor is a lowly status. Until the end of the 19th century, medical degrees could be acquired at minimum cost with little effort and required but a brief apprenticeship.[1] Attracting large numbers of young men, the profession became overcrowded, resulting in keen competition for paying patients. Students often supplemented their income by farming or operating a small business. (What else is new!) Practitioners with lucrative practices among the well-to-do tended to come from an affluent background, as in Britain, had taken liberal arts degrees at well-known colleges and their medical degree from one of the colleges' medical schools. Status related far more to social class than membership in a supposedly learned profession. The lack of licensure laws allowed a host of quacks, empirics, folk doctors, and other irregulars to flourish and assume the title of doctor. (Current moves to deregulate medicine will no doubt result once again in this phenomenon.)

In the 17th century, physicians were well-regarded and respected members of their community, but in the 18th century the profession came under attack, for over the years the number of practitioners with university backgrounds declined while more were the products of apprenticeships, and this resulted in quarrels in the profession. When the demand for doctors increased with increasing population, the proprietary medical schools also expanded, although the graduates were often barely literate. (Note the current concern with offshore medical schools.) Medicine was characterized by neither professional courtesy nor etiquette, and practitioners were not noted for their culture and refinement. (It is perhaps extreme, to agree with Daniel Drake that medical students were often too stupid for the bar and too immoral for the pulpit.) Respect for the medical profession grew as science advanced, as medical education was reformed, and as licensure laws became effective. Though public health measures played a major role in reducing morbidity and mortality, doctors

---

[1]J. Duffy, "American Perceptions of the Medical, Legal and Theological Professions," *Bulletin of the History of Medicine* 58 (1984), pp. 1–15.

got much of the credit. As it became harder to enter the profession, the ratio of physicians to population decreased, making the fee system more lucrative and enhancing the financial position of physicians to its current admired status. But the true doctor still felt as Edward Keyes described to Cornell students in a 1926 address: "Ours is a profession, never a business. Those of us who are the greatest of surgeons and the happiest men make no more than a bare living."

It is an irony that as medicine has become more technologically effective, the physician has come under increasing attack, perhaps because of an abrogation of the doctor's traditional role of healer, a role which placed as much attention on the person as on the disease. The physician is somewhat to blame for the change in attitude; with the pressures of competition and the threat of litigation, doctors have become more concerned with processes than people. Yet, equally ironic, the very narrowness of physicians' definition of their role as treating disease in individuals contains the seed of the end of doctoring. For illness is more than physical cause, and health much more. As the nature of the tasks facing medicine alter, the educated capacities of the physician become less central and their educated incapacities more glaring.

The definition of disease is not medical alone, but social and moral, and it changes from time to time. Alcoholism is no longer a criminal offense, but a medical condition. Homosexuality is no longer an illness. Yet those who define, control, and physicians in many countries still control who works and who does not, for they define sickness. Consumers are rebelling against that control, and yet, also ironically, once a physician is divested of authority, he or she becomes merely a technician whose healing words and presence no longer carry benefit. Disease theories may have produced a kind of medical tunnel vision, and perhaps many doctors have not cared to see sick persons in all their wholeness and variability. But if, as one author urges, "we must become the masters of medicine and not its servants; in the politics of medicine it is we who must set the policies,"[2] we may be throwing out the baby with the bath water. For all the inadequacies of many physicians, for all their arrogance, sickness is often

---

[2]I. Kennedy, *The Unmasking of Medicine* (Boston: George Allen, 1981).

a mystery for which we need consolation. Once the physician is divested of his magic, to whom shall we turn?

> The patient has to believe in the physician, to have confidence in their advice and reassurance and in their selection of a pill that is helpful. The patient must have a conviction that the physician not only can be trusted but does have some special knowledge and if the treatment is to succeed, he invests that physician with authoritative experience and competence.[3]

Certainly the physician should involve the patient, should list alternatives, but the physician should not shirk his responsibility to recommend a course of action which the patient is free to refuse. It is easy in today's climate to understand why doctors have moved away from this, for once they shift responsibility to the patient, they cannot be held responsible and therefore liable.

Doctors must resist plupractice and becoming super doc. They must resist the demands placed on them in part by their own self-serving and ill-advised public relations. It is understandable that in the Western World an aging population resents the creaks and groans of age. (We accept cars that leak oil and have rust spots, but cannot accept that we have age blemishes and leak urine as we reach our 50s. This is not the doctors' business, it is for this that people buy Oil of Olay.) The paradox is that if doctors stick to what they know and can do, their role will diminish and they must become technicians. Or they can assume an altered role in the health system of the future in which they bring to bear their training and experience to influence health policies and health systems. But regardless of the choice they make, they cease to be doctors and have to become something else. Their profession has been overtaken by events, for a profession has a definite subject matter and a technology used to approach it. Other fields have experienced similar changes. Once anthropology went beyond the content matter of the primitive and the technology of participant observation, it became something other than anthropology. Its practitioners might have had more interesting content areas to investigate and a broader range of technologies with which to do it, but they were no longer anthropologists. So it is with doctors. To retain power and control they must assume a broader social and organizational role,

[3]F. J. Ingelfinger, "Arrogance," *New England Journal of Medicine* 303, no. 26 (1980), pp. 1507–11.

i.e., become physician managers, whether entrepreneurs or bureaucrats. To retain the content area of disease, they must revert to becoming technicians. Either way, doctoring ends. As with the crafts, there will always be isolated pockets of caring doctors practicing their craft in an era of industrialization. They will be valued anomalies, and rare, like unicorns. Today, the doctor is like the blacksmith regarding the assembly line. The pain lies in seeing the end of what one had been trained for and wanted. Future generations will not know that pain because they will have been brought up with different expectations.

But now, for doctors trained in a different era, is a time to remember what the profession was like. What it was like to practice medicine when you were respected and your authority was unquestioned. What it was like when you could do what you felt was best for your patients without worrying about what it would cost. What it was like when you had to treat many patients, who, if you were a general practitioner, or lived in the country or in a poor part of town, could not pay your bills. What it was like to always be on call.

The phenomenon of change is not restricted to the United States. With WHO's call for health for all through primary health care, there is a demand for a reorientation of health training, and physician training in particular. Primary health care represents a totally new approach to health development. It involves the total reorientation of health systems. Its characteristics are: reorientation of health services so that secondary and tertiary care are geared to supporting the first-contact-level care and the entire health system is working to provide backup for the grass-roots level; a more even distribution of health resources, meaning in most cases, a neat redistribution toward the first contact at the supervisory level and toward promotive, preventive, and rehabilitative care; a multisectoral character; and community participation.[4]

The role of health personnel is a function of their competence to perform the tasks assigned to them. Community health workers, for instance, are qualified when they have been properly

---

[4]T. Fulop, "Health Manpower for Health for All" (Paper presented at Towards Future Health and Medical Manpower: New Strategies and Education for the 21st Century, Tokyo, Japan, April 1985).

trained to carry out their tasks. A physician in charge of a district or rural hospital is qualified when, in addition to the traditional task of treatment and prevention, he or she has learned how to organize, supervise, and monitor the health personnel posted to health centers or dispensaries under that physician's supervision. Qualification therefore depends on competence and not on a certificate or diploma issued by a training center, whatever its reputation may be. Paper qualifications can be equated with competence only when they are the result of proper preparation, training, and experience that enable health workers to efficiently perform the tasks they have to carry out.

Health training therefore must be competency based, community oriented, community based, multiprofessional, integrated on a problem basis, student centered, and adapted to the development of sciences and of local needs and resources.[5]

The Tokyo Declaration, a statement issued by a WHO regional conference titled "Towards Future Health and Medical Manpower: New Strategies in Education for the 21st Century," suggested that health personnel in the future will need to possess at least the following skills and attributes:

To be responsive to the needs of communities.

To work as effectively in complex organizations, communities, and groups as alone, with appropriate managerial capabilities.

To function effectively in multidisciplinary teams, as members as well as leaders.

To communicate and negotiate with community leaders, the public, and consumers to obtain their involvement in the health program and activities.

To promote healthy lifestyles through health-promotion, disease-prevention, and health-education programs on an individual and community basis.

To be informed about the latest developments in health sciences and to critically assess the appropriateness of technology.

---

[5]Ibid.

To make complex clinical and managerial decisions, balancing individual expectations, cost for society, and ethics.

To give comprehensive individual care that considers the total needs of the patient.

The training of such future workers in the health system of tomorrow, including physicians, involves fundamental changes. There must be more community involvement; more communication between medical schools, health delivery organizations, government agencies, and communities; more faculty involvement in relevant practice and research; and curriculum change and problem-based learning. Many of these changes lie in the future. WHO called this regional conference recognizing that the major impediment to the achievement of its goal of health for all was the failure of health training institutions in general, and medical schools in particular, to alter their educational processes and content and therefore produce the kinds of workers needed by such new health systems. However, some steps already have been made in institutions such as the University of Limburg in the Netherlands.[6] And changes in medical school curricula and processes have been called for by many groups.[7,8]

It is noteworthy that trends in the United States parallel these developments. Indeed, some believe that such changes could once again restore the role of the physician as patient advocate. For the problem with traditional medical education is that it has long turned out artistes rather than technicians, doctors, or sociomedical scientists.[9] Selection by a medical school is often guided by socioeconomic criteria rather than the academic ability of the applicant, and matriculation brings isolation from any but professional contacts. While lower-class backgrounds have been found to correlate with superior academic perfor-

---

[6]J. M. Greep, "Change in Established Schools for Health Sciences" (Paper presented at Towards Future Health and Medical Manpower: New Strategies for the 21st Century, Tokyo, Japan, April 1985).

[7]"Report of Fifth Regional Meeting of Deans of Medical Schools" (WHO Regional Office for the Western Pacific, Manila, Philippines, December 1983).

[8]J. J. Guilbert, ed., *Nurses and Physicians of Tomorrow* (International Council of Nurses and World Federation for Medical Education, 1984).

[9]M. Oppenheim, *Healers, New England Journal of Medicine* 19 (1980), pp. 1117–20.

mance (in Britain), 78.3 percent of those applying to medical schools from state-financed institutions were rejected compared with 20.5 percent of those applying from private schools! In addition, 21 percent of medical students in Britain have a father practicing medicine while 68 percent of such students in the United States have a relative in the medical profession. Class plays an acknowledged role. According to the Royal College of Surgeons in England:

> There has always been a nucleus in medical schools of students from cultured homes . . . this nucleus has been responsible for the continued high social prestige of the profession as a whole and for the maintenance of medicine as a learned profession. Medicine would lose immeasurably if the proportion of such students in the future were to be reduced in favor of the precocious children who are qualified for subsidies from local authorities and the state purely on examination results.

So a group of prospective physicians is created with social and educational origins that are totally unrepresentative of those to whom their skills are to be directed. Professional socialization therefore builds an identity with the profession that is antithetical to the formation of relationships with the patient and inimical to the role of the physician as advocate of the patient if that patient is poor or of the working class. It is not surprising that the identification of the doctor is with the middle class rather than with the working class. It is also not surprising that doctors still mystify and use medical jargon as a way to avoid offering knowledge to patients. Given that lay management, at least in the National Health Service in Britain, also tends to be from the upper classes, the problem is perpetuated. The shift from publicly financed and delivered health care to the private sector (i.e., proprietary health systems), which is a growing phenomenon in Britain as in the United States, does not change this balance of power, for its market is also the middle class. The result is two classes of service. As already noted, the disappearance of traditional sources of funding for the poor and those in need in the United States is shifting many community and teaching hospitals from their traditional role of providing at least in part for the indigent toward the private pay patient.

The recommendations of WHO were meant to prevent the possibility of a two-class system. They have prompted further recommendations from the Association of American Medical

Colleges (AAMC) and Harvard University. An AAMC report asserts that:

> Every physician should be caring, compassionate, and dedicated to patients—to keeping them well and to helping them when they are ill. Each should be committed to work, to learning, to rationality, to science, and to serving the greater society. Ethical sensitivity and moral integrity, combined with equanimity, humility, and self-knowledge, are quintessential qualities of all physicians. The ability to weigh possibilities and devise a plan of action responsive to the personal needs of each patient is vital. . . . The goal of a general professional education of physicians comprises both the acquisition of these attributes and the preparation for specialized education in medicine, and these two purposes are not only compatible but usually supportive. Although in social practice persons may be categorized and dealt with in various groupings, it nevertheless remains true that the evolution of each person is unique. The physician's general professional preparation must respond to the interdependence of the development both of the whole person and the specialized professional.[10]

Such professionals must be able to deal with:

Rapid advances in biomedical knowledge and technology.

Chemical, mechanical, and electronic technologies available for prevention and treatment of disease.

Medical practice that will become ever more highly specialized.

The increasing recognition that many factors determine health and illness which are the consequences of lifestyle, environmental factors, and poverty.

The need of patients for advice and counsel about how to use special medical services.

The fact that physicians will generally be employed by large corporations or by health service organizations covering specific population groups.

The fact that the environment of medical education will be heavily influenced by the agencies that pay for medical services and that will shape the nature of these services.

---

[10] "Physicians for the 21st Century" (Report of the Project Panel on the General Professional Education of the Physician and College Preparation of Medicine, Association of American Medical Colleges, 1984).

The president of Harvard echoed the concerns voiced by others that the psyche, the preventive, and costs are all but ignored and ethics, history, behavioral science, and organization are neglected in medical education.[11] Disease is regarded as a scientific phenomenon rather than a deviation from a biomedical norm. Facts are truths rather than problems. Psychological and behavioral factors, though influencing health, are regarded as unscientific. It is necessary for the physician to be effective not only for the patient but also for society in avoiding unnecessary tests and procedures. Doctors must therefore be proficient in the uses and limitations of statistics, computer analysis, and decision making. Effective practice must require psychological as well as scientific understanding. It is the doctors' role—while delegating some responsibilities to others such as psychiatrists, social workers, clergy, skillful administrators, lobbyists, and computer analysts—to take the pieces, fit them together, and form a coherent plan of action. The physician fulfills this role because he or she will normally know more than anyone else about the patient's condition and thus will best be able to prepare the patient to make intelligent judgments about alternative treatments.

Moreover, as health delivery organizations employ an increasing share of this nation's doctors, they will want to hire practitioners trained to gather information economically, to make cost-effective decisions, and to motivate patients to comply more willingly with health-preserving regimens. Education must be directed toward that end. Harvard President Bok recommends not only content changes, but also process changes in the nature of instruction, much along the lines suggested by WHO. Yet neither the AAMC nor Harvard apparently recognizes that what they are recommending is the physician manager if not super doc, and that traditional doctoring and these roles are incompatible. The problem of changing needs and changing demands may be mitigated by changing curriculum content or the process by which it is taught, but the doctor's role will be inevitably altered to something other than what it was. It may be neither better nor worse, but it certainly will be different,

---

[11] D. Bok, "Needed: A New Way to Train Doctors," *Harvard Magazine*, May–June 1984, pp. 32–71.

and it is over this change that many physicians today are grieving.

The industrialization of medicine is inevitable, though it may go faster or slower here or there.[12] Attempts to reify physicians in the old mold are doomed to failure. The advance of capitalism, i.e., industrialization, results in bringing under organizational control a number of prerogatives that once belonged to the medical profession. These include the criteria for entrance, the content of training, autonomy regarding terms and content of work, the objects of labor, the tools of labor, the means of labor, and the amount and rate of remuneration for labor. While the process is slow and has only just started, the absolute number of physicians increased in the last 20 years in the United States, yet the number of self-employed physicians dropped and there was a rapid rise in the number of salaried physicians. More doctors also entered hospital-based practice and other bureaucratic activities such as teaching, research, and administration. In summary, 45 percent of active physicians in 1963 were salaried, while 58 percent were salaried in 1973. This is due to the bureaucratization of medical practice.[13] Even solo physicians are receiving a larger proportion of their income from personal investments while there has been a drop in the proportion they receive from professional activities. With this trend toward bureaucratization, physicians' goals are changing and doctors are becoming interested in ascending the managerial hierarchy and advancing the status of their organization, because power and prestige are no longer a function of personal attributes or professional expertise but a result of position in the organization.

"The physician will . . . become an historical anachronism." It is already possible to perform six of the major tasks now commonly performed by physicians more efficiently and reliably and often in a manner actually preferred by patients by using technology. (These tasks are the medical history, the physical examination, the ordering of ancillary tests, the formulation of a diagnosis, the institution of some treatment, and the determination

---

[12]J. B. McKinley and J. Arches, "Towards the Proletarianization of Physicians," *International Journal of Health Services* 15, no. 2 (1985), pp. 161–95.

[13]Ibid.

of a prognosis.)[14] Because medical treatment often involves matching some supposed condition with available treatment, it often is someone other than the physician who is responsible for dispensing the agent that arrests or alleviates symptoms. This is a function of technology in the United States and other Western countries, and of policy in Third World countries. In the past, the physician was credited with the cure when nature was, in fact, responsible. Today, it is technology that does the diagnosis and the curing, tomorrow it will be the computer.

Given that the power of the medical profession lies in its monopoly over a content area and a technology, the shift in the locus of such control from the physician to the organization may mean that the rationale for the profession of medicine is being eroded and may no longer exist. It is not simply technology that spurs this process, but (in the United States) the need for and capability of measuring diagnosis and treatment through such instruments as protocols. With the advent of sets of rules, which is what protocols are, judgment is no longer required. While protocols are being developed to ensure standard treatment and reduce litigation liability, or to reduce costs by avoiding unnecessary testing and treatment, they do make it easier for unskilled workers to apply such rules. And, of course, the existence of protocols suggests that computerization is merely the next step. The physician's assistant, the nurse practitioner, or the EMS (Emergency Medical Services) technician can or will be able to do much of what has previously been the prerogative of the doctor.

As already noted, recruitment, while still largely determined by physicians, is increasingly of interest to managers who, in organizations such as HMOs, must be concerned with balancing specialties and engaging doctors who will practice with cost-effective quality styles compatible with organizational interests. So control will shift toward management. In addition, government actions in the United States and elsewhere are limiting part or all of physicians' income.

Physicians in the United States are by no means blind to these trends, though they do not as yet appreciate their fundamental nature or necessarily correctly attribute them to the proper profound and underlying causes, but they sense the gist.

[14] J. S. Maxmen, "Good-by Dr. Welby," *Social Policy* 3 (1972), pp. 97–106.

In the 10-hospital study, of 100 doctors interviewed about how they felt about doctoring, approximately one third said that if they had to do it all over again, they would not enter medicine, and a further third would only do so with grave doubts.

Doctors do see all too clearly their loss of independence, which they attribute to government control and regulation, the effects of competition, malpractice, economics, technology, and the physician glut.

What is changing?

> The entire model of the solo practitioner, free spirit, private practitioner, is a thing of the past. Doctors must now think of survival, joining groups, an employee concept that is totally different from the environment I was trained in.
>
> Government is getting a bigger hand in regulating physicians. We no longer are at liberty to say when a patient needs to be admitted, how long they need to stay; there is pressure to get the patient home, sometimes when it might medically be better for them to stay a little longer.
>
> The concept of health care is a team effort. The physician is losing some of his position, not being identified outside the team, he will lose his boundaries. He will have a few special gimmicks he will be able to perform.
>
> The depersonalization of health care with the use of physician extenders, computers, multiphasic lab tests, these are intervening between the patient and the doctor.
>
> Regulations, DRGs, lab repayment schedules are causing paperwork and expense and work.
>
> Competition is one, so people may have to see more patients.
>
> There's more competition. I did not go into medicine to be a businessperson. Essentially that's what I have to become to keep my head above water.
>
> Malpractice separates the doctor from the patient because you're afraid of it.
>
> Medicare asks us to sign a contract that cuts our fees by one third and pays us our costs so we see patients for free. I don't know how you can do that for a quarter or a third of your practice.
>
> Costs—people cannot afford it. Expectations—it was a lot easier when people didn't have them.
>
> The skill of a physician used to be based on his clinical acumen. Now it's based on scientific tests.

While some physicians welcome more realism on the part of the patient and the possibility of cure brought by new technologies, for the most part, they experience practice as less fun, more burdensome, and more like a business.

In the same fashion, while some doctors see the impact of these changes as essentially positive, with a tightening of standards, better care due to competition, and more realism in expectations, most see the consequences as adverse both for doctoring and for patients. They do not like having to practice defensive medicine, and "in time you will find most doctors will be practicing a quality of medicine that will be very depressing in general."

> It may change the quality of people who go into medicine.
>
> The physician's response to the patient will change, it will be handled more as a job. Today instead of spending 30 minutes listening to patients' problems, it's going to be about 15 minutes, take care of the problem and out.

Doctors will handle this differently.

> For some it will be a retreat into intellectualism and a more contemplative life, accepting a lower standard of living, refusing to compete, going into teaching. For others it will be rejection of the old values and a joining in the entrepreneurial, business-oriented corporate world which we're being presented with. For yet others it will be a dogged clinging to the vestiges of what it once was, the last angry man.

But many share disillusionment.

> Practicing medicine is more disappointing than it was a few years ago.
>
> You get undercut in your care. You can try to make the best decisions, and all of a sudden the patient says, "Hey, wait a minute," and they've gone to another doctor.
>
> You are not able to weigh your advice as much as you could before.
>
> The presumption of guilt evident in the media and the political area that doctors are bad guys who are responsible for high costs is bad.
>
> When half your overhead is malpractice insurance, it does not make any sense.
>
> A lot of physicians are thinking about early retirement, taking administrative jobs. I have never seen people so discouraged with the day-to-day practice of medicine. They feel under attack, and at a time when we can do more for people than ever before.
>
> You wake up each morning praying that some patient won't get pissed off at you and ruin your life for the next five years for something that may be the best possible medicine, but that someone from an ivory tower will say they would have done differently.
>
> Not it is not uncommon to talk to someone and as soon as they find out you're a doctor, they say—I hate doctors, they are hungry for money, you can't get them when you have an emergency. They are negligent, they are not good, they lie to you.

> Other people are making decisions that physicians should make. The thing that is being focused on is being efficient; but when you're too efficient, you are not doing your job.
>
> It takes a lot of the fun out of medicine. Nobody remembers how to do a physical examination. I think we're getting to "Star Trek" medicine—we buzz the patient with a scanner and it tells us what's wrong with him and what to do for him.
>
> They're going to put physicians in a position where they're going to be least effective because they're going to be worrying about costs, rationing, malpractice, and all of this is going to affect the way they practice medicine. Rather than doing what you think is best, you do what you think will protect you in a court of law which is absolutely ridiculous, but there are no alternatives.

How will these changes affect patients? Some will benefit, as they may get more medicine and good care. There will be more ways to make diagnoses and treat patients. Costs may come down. But patients may suffer from the decreasing interest and involvement of the physician, which will hurt the quality of care, or may be discharged too soon. "They have lost the trust in doctors and doctors have lost closeness to the patient. It's become more expensive because of that." The main concerns are with diminished caring and with the possible effect of rationing.

While doctors currently practicing may regret or be disquieted by the changes they are experiencing and the effects they foresee, organizational medicine will attract a different kind of person to doctoring. With less freedom and less challenge, the brightest of future generations are already going elsewhere, and those who enter the profession will seek the regularities of a secure life or be entrepreneurs eager to enter the business of medicine.

What does all this mean for the physician of the future in the health delivery organization of the future? With more relevant training and more consonant values and desires, future physicians may better fit into the organizational life that is ahead, and thus, some of the sharp conflicts now being experienced may well be reduced. But to the extent that a doctor, as a healer, must be an advocate for his or her patients, for their pain and their suffering, some conflicts should remain inviolable if doctoring is to survive even in some attenuated fashion. The traditional doctor's unique contribution lies in the care of the sick, as decision maker for the patient. The indispensable nature of the doctor in decision making in the presence of uncertainty lies in his or her role as advocate for the patient, for the physician's cause is the patient's welfare as perceived by the patient and not the promotion of a particular intervention, even if organizationally sanctioned. Doctors must make assessments that are based on their appreciation of the complex interactions between the patient, the environment, and the disease.[15]

In an organizational setting, employees can express the dissatisfaction they feel with the organization's policies through exit, voice, or loyalty; they can leave, they can speak up, or they can stay silent.[16] But those who speak up may face retaliation in an organization in which they must remain, especially if alternative employment (exit) is realistically unavailable. (In Italy there are 30,000 unemployed doctors.) In an era of physician glut and limited employment alternatives, how easy will it be for physicians to speak up for the patient against the organization?

Medicine is, in a sense, both science and art—in a looser sense, science and poetry. Perhaps this phase—the end of doctoring—is a temporary ascendance of the scientific over the poetic, the technical over art, but there is a disquieting element. It is not simply a change in the balance of the faculties with which the individual practitioner applies his art or science to the individual patient, it is also a change in the way in which doctoring itself is organized and practiced. The fact that the product can more easily be measured and needs to be measured for economic reasons, the fact that competition requires the aggregation of resources and therefore organization, the fact that organizational interests require economy, place different pressures on the way in which doctoring is carried out, and to some degree on the choices available to the individual practitioner.

The choices are not necessarily detrimental either to the patient or to the physician. The patient may well have more efficacious treatment, more available choice, and potentially less-expensive care. Caring may no longer reside in the individual medical practitioner; there is no reason why it should not be ob-

---

[15] H. M. Schoolman, "The Role of the Physician as Patient Advocate," *New England Journal of Medicine* 296 (1977), pp. 103–4.

[16] A. O. Hirschman, *Shifting Involvements: Private Interest and Public Action* (Princeton, N.J.: Princeton University Press, 1983).

tainable, and it often is, in others, such as the nurse, the nurse practitioner, or the physician's assistant. But whether caring has the same meaning and value when it resides in other professionals is not yet clear. Perhaps this is a matter of habit. But it is undisputed that caring has an extra value when associated with authority, and other professionals, however competent, lack the authority of the doctor. Moreover, caring carries some quality connotations, for it is in a profound understanding of the individual that the unusual condition is detectable.

Here is where art resides and the computer cannot compete. For most conditions, the medicine of the future may do and do well. For some it may not. The ultimate management challenge perhaps lies in how to retain the essence of doctoring—advocacy for patients—in the complex bureaucratic systems that lie ahead, or the end of doctoring is truly in sight, with the advent of machine medicine.

REFERENCES

Bosk, C. L. *Forgive and Remember: Managing Medical Failure.* Chicago, Ill.: University of Chicago Press, 1979.

Browdy, J. D. *Health Care Executive Compensation: Principles and Strategies.* Rockville, Md.: Aspen Systems Corporation, 1983.

Carels, E. J.; D. Neuhauser; and W. B. Stason, eds. *The Physician and Cost Control.* Cambridge, Mass.: Oelgeschlager, Gunn & Hain, 1980.

Carroll, T. G. *Restructuring Hospital Quality Assurance.* Homewood, Ill.: Dow Jones-Irwin, 1984.

Cooper, P. D., ed. *Health Care Marketing: Issues and Trends.* Germantown, Md.: Aspen Systems Corporation, 1979.

Craddick, J. W. *Medical Management Analysis: A Systematic Approach to Quality Assurance and Risk Management,* 1983.

Freidson, E. *Doctoring Together: A Study of Professional Social Control.* New York: Elsevier, 1975.

Freidson, E. *Professional Dominance: The Social Structure of Medical Care.* New York: Atherton, 1970.

Fry, J. *Medicine in Three Societies: A Comparison of Medical Care in The USSR, USA, and UK.* New York: American Elsevier, 1969.

Gallagher, E. B., ed. *The Doctor-Patient Relationship in the Changing Health Scene.* Washington, D.C.: U.S. Department of Health, Education and Welfare, 1976.

Goldsmith, J. C. *Can Hospitals Survive? The New Competitive Health Care Market.* Homewood, Ill.: Dow Jones-Irwin, 1981.

Gordon, F. *Doctors and State Medicine: A Study of the British Health Service.* London: Pitman Medical, 1973.

Goss, M. E. *Physicians in Bureaucracy: A Case Study of Professional Pressures on Organizational Roles.* New York: Arno Press, 1980.

Gray, B. H., ed. *The New Health Care For Profit.* Washington, D.C.: National Academy Press, 1983.

Hirschman, A. O. *Shifting Involvements: Private Interest and Public Action.* Princeton, N.J.: Princeton University Press, 1982.

Jacques, E., ed. *Health Services: Their Nature and Organization, and the Role of Patients, Doctors, Nurses, and the Complementary Professionals.* London: Heinemann, 1978.

Kelman, S. *Improving Doctor Performance: A Study in the Use of Information and Organizational Change.* New York: Human Sciences Press, 1980.

Kennedy, I. *The Unmasking of Medicine.* Boston: George Allen & Unwin, 1981.

Mechanic, D. *The Growth of Bureaucratic Medicine.* New York: John Wiley & Sons, 1976.

Medawar, P. B. *The Hope of Progress.* London: Methuen, 1972.

Millman, M. *The Unkindest Cut.* New York: Morrow, 1977.

Pauly, M. V. *Doctors and Their Workshops: Economic Models of Physician Behavior.* Chicago: University of Chicago Press, 1980.

Reader, W. J. *Professional Men: The Rise of the Professional Classes in Nineteenth Century England.* New York: Basic Books, 1966.

Rogers, D. *American Medicine: Challenge for the 1980s.* Cambridge, Mass.: Ballinger, 1978.

Rubright, R. *Persuading Physicians: A Guide for Hospital Executives.* Rockville, Md.: Aspen Systems, 1984.

Schenke, R., ed. *The Physician in Management.* Washington, D.C.: Artisan, 1980.

Snook, I. *Building a Winning Medical Staff.* Chicago: American Hospital Publishing, 1984.

Starr, P. *The Social Transformation of American Medicine.* New York: Basic Books, 1982.

Thornton, A. P. *The Habit of Authority.* London: George Allen and Unwin, 1966.

Wechsler, H. *Handbook of Medical Specialties.* New York: Human Sciences Press, 1976.

Weed, L. L. *Medical Records, Medical Education and Patient Care: The Problem-Oriented Record as a Basic Tool.* Cleveland: Case Western Reserve, 1970.

INDEX

A

Abbot, J., 149 n, 157 n
Abramowitz, K. S., 1 n, 5 n, 14 n, 15 n, 16 n, 17, 22 n, 30 n
Absolute costs, 167
Academicians, 204, 206, 208
Academic medical centers, 209–10
  compared to teaching hospitals, 210
  loyalty, 125
Admissions, 108, 112–13
  high-volume doctors, 115–16, 124–25
  HMOs, 7–8
  location options, 196
  loyalty, 106
Adolfi, H., 158 n
Aetna Insurance Company, 16
Alcoholism, 245
Alma Alta Convention, 243
Alternate health care systems, 5, 136
Ambulatory care, 3, 5, 18, 21
  clinical outcomes, 138–39
  freestanding, 222
  HMOs, 136
  hospitals, 7, 8, 28, 30, 68, 210, 218
  nonphysician management, 6
  surgery centers, 6
American Federation of Dentists and Physicians, 98
American Federation of Labor-Congress of Industrial Organizations, 98
American Federation of Physicians and Dentists, 98
American Medical Association, 92, 173
Anderson, A., 11 n, 18 n, 23 n, 26 n, 72 n
Anderson, M., 150 n
Arches, J., 35 n, 44 n, 253 n
Association of American Medical Colleges (AAMC), 101, 251, 252
Attending Physicians Association of the City Hospital Center in Elmhurst, Long Island, 93
Autonomy of physicians, 4, 10, 12, 13, 43, 53, 60, 202

B

Bad medicine, 131
Bag ladies, 139
Barnard, K., 46 n
Becker, S., 74 n
Beinfield, M., 150 n
Belloc, Hilaire, 106
Bergman, J., 150 n
Berk, A. A., 138 n
Beverly Enterprises, 17
Bianchi, R., 154 n
Blair, C. W., 150 n
Bloom, B., 149 n
Blowers, L., 158 n
Blue Cross/Blue Shield, 10, 16, 134
Blum, A., 151 n
Blum, B., 152 n
Board, 72
  representation of physicians, 72–74
Bok, D., 252
Bole, G., 154 n
Bosk, C. L., 57 n, 158 n
Brand, D., 155 n
Braunwald, E., 154 n

Brennan, P. J., 150 n
British Medical Association, 102
British National Health Service; *see* National Health Service (Great Britain)
Brook, R., 155 n
Browdy, J. D., 160 n
Brunwald, E., 157 n
Buck, C., 155 n, 156 n
Bureaucratic medical settings, 13
Bureaucratization of medicine, 43, 253
Business-sponsored health care coalitions, 9

C

Campbell, P., 20 n
Capitated system, 129, 136
Capitation fee, 102, 135, 165, 220
Carels, E., 149 n, 150 n, 152 n
Carroll, T. G., 166 n
Carstairs, V., 148 n
CEO; *see* Chief executive officer
Chalmers, T. C., 138 n
Change management, 175
Charache, P., 154 n, 157 n
Charity care, 24; *see also* Indigent
Cherkin, D., 150 n
Chester, T. E., 72 n
Chief executive officer (CEO), 108
  conflict management, 177, 179, 183
  cost and quality management, 132–33, 142, 145, 146, 164
  HCA hospital, 213–14
  loyalty, 124–25
  manager's skill and style influencing doctors, 226–33
  10-hospital study, 113–27, 131, 226–33
CIGNA health system, 16
Clayton, P. S., 156 n
Clinical autonomy, 38–39
Clinical information systems, 152
Clinical judgement, 34, 37–38, 254
Cobo, A., 149 n, 158 n
Colding Health Services, 70–71
Collegium, 38, 57, 63, 181
Colton, T., 149 n
Committee on Interns and Residents (CIR), 98
Communication
  conflict management, 184
  technology, 79
Community health workers, 247–48
Community hospitals, 17, 18, 22, 207–8, 209
  acquisition by for-profit hospitals, 211
  loyalty, 121, 125
Community mental health movement, 139
Compensation, 92, 158–66
  direct expense profit center plan, 160
  employer-employee relationships, 160
  fixed, 159
  independent contract, 159–60
  performance-based incentives, 159
  physician behavior influenced by, 225
  relative value scale, 161
  salary, 158
  variable, 159
Competition, 27
Computerization, 3, 36, 44, 45, 54
Condominium style of hospital organizational structure, 75
Confidentiality, 35
Conflict management, 175–86
  communication, 184
  interpersonal conflict, 182
  types of physical conflict, 176
Consults, 108
Coombs, R., 47
Cooper, J., 154 n
Cooper, John A. D., 101
Cooper, P. D., 259
Cooper, R., 159 n
Corporate model of hospital organizational structure, 73–74, 75–76

Cost leadership strategy, 120–21
Cost management, 131, 145–48
  Doctor's Health Services, 133–35
  DRGs, 145, 156–57
  hospitals, 146–47
  HMOs, 135–37, 146, 151–52, 156–57
  physician's involvement, 146–58
    administrative changes, 155
    attitudes, 146–48
    changing behavior, 148–72
    economic sanctions, 155
    education, 152–54
    financial incentives, 146, 156, 158–68
    information feedback, 169
    peer reviews, 146, 152, 154–55
  productivity, 167
  quality/cost tradeoffs, 131–40
  summary of M.D. behavior-change programs
    assumptions, 171
    incentives, 171
    measures used, 170–71
    policies for deviance, 171–72
Cost per unit of resource, 166
Cost reimbursement, 138
Cotner, R., 160 n
Cox, A. G., 150 n
Craddick, J. W., 259
Craig, W., 150 n, 155 n
Crane, D., 34 n
Credential files, 141
Croen, L., 100 n
Cunnington, A., 150 n

D

Dalton, Tom, 70
Daniels, M., 150 n
Daniels, N., 93 n, 98 n, 99 n
Davis, C., 149 n, 157 n
Defensive medicine, 37, 147, 256
Deprofessionalization, 36, 44
Detmer, D., 147 n, 158 n
Deviant behaviors, 35
Deviant mistakes, 37
Devotion; *see also* Loyalty
  compensation, 158
  definition, 105
  enhancement, 108, 120
  expectations leading to, 114
  physician-management relations questionnaire, 198–200
Diagnosis Related Grouping (DRG), 17, 25, 30, 109, 145, 183, 255
  divisional model of hospital organization, 77
  generational problems, 183
  patient stay lengths, 167
Diagnostic techniques and tests, 150–51
Dickens, Charles, 131
Differentiation strategy, 20–21
Direct expense profit center plan, 160
Disease, definition of, 245
Diversification, 24
Divisional model of hospital organization, 75, 76–77
  cost management, 163
Dixon, R., 150 n
Doctor
  authority, 34–35, 259
  autonomy; *see* Autonomy of physicians
  choice of profession, 46–47
  clinical judgement, 34, 37–37
  compensation; *see* Compensation
  control over profession, 57, 60–65
  cost containment
    attitudes, 147–48
    changing behaviors, 148–72
  credential files, 141
  death of the medical profession, 243
  errors, 37, 55–56
  generational problems, 183
  historical status of profession, 244–45
  HMO relations, 30–33, 205–6
  hospitals, 28–30, 68–89
  income, 4, 8; *see also* Compensation
  as independent contractors, 103
  as interns and residents, 103–4

Doctor—*Cont.*
joint financial ventures with organization, 90–91
litigation; *see* Litigation
manager's influence on, 3, 224–42
overloads, 220, 221
plupractice, 65, 243, 246
private practice; *see* Private practice
relations to health care organizations, 1–3, 224–42
adversarial relationship, 41
clinical judgement replaced by managerial, 34, 37, 39
consultant, 39–40
future prospects, 257–58
goals, 40
joint ventures, 90–92
patient relationship affected, 35
true partnership, 89–92
voice in management and governance, 67–103
responsibilities, 56–57
salaried, 11, 97–98
self-employed, 11
specialties; *see* Specialties
as staff physicians, 103
surplus of, 9, 10, 27
technology, 35–36
training, 46–52, 248–53
unions; *see* Unionization of doctors
value chain, 29
values, 52–56, 202
voice; *see* Physician voice
work settings; *see* Work settings
Doctor-patient relationship, 1, 35, 42–46, 54, 106
fiduciary, 165
HMOs, 45–46
limiting duration of encounters, 161
weakening of, 45
Doctor's Health Services, 133–35
Drake, David, 244
Dresnick, S., 151 n
DRG; *see* Diagnosis Related Grouping
Dryden, John, 242
Duffy, J., 244 n
Dunn, W., 5 n
Dyck, F., 155 n
Dzau, V., 154 n, 157 n

E

Echeverri, O., 149 n, 158 n
Ecker, M., 155 n
Egan, L., 155 n
Egdahl, R. H., 7 n, 9 n
Eiland, G., 163 n
Eisenberg, H., 9 n, 12 n
Eisenberg, J., 149 n, 152 n, 156 n
Employer-employee relationship, 104–5, 160
Engel, G. V., 93 n
Entrepreneurial physician, 207
Erickson, S., 150 n
Errors, 55–56, 65
deviant, 37
HMOs, 65
interpersonal, 58
judgmental, 65
normal, 37, 58
Evashwick, C., 209

F

Family practitioner, 9, 204, 206
Fee-for-service, 9, 10, 11, 22, 202, 205, 207
cost management, 149
doctor-patient relationship, 54, 106
hospitalization rates, 151
managed care plan, 15
patient days per thousand, 1
Fiduciary relationship of doctor to patient, 165
Fielding, Henry, 202
Fifer, W. R., 137 n
Fineberg, H., 151 n
Fletcher, John, 20
Focus group, 188
Focus strategy, 20–21

Ford Hospital; *see* Henry Ford Hospital
Foreman, J., 12 n
For-profit health care facilities, 5, 13, 14, 33, 211, 218–19, 250
  doctor involvement, 80
  goals, 74
  multihospital systems, 15
Fox, R., 35 n
Fox, Sir Theodore, 102
France, physician authority, 42
Frazier, W., 155 n
Freidson, E., 37 n, 38 n, 57 n, 58 n, 61 n, 219 n, 220 n
Friedman, E., 6 n, 12 n
Fry, J., 259
Full Time Equivalents, (FTEs), 167
Fulop, T., 247

G

Gallagher, E. B., 35 n, 42 n, 43 n
Gelbach, S., 154 n
Generational problems among doctors, 183
Germany, physician authority, 42
Gittlesohn, A., 158 n
Goldsmith, J. C., 22 n, 28 n, 29 n, 66 n, 67 n, 174 n
Gomez, A., 149 n, 158 n
Gordon, F., 260
Goss, M., 234 n
Graham, F. E., 219 n
Grand rounds, 144
Grant, A., 150 n
Gray, B., 40 n, 156 n, 164 n, 165 n
Gray, G., 150 n
Great Britain
  clinical autonomy, 38–39
  malpractice litigation, 42
  medical education, 250
  mental health, 139
  status of physicians, 244
Greenland, P., 154 n
Greep, J. M., 249 n
Grimes, D., 72 n
Griner, P., 150 n, 154 n, 155 n
Group Health Association (GHA) (Washington, D.C.), 7, 71
  financial incentives for productivity, 162
  unionization, 59, 93–98
Group model HMO, 75, 220
Group practice, 59, 63, 219–20
  doctor-management relations, 68–69
Guilbert, J. J., 249 n

H

Hall, R. H., 93 n
Harris, J., 154 n
Harris, Lou, 10, 30 n, 31 n, 33 n, 173 n
Harrison, D. H., 221 n
Harris poll, 10, 173
Harvard University, 251–52
Harwood, Michael, 49
Hauck, W., 149 n
Haug, M. R., 36 n, 43 n, 44 n, 45 n
HCA; *see* Health Corporation of America
Head, J., 164 n
Health Care Financing Administration (HCFA), 17
Health care organizations
  competitive environment, 1
  future prospects, 243–59
  HMOs; *see* Health maintenance organizations
  hospitals; *see* Hospitals
  managing the doctor, 2
  organizational imperatives, 25–28
  physician relationship, 1–3, 34–41, 67–103, 224–42
  strategic planning, 20–25
    cost leadership, 20–21
    differentiation, 20–21
    diversification, 24
    focus strategy, 20–21
    objectives, 23
    physician input, 21–25
  value chain, 128–30

Health care personnel, 247
  skills required, 248
  training, 248–53
Health care training, 46–52, 248–53
Health Corporation of America (HCA), 28, 29, 73, 115, 120, 166, 211–18
  doctor's view of, 216–17
Health Corporation of the Archdiocese of Newark (HCAN), 109–12
Health insurance carriers; *see* Insurance carriers
Health maintenance organizations (HMOs), 1, 5, 14–16, 220–21
  admission rates, 1–8
  AMA imprimatur, 11
  compensation mechanisms, 72
  cost and quality tradeoffs, 135–37
  cost management, 151–52, 156–57, 165
  costs compared to traditional delivery services, 7–8
  definition, 7
  doctor relationship, 2, 30–33, 71
  errors, 65
  freestanding outpatient center affiliation, 27
  future prospects, 17
  group model, 75, 220
  growth, 32
  limiting duration of patient-doctor encounters, 161–62, 175
  managing change and conflict, 181, 184, 185
  multisite, 78
  recruitment, 172–74
  staff model, 220
  value chain analysis, 128
Health Watch (Rochester, New York), 33
Heasman, M. A., 148 n
Henry Ford Hospital, 21, 68, 78
  cost/quality management, 138–40
Henteleff, P., 148 n
Herzlich, C., 43 n
Hiatt, H. H., 5 n
High-technology organization, 20–22, 78, 79, 120, 121, 125
High-volume admitters, 115–16, 124
Hirsch, E., 154 n
Hirschman, A. O., 258 n
Hitt, D. H., 184 n, 185 n
HMOs; *see* Health maintenance organizations
Hoefer, A., 155 n
Homeless, 139
Homosexuality, 245
Hooper, D., 165 n
Horder, Lord, 46
Hospital-based outpatient medical practice, 28–29
Hospital Corporation of America, 14, 17
  quality management, 144
  value chain analysis, 129–30
Hospital management companies, 15
Hospitals, 1
  admissions; *see* Admissions
  alternative services, 5, 136
  bankruptcy, 18
  corporation model, 73–74
  costs, 146–47
  for-profit; *see* For-profit health care facilities
  future prospects, 16–18
  gross revenue per patient day, 17
  HMOs and PPOs, 17, 30
  length of stay, 17, 149
  loyalty and devotion of doctors; *see* Devotion *and* Loyalty
  nonprofit, 17, 80–81
  occupancy, 16
  organizational structure
    corporate model, 73–74, 75–76
    divisional model, 75, 76–77
    functional lines, 74–75
    parallel model, 77–78
  overbuilding, 16
  physician choice, 106–7, 125
  price war, 17
  proprietary, 5
Howat, H., 73 n
Hsiao, W. C., 161 n

Humana, 120, 218–19
Hunt, K., 10 n, 187 n

I

Idaho Health Plan (IHP), 133–34
Independent contract system, 159–60
Independent practice, 38, 63; *see also* Private practice
Independent Practice Associations (IPAs), 5, 11, 12, 31, 32, 33, 221
  capitated system, 129
  cost management, 156, 157
  Doctor's Health Service, 133–35
  loyalty to organization, 115, 127, 128
Indigent care, 8, 17, 24, 218, 221, 250
Industrialization of health care, 44, 46, 243, 253
Industrialized nations, health problems, 243
Influential doctors, 87–89
Information feedback in cost management, 169
Informing, 83–87
Ingelfinger, F. J., 246 n
Innes, A., 150 n
Insurance carriers; *see also* Medicaid *and* Medicare
  competition, 15
  future prospects, 17
  HMOs, 16
  hospital management companies, 15
  managed care plan, 15–16
  reimbursement, 15
Internal Revenue Service ruling 66-74, 104
Internists, 203–4, 205
Internship, 50–52
  unions, 103–4
Investor-owned health care chains, 5
Involving doctors in management, 83–87
IPAs; *see* Independent Practice Associations

J

Jacques, E., 260
Jessee, W., 154 n
Johannes, R., 154 n, 157 n
John Hancock Insurance Company, 16
Johns, R., 153 n
Johnson, K., 159 n
Johnson, M. L., 38 n, 46 n
Johnson, R., 73 n
Johnson Foundation, 28
Joint ventures between organizations and doctors, 29, 90–92, 112, 114, 116, 146, 207
Joskow, P. L., 138 n

K

Kaiser, L., 12 n, 23 n, 236 n
Kaiser Health Plan, 7, 14, 94, 97, 134
Kaskiw, E. A., 164 n
Keck, R. K., 156 n
Kelman, S., 152 n
Kenders, K., 154 n
Kennedy, I., 245 n
Kessler, M., 73 n, 209 n
Keyes, Edward, 245
Kimberly, J. R., 221 n
Klein, L., 154 n, 157 n
Knutson, Richard, 98
Kohlhepp, F. W., 158 n
Kornguth, P., 155 n
Krishan, I., 149 n, 157 n
Kunin, C., 150 n
Kurtz, M., 237 n

L

Lancet, 102
Larson, J., 73 n
Laszio, J., 150 n
Lavin, B., 44 n
Lawrence, M., 157 n, 164 n
Lawrence, R., 154 n
Leadership groups in health delivery organizations, 72
Lee, J. A., 150 n

Lee, K., 46 n
Leist, E., 154 n
Leopoid, E. T., 155 n
Light, T., 155 n
Linn, B., 151 n
Liptzen, B., 150 n, 155 n
Litigation, 36
  influence on doctor behavior, 225
  malpractice, 42, 100, 147, 151, 255
  protocols, 254
Low-cost versus high technology system, 20–22, 78–79
Loyalty
  defined, 106
  enhancement, 108–13, 121
  expectations of physicians, 114
  fund raising, 124
  "good hotel" service, 118
  multiple affiliation affecting, 115
  patient to doctor, 107
  physician-management relations questionnaire, 198–200
  physician to hospital, 106
  physician voice, 119
  rewards, 127
  teaching versus community hospitals, 125–26
  10-hospital study, 113–27
  value chain analysis, 127–30
Luft, H. S., 7 n, 8 n, 156 n, 164 n
Lyle, C., 154 n

M

Malfeasance, 37, 65
Malpractice litigation, 42, 100, 147, 151, 255
Managed care plan, 15–16
Management contracting, 211
Manager of health organization, 62–65
  control over physicians, 62–65
  defined, 62
  lay manager
    influence on physician behavior, 225–33
    style and skills, 224–33
  loyalty expectations, 118–19
Manager of health organization—*Cont.*
  physician manager, 233–42
  style and skills, 224–42
  understanding doctors, 202
Manzano, C., 149 n, 158 n
Marcus, S. A., 100 n, 105 n
Marion, R., 150 n
Martin, A. R., 154 n, 157 n
Matsumoto, M., 150 n
Maxmen, J. S., 36 n, 254 n
McClure, W., 149 n, 152 n, 157 n
McKinley, J. B., 35 n, 44 n, 253 n
McNamara, M., 150 n
Meade, T. W., 150 n
Mechanic, D., 13 n, 35 n, 43 n, 62 n
Medawar, P. D., 56 n
Medicaid, 10, 15
  cost/quality tradeoffs, 137–38
  Massachusetts legislation, 39
  prospective payment system, 17
Medical costs, 5
Medical schools, 9
  failure to educate for new health systems, 249, 252
  health organization management training, 222–23
Medical students, 46–52
  choice of profession, 46
  clinical experience, 48
  internship, 49–52
  residencies, 49–52
  rewards, 47
  specialties, 47, 50, 52
  training standards, 50–52
Medicare, 10, 15, 255
  cost/quality tradeoffs, 137–38
  fixed-rate DRGs, 17
  hospital length of stay, 17
Mental health, 139
Midwife, 45, 148
Miles, Peter, 134, 135
Miller, Bob, 101
Miller, F. H., 165 n
Millman, M., 184 n
Mohler, E., 149 n, 157 n
Moore, S., 156 n
Morell, J., 164 n
Moxley, J., 6 n

Multihospital systems, 5, 15, 22
Multiple hospital affiliations, 107, 115
Multiple tier service, 8–9, 23, 138, 250
Multisite HMOs, 78
Mushlin, A., 154 n
Myers, L., 149 n, 157 n

N

National Health Service (Great Britain), 43, 45, 57
  administration, 63
  physician involvement in conflicts, 73, 102
  upper class management, 250
National Industrial Council for HMO, 15
National Labor Relations Act, 105
National Labor Relations Board, 94, 96, 104
National Physicians Council (AFL-CIO), 98
Neighborhood health centers, 28, 221–22
Networking of organizations, 23
Neuhauser, D., 74 n, 152 n
New England Journal of Medicine, 104
New York's League of Voluntary Hospitals, 98
Nickerson, R., 149 n
"Noise" in organizations, 197–98
Nole, N., 98 n, 101 n
Noninvasive technologies, 8
Nonprofit hospitals, 17; *see also* Hospitals
  goals, 74
  physician influence, 80–81
Norbrega, F., 149 n, 157 n
Normal mistakes, 37
Not-for-profit health care chains, 5
Nurse practitioner, 11, 45, 148

O

Obstetricians, 203, 204
Occupational medical clinic, 6
Ochsner Clinic, cost management, 162
Ohio Valley Hospital Association (NLRB case), 104
Oppenheim, M., 249 n
Organizational incentives to control costs, 136
Ottensmeyer, D., 13 n
Outpatient centers, 26–27
Outpatient surgical procedures, 6
Overloads, 220
  HMOs, 221
Owen, John, 34

P

Pais, M. J., 155 n
Parallel model of hospital organization, 77–78
Paraprofessional, 45
Parker, R., 158 n
Partnership relationship between doctor and organization, 89–92
Pathologist, 204
Patient care protocols; *see* Protocols
Patient care review procedures, 135
Patient incentives for cost control, 136
Patient-physician relationship; *see* Doctor-patient relationship
Pauly, M. V., 260
Pediatricians, 203, 204
Perlman, L., 151 n
Peterson, O., 149 n
Pflanz, M., 42 n
Physician; *see* Doctor
Physician assistant, 11, 45, 148
Physician corporations, 76
Physician incentives to control costs, 136
Physician involvement in organization; *see* Physician voice
Physician-management relations monitoring (PMRM), 197–201
Physician's National Housestaff Association, 93
Physician voice, 67, 198, 200
  communication, 80, 83–84

Physician voice—*Cont.*
governance and the board, 71–81
influence, 81–82
influential doctor, 87–88
informing, 83–84
involving, 85–86
managing loyalty, 114, 119
10-hospital study, 79–80, 114–15
unions; *see* Unionization of doctors
Piemme, T., 148 n, 150 n, 154 n
Plupractice, 65, 243, 246
Pope, Alexander, 175
Porter, M. E., 20 n, 29 n, 128 n
PPO; *see* Preferred Provider Organization
Practice pattern impact study, 106, 108, 186–97
focus group, 188, 197
interviewing, 190–92, 197
key findings, 192–96
questionnaire, 189, 197
Pratt, T., 151 n
Preferred Provider Organization (PPO), 5–6, 10, 12, 15
managed care plan, 16
Prepaid group practice, 8
HMOs; *see* Health maintenance organizations
hospitalization rate, 151
Primary care physicians, 9, 172–73
Private-pay patients, 18
Private practice, 11, 18, 120, 205, 208; *see also* Fee-for-service
Productivity, 27, 146
group practice, 162–63
incentive bonuses, 159, 161
Profession, 36, 56
dominant, 38, 61
Professional authority, 60
Professional dominance, 38, 61
Professionalism, 99, 105
definition, 103
Professional Standards Review Organization (PSRO), 155
Profit-making hospitals; *see* For-profit health care facilities
Proletarianization, 35, 44
Proprietary health care facilities; *see* For-profit health care facilities
Prospective reimbursement systems, 117, 132, 138
Protocols, 3, 27, 62, 155, 254
Prudential Insurance Company, 16
Psychiatrists, 203

Q–R

Quality, 131, 132
cost/quality tradeoffs, 131–40
eradicating bad medicine, 131–32
HMOs, 135–37, 172–73
hospital standards, 132
Quality assurance procedures, 137, 140, 144
Quintero, M., 149 n, 158 n
Radiologists, 204
Ramgopal, V., 155 n
Reader, W. J., 36 n
Recruitment
HCA hospitals, 215
HMOs, 172–73
organization management, 254
physician involvement, 172
Referrals, 108
Registered nurses, 104
Regulation of physicians, 4
Reimbursement system, 8–10, 147, 225
cost, 138
cost-plus, 15
medicare, 17
prospective, 117, 138
Relative value scale of compensation, 161
Relman, A. S., 13 n
Residency, 49–52
unions, 103–4
Rhyne, R., 154 n
Rice, J. A., 156 n
Richards, I. A., 56 n
Right of control test of National Labor Relations Act, 105
Roeder, P., 6 n
Rogan, P., 164 n

Rogers, D. E., 10 n, 290 n
Roos, L., 148 n
Roos, N., 148 n
Rossoff, A., 149 n, 152 n, 156 n
Roth, W., 151 n
Rowbottom, R., 62 n, 64 n
Royal College of Surgeons, (Great Britain), 250
Royer, J., 235 n
Rubin, I., 235 n
Rubright, R., 260
Russia, doctor-patient relationship, 45

S

St. Joseph's Hospital (Toronto), 101
Saint Mary's Hospital (East Orange, N. J.), 109–13
Salary system, 11, 97–98, 136, 253
Saltman, R. B., 62 n, 155 n
Samaritan Hospital Group, 29
Sandrick, K., 73 n
Schenke, R., 236 n
Schliftman, A., 148 n, 150 n
Schneeweiss, R., 150 n
Schoolman, H. M., 258 n
Schroeder, S., 148 n, 149 n, 150 n, 154 n, 156 n, 157 n
Schulz, R., 71, 72 n
Schwartz, W. B., 138 n
Self-employed doctors; *see* Private practice
Senior doctor, 163
Shaw, W., 155 n
Shea, K., 155 n
Sheldon, Alan, 2 n, 52 n, 165 n
Shortell, S. M., 40 n, 67 n, 74, 75 n, 185 n, 209 n
Showstack, J., 150 n, 156 n
Siegel, B., 100 n
Simpson, J. E., 150 n
Skipper, J. K., 103 n
Slater, C., 235 n
Smoldt, R., 149 n, 157 n
Snook, I., 260
Specialties
  internists, 203
  obstetricians, 203
  pediatricians, 203, 204
  psychiatrists, 203
  selection, 47, 50, 52
  subspecialties, 210
  surgeons, 203, 205
Starr, P., 5 n
Stason, W. B., 152 n, 161 n
Stilwell, J. A., 150 n
Stimpson, G. V., 43 n
Stollwinder, J. U., 156 n
Stross, J., 154 n
Subspecialties, 210
Surgeons, 203, 205
Swiercz, P. M., 103 n

T

Tabatabai, C., 149 n, 150 n
Taylor, Lord, 102
Teaching hospital, 8
  academic hospital compared, 210
  community hospitals compared, 125–26
  high-technology, 125
  incentive plans, 163
  loyalty to, 125
  managerial characteristics, 144, 209–10
Technology, 5, 215–16; *see also* High-technology organization
  communication, 79
  cost effectiveness, 138
  displacing doctors, 243, 235–46, 253–54
  doctor-patient relationship, 45
  expectations of patients, 65
  high-technology versus low-cost, 20–22, 78–79
  hospital costs, 147
  surgeons, 203
  variation in use by physicians, 165
Tell, E., 148 n, 152 n
10-hospital study, 10, 39, 46, 79, 108, 113–27, 131, 140, 226–33

10-hospital study—*Cont.*
  CEO; *see* Chief executive officer
Tests, 150
Thibodeau, L., 154 n, 157 n
Third-party payment system, 9–10, 147
Third World health problems, 243
Thornton, A. P., 45 n, 260
Tokyo Declaration, 248
Tolliday, H., 38 n, 64 n
Trenz, P., 159 n
Tupasi, T., 150 n
Two-tier medicine, 8–9, 23, 138, 250
Tyson, T., 149 n, 158 n

U

Uman, S., 155 n
Unionization of doctors, 12, 36, 44, 92–105
  arguments for and against, 98–103
  background, 92–98
  Group Health Association (Washington, D.C.), 93–98
  house staff, 104
Union of American Physicians, 98
University of Limburg (Netherlands), 249
Urgent care centers, 6

V

Value chain, 29, 128–30
Values of physicians, 52–56, 202
Veatch, R. M., 165 n
Voluntary Hospitals of America (VHA), 16

W–Y

Wassertheil-Smoller, S., 100 n
Webster, John, 67
Wechsler, H., 203 n
Weed, L. L., 260
Wenberg, J. E., 4 n
Wennberg, J., 148 n, 158 n
White, K., 155 n, 156 n
Williams, K., 155 n
Williams, S., 156 n
Wolcott, B., 150 n
Wolf, M., 154 n, 157 n
Wolfe, S., 98 n, 99 n
Wolinsky, F. D., 8 n, 32 n, 136 n
Women
  entering medical profession, 11, 35
  medical school experience, 48
Wood, Z., 154 n
Woods, D., 93 n, 101 n, 103 n
Work settings, 202, 207–22; *see also under individual types*
  academic medical centers, 208–10
  bureaucratic, 13
  community hospitals, 207–8, 210
  for-profit health systems, 211–18
  freestanding ambulatory centers, 222
  group practice, 219–20
  HMOs, 220–21
  neighborhood health centers, 221–22
World Health Organization (WHO), 64, 243, 247, 249, 250
  Alma Alta Convention, 243
  Tokyo Declaration, 248
Young, D., 150 n
Young, D. Y., 62 n